KU-774-555

THE DYNASTS

AN EPIC-DRAMA
OF THE WAR WITH NAPOLEON
PARTS I AND II

MACMILLAN AND CO., Limited
LONDON · BOMBAY · CALCUTTA · MADRAS
MELBOURNE

THE MACMILLAN COMPANY
NEW YORK · BOSTON · CHICAGO
DALLAS · SAN FRANCISCO

THE MACMILLAN CO. OF CANADA, Ltd.
TORONTO

THE DYNASTS

AN EPIC-DRAMA
OF THE WAR WITH NAPOLEON

PARTS I AND II

BY

THOMAS HARDY

And I heard sounds of insult, shame, and wrong,
And trumpets blown for wars.

MACMILLAN AND CO., LIMITED
ST. MARTIN'S STREET, LONDON
1924

PRINTED IN GREAT BRITAIN

THE DYNASTS

AN EPIC-DRAMA OF THE WAR WITH NAPOLEON, IN THREE PARTS, NINETEEN ACTS, AND ONE HUNDRED & THIRTY SCENES

THE TIME COVERED BY THE ACTION BEING ABOUT TEN YEARS

And I heard sounds of insult, shame, and wrong,
And trumpets blown for wars.

PREFACE

THE Spectacle here presented in the likeness of a Drama is concerned with the Great Historical Calamity, or Clash of Peoples, artificially brought about some hundred years ago.

The choice of such a subject was mainly due to three accidents of locality. It chanced that the writer was familiar with a part of England that lay within hail of the watering-place in which King George the Third had his favourite summer residence during the war with the first Napoléon, and where he was visited by ministers and others who bore the weight of English affairs on their more or less competent shoulders at that stressful time. Secondly, this district, being also near the coast which had echoed with rumours of invasion in their intensest form while the descent threatened, was formerly animated by memories and traditions of the desperate military preparations for that contingency. Thirdly, the same countryside happened to include the village which was the birthplace of Nelson's flag-captain at Trafalgar.

When, as the first published result of these accidents, *The Trumpet-Major* was printed, more than twenty years ago, I found myself in the tantalizing position of having touched the fringe of a vast international tragedy without being able, through limits of plan, knowledge, and opportunity, to enter further into its events; a restriction that prevailed for many years. But the slight regard paid to English influence and action throughout the struggle by those

Continental writers who had dealt imaginatively with Napoléon's career, seemed always to leave room for a new handling of the theme which should re-embody the features of this influence in their true proportion ; and accordingly, on a belated day about six years back, the following drama was outlined, to be taken up now and then at wide intervals ever since.

It may, I think, claim at least a tolerable fidelity to the facts of its date as they are given in ordinary records. Whenever any evidence of the words really spoken or written by the characters in their various situations was attainable, as close a paraphrase has been aimed at as was compatible with the form chosen. And in all cases outside oral tradition, accessible scenery, and existing relics, my indebtedness for detail to the abundant pages of the historian, the biographer, and the journalist, English and Foreign, has been, of course, continuous.

It was thought proper to introduce, as supernatural spectators of the terrestrial action, certain impersonated abstractions, or Intelligences, called Spirits. They are intended to be taken by the reader for what they may be worth as contrivances of the fancy merely. Their doctrines are but tentative, and are advanced with little eye to a systematized philosophy warranted to lift "the burthen of the mystery" of this unintelligible world. The chief thing hoped for them is that they and their utterances may have dramatic plausibility enough to procure for them, in the words of Coleridge, "that willing suspension of disbelief for the moment which constitutes poetic faith." The wide prevalence of the Monistic theory of the Universe forbade, in this twentieth century, the importation of Divine personages from any antique Mythology as ready-made sources or channels of Causation, even in verse, and excluded the celestial machinery of, say, *Paradise Lost*, as peremptorily as that of the *Iliad* or the *Eddas*. And the abandonment of the masculine pronoun in allusions to the First or Fundamental Energy seemed a necessary and logical consequence of the long abandonment by thinkers of the anthropomorphic conception of the same.

These phantasmal Intelligences are divided into groups, of which one only, that of the Pities, approximates to "the Universal Sympathy of human nature—the spectator idealized"[1] of the Greek Chorus; it is impressionable and inconsistent in its views, which sway hither and thither as wrought on by events. Another group approximates to the passionless Insight of the Ages. The remainder are eclectically chosen auxiliaries whose signification may be readily discerned. In point of literary form, the scheme of contrasted Choruses and other conventions of this external feature was shaped with a single view to the modern expression of a modern outlook, and in frank divergence from classical and other dramatic precedent which ruled the ancient voicings of ancient themes.

It may hardly be necessary to inform readers that in devising this chronicle-piece no attempt has been made to create that completely organic structure of action, and closely-webbed development of character and motive, which are demanded in a drama strictly self-contained. A panoramic show like the present is a series of historical "ordinates" (to use a term in geometry): the subject is familiar to all; and foreknowledge is assumed to fill in the junctions required to combine the scenes into an artistic unity. Should the mental spectator be unwilling or unable to do this, a historical presentment on an intermittent plan, in which the *dramatis personæ* number some hundreds, exclusive of crowds and armies, becomes in his individual case unsuitable.

In this assumption of a completion of the action by those to whom the drama is addressed, it is interesting, if un-

---

[1] Schlegel.

necessary, to name an exemplar as old as Aeschylus, whose plays are, as Dr. Verrall reminds us,[1] scenes from stories taken as known, and would be unintelligible without supplementary scenes of the imagination.

Readers will readily discern, too, that *The Dynasts* is intended simply for mental performance, and not for the stage. Some critics have averred that to declare a drama[2] as being not for the stage is to make an announcement whose subject and predicate cancel each other. The question seems to be an unimportant matter of terminology. Compositions cast in this shape were, without doubt, originally written for the stage only, and as a consequence their nomenclature of "Act," "Scene," and the like, was drawn directly from the vehicle of representation. But in the course of time such a shape would reveal itself to be an eminently readable one; moreover, by dispensing with the theatre altogether, a freedom of treatment was attainable in this form that was denied where the material possibilities of stagery had to be rigorously remembered. With the careless mechanicism of human speech, the technicalities of practical mumming were retained in these productions when they had ceased to be concerned with the stage at all.

To say, then, in the present case, that a writing in play-shape is not to be played, is merely another way of stating that such writing has been done in a form for which there chances to be no brief definition save one already in use for works that it superficially but not entirely resembles.

Whether mental performance alone may not eventually be the fate of all drama other than that of contemporary or frivolous life, is a kindred question not without interest. The mind naturally flies to the triumphs of the Hellenic and Elizabethan theatre in exhibiting scenes laid "far in the

---

[1] Introduction to the *Choephori*.
[2] It is now called an Epic-drama (1909).

Unapparent," and asks why they should not be repeated. But the meditative world is older, more invidious, more nervous, more quizzical, than it once was, and being unhappily perplexed by——

Riddles of Death Thebes never knew,

may be less ready and less able than Hellas and old England were to look through the insistent, and often grotesque, substance at the thing signified.

In respect of such plays of poesy and dream a practicable compromise may conceivably result, taking the shape of a monotonic delivery of speeches, with dreamy conventional gestures, something in the manner traditionally maintained by the old Christmas mummers, the curiously hypnotizing impressiveness of whose automatic style—that of persons who spoke by no will of their own——may be remembered by all who ever experienced it. Gauzes or screens to blur outlines might still further shut off the actual, as has, indeed, already been done in exceptional cases. But with this branch of the subject we are not concerned here.

                                                              T. H.

September 1903.

CONTENTS

THE DYNASTS: AN EPIC-DRAMA OF THE WAR WITH NAPOLEON

PART SECOND

CONTENTS

PART FIRST

CHARACTERS

I. Phantom Intelligences

{ THE ANCIENT SPIRIT OF THE
    YEARS.
{ CHORUS OF THE YEARS.

{ THE SPIRIT OF THE PITIES.
{ CHORUS OF THE PITIES.

{ SPIRITS SINISTER AND IRONIC.
{ CHORUSES OF SINISTER AND
    IRONIC SPIRITS.

{ THE SPIRIT OF RUMOUR.
{ CHORUS OF RUMOURS.

THE SHADE OF THE EARTH.

SPIRIT-MESSENGERS.

RECORDING ANGELS.

II. Persons

The names printed in italics are those of mute figures.

MEN

GEORGE THE THIRD.
The Duke of Cumberland.
PITT.
FOX.
SHERIDAN.
WINDHAM.
WHITBREAD.
TIERNEY.
BATHURST AND FULLER.
Lord Chancellor Eldon.
EARL OF MALMESBURY.
LORD MULGRAVE.
ANOTHER CABINET MINISTER.
Lord Grenville.
Viscount Castlereagh.

Viscount Sidmouth.
ANOTHER NOBLE LORD.
ROSE.
Canning.
Perceval.
Grey.
Speaker Abbot.
TOMLINE, BISHOP OF LINCOLN.
SIR WALTER FARQUHAR.
Count Munster.
*Other Peers, Ministers, ex-Ministers,
    Members of Parliament, and
    Persons of Quality.*

NELSON.
COLLINGWOOD.
HARDY.
SECRETARY SCOTT.
DR. BEATTY.
DR. MAGRATH.
DR. ALEXANDER SCOTT.
BURKE, PURSER.
Lieutenant Pasco.
ANOTHER LIEUTENANT.
POLLARD, A MIDSHIPMAN.
ANOTHER MIDSHIPMAN.
Captain Adair.
Lieutenants Ram and Whipple.
Other English Naval Officers.
Sergeant-Major Secker and Marines.
*Staff and other Officers of the English
    Army.*
A COMPANY OF SOLDIERS.
*Regiments of the English Army and
    Hanoverian.*
SAILORS AND BOATMEN.
A MILITIAMAN.
Naval crews.

———

*The Lord Mayor and Corporation of
    London.*
A GENTLEMAN OF FASHION.
WILTSHIRE, A COUNTRY GENTLE-
    MAN.
A HORSEMAN.
TWO BEACON-WATCHERS.
ENGLISH CITIZENS AND BURGESSES.
COACH AND OTHER HIGHWAY
    PASSENGERS.
MESSENGERS, SERVANTS, AND
    RUSTICS.

———

NAPOLÉON BONAPARTE.
DARU, NAPOLÉON'S WAR SECRE-
    TARY.
LAURISTON, AIDE-DE-CAMP.
MONGE, A PHILOSOPHER.
BERTHIER.
MURAT, BROTHER-IN-LAW OF
    NAPOLÉON.
SOULT.
NEY.
LANNES.
Bernadotte.
Marmont.

Dupont.
Oudinot.
Davout.
Vandamme.
Other French Marshals.
A SUB-OFFICER.

———

VILLENEUVE, NAPOLÉON'S ADMIRAL.
DECRÈS, MINISTER OF MARINE.
FLAG-CAPTAIN MAGENDIE.
LIEUTENANT DAUDIGNON.
LIEUTENANT FOURNIER.
DE PRIGNY, HEAD OF STAFF.
Captain Lucas.
OTHER FRENCH NAVAL OFFICERS
    AND PETTY OFFICERS.
*Seamen of the French and Spanish
    Navies.*
Regiments of the French Army.
COURIERS.
HERALDS.
Aides, Officials, Pages, etc.
ATTENDANTS.
French Citizens.

———

CARDINAL CAPRARA.
Priests, Acolyths, and Choristers.
*Italian Doctors and Presidents of
    Institutions.*
Milanese Citizens.

———

THE EMPEROR FRANCIS.
THE ARCHDUKE FERDINAND.
Prince John of Lichtenstein.
PRINCE SCHWARZENBERG.
MACK, AUSTRIAN GENERAL.
JELLACHICH.
RIESC.
WEIROTHER.
ANOTHER AUSTRIAN GENERAL.
TWO AUSTRIAN OFFICERS.

———

The Emperor Alexander.
PRINCE KUTÚZOF, RUSSIAN FIELD
    MARSHAL.
COUNT LANGERON.
COUNT BUXHÖVDEN.

Count Milorádovich.
Dokhtórof.

Giulay, Gottesheim, Klenau, and
    Prschebiszewsky.
Regiments of the Austrian Army.
Regiments of the Russian Army.

WOMEN

Queen Charlotte.
English Princesses.
Ladies of the English Court.
Lady Hester Stanhope.
A Lady.
Lady Caroline Lamb, Mrs. Damer,
    and other English Ladies.

The Empress Joséphine.
Princesses and Ladies of Joséphine's
    Court.
Seven Milanese Young Ladies.

City- and Towns-women.
Country-women.
A Militiaman's Wife.
A Street-woman.
Ship-women.
Servants.

FORE SCENE

THE OVERWORLD

Spirit and Chorus of the Years, the Spirit and Chorus
e of the Earth, the Spirits Sinister and Ironic with their
Spirit-Messengers, and Recording Angels.

SHADE OF THE EARTH

of the Immanent Will and Its designs?

SPIRIT OF THE YEARS

IT works unconsciously, as heretofore,
Eternal artistries in Circumstance,
Whose patterns, wrought by rapt æsthetic rote,
Seem in themselves Its single listless aim,
And not their consequence.

CHORUS OF THE PITIES (aerial music)

> *Still thus?   Still thus?*
> *Ever unconscious!*
> *An automatic sense*
> *Unweeting why or whence?*
> *Be, then, the inevitable, as of old,*
> *Although that SO it be we dare not hold!*

SPIRIT OF THE YEARS

Hold what ye list, fond unbelieving Sprites,
You cannot swerve the pulsion of the Byss,
Which thinking on, yet weighing not Its thought,
Unchecks Its clock-like laws.

SPIRIT SINISTER (aside)

>   *Good, as before.*
> *My little engines, then, will still have play.*

SPIRIT OF THE PITIES

Why doth It so and so, and ever so,
This viewless, voiceless Turner of the Wheel?

SPIRIT OF THE YEARS

As one sad story runs, It lends Its heed
To other worlds, being wearied out with this;
Wherefore Its mindlessness of earthly woes.
Some, too, have told at whiles that rightfully
Its warefulness, Its care, this planet lost
When in her early growth and crudity
By bad mad acts of severance men contri
Working such nescience by their own de
Yea, so it stands in certain chronicles,
Though not in mine.

SPIRIT OF THE PITIES

       Meet is it, none the less,
To bear in thought that though Its consciousnes
May be estranged, engrossed afar, or sealed,
Sublunar shocks may wake Its watch anon?

SPIRIT OF THE YEARS

Nay.   In the Foretime, even to the germ of Being,
Nothing appears of shape to indicate
That cognizance has marshalled things terrene,
Or will (such is my thinking) in my span.
Rather they show that, like a knitter drowsed,
Whose fingers play in skilled unmindfulness,
The Will has woven with an absent heed
Since life first was; and ever will so weave.

SPIRIT SINISTER

Hence we've rare dramas going—more so since
It wove Its web in that Ajaccian womb!

SPIRIT OF THE YEARS

Well, no more thus on what no mind can mete.
Our scope is but to register and watch
By means of this great gift accorded us—
The free trajection of our entities.

SPIRIT OF THE PITIES

On things terrene, then, I would say that though
The human news wherewith the Rumours stirred us
May please thy temper, Years, 'twere better far
Such deeds were nulled, and this strange man's career
Wound up, as making inharmonious jars
In her creation whose meek wraith we know.
The more that he, turned man of mere traditions,
Now profits naught. For the large potencies
Instilled into his idiosyncrasy—
To throne fair Liberty in Privilege' room—
Are taking taint, and sink to common plots
For his own gain.

SHADE OF THE EARTH

And who, then, Cordial One,
Wouldst substitute for this Intractable?

CHORUS OF THE PITIES (aerial music)

We would establish those of kindlier build,
In fair Compassions skilled,
Men of deep art in life-development;
Watchers and warders of thy varied lands,
Men surfeited of laying heavy hands
Upon the innocent,
The mild, the fragile, the obscure content
Among the myriads of thy family.
Those, too, who love the true, the excellent,
And make their daily moves a melody.

SHADE OF THE EARTH

They may come, will they. I am not averse.
Yet know I am but the ineffectual Shade
Of her the Travailler, herself a thrall
To It; in all her labourings curbed and kinged!

SPIRIT OF THE YEARS

Shall such be mooted now? Already change
Hath played strange pranks since first I brooded here.
But old Laws operate yet; and phase and phase
Of men's dynastic and imperial moils
Shape on accustomed lines. Though, as for me,
I care not how they shape, or what they be.

SPIRIT OF THE PITIES

You seem to have small sense of mercy, Sire?

SPIRIT OF THE YEARS

Mercy I view, not urge;—nor more than mark
What designate your titles Good and Ill.
'Tis not in me to feel with, or against,
These flesh-hinged mannikins Its hand upwinds
To click-clack off Its preadjusted laws;
But only through my centuries to behold
Their aspects, and their movements, and their mould.

SPIRIT OF THE PITIES

They are shapes that bleed, mere mannikins or no,
And each has parcel in the total Will.

SPIRIT OF THE YEARS

Which overrides them as a whole its parts
In other entities.

SPIRIT SINISTER (aside)

　　　　　Limbs of Itself:
Each one a jot of It in quaint disguise?
I'll fear all men henceforward!

SPIRIT OF THE PITIES

Go to.　Let this terrestrial tragedy—

SPIRIT IRONIC

Nay, comedy—

SPIRIT OF THE PITIES

　　　　　　Let this earth-tragedy
Whereof ye spake, afford a spectacle
Forthwith conned closelier than your custom is.—

SPIRIT OF THE YEARS

How does it stand?　(To a Recording Angel)
　　　　　　Open and chant the page
Thou'st lately writ, that sums these happenings,
In brief reminder of their instant points
Slighted by us amid our converse here.

RECORDING ANGEL (from a book, in recitative)

Now mellow-eyed Peace is made captive,
    And Vengeance is chartered
To deal forth its dooms on the Peoples
    With sword and with spear.

Men's musings are busy with forecasts
    Of musters and battle,
And visions of shock and disaster
    Rise red on the year.

The easternmost ruler sits wistful,
    And tense he to midward;
The King to the west mans his borders
    In front and in rear.

While one they eye, flushed from his crowning,
    Ranks legions around him
To shake the enisled neighbour nation
    And close her career!

SEMICHORUS I. OF RUMOURS (aerial music)

O woven-winged squadrons of Toulon
    And fellows of Rochefort,
Wait, wait for a wind, and draw westward
    Ere Nelson be near!

For he reads not your force, or your freightage
    Of warriors fell-handed,
Or when they will join for the onset,
    Or whither they steer!

SEMICHORUS II

O Nelson, so zealous a watcher
    Through months-long of cruizing,
Thy foes may elude thee a moment,
    Put forth, and get clear;

And rendezvous westerly straightway
    With Spain's aiding navies,
And hasten to head violation
    Of Albion's frontier!

Spirit of the Years

Methinks too much assurance thrills your note
On secrets in my locker, gentle sprites;
But it may serve.—Our thought being now reflexed
To forces operant on this English isle,
Behoves it us to enter scene by scene,
And watch the spectacle of Europe's moves
In her embroil, as they were self-ordained
According to the naïve and liberal creed
Of our great-hearted young Compassionates,
Forgetting the Prime Mover of the gear,
As puppet-watchers him who pulls the strings.—
You'll mark the twitchings of this Bonaparte
As he with other figures foots his reel,
Until he twitch him into his lonely grave:
Also regard the frail ones that his flings
Have made gyrate like animalcula
In tepid pools.—Hence to the precinct, then,
And count as framework to the stagery
Yon architraves of sunbeam-smitten cloud.—
So may ye judge Earth's jackaclocks to be
Not fugled by one Will, but function-free.

The nether sky opens, and Europe is disclosed as a prone and emaciated figure, the Alps shaping like a backbone, and the branching mountain-chains like ribs, the peninsular plateau of Spain forming a head. Broad and lengthy lowlands stretch from the north of France across Russia like a grey-green garment hemmed by the Ural mountains and the glistening Arctic Ocean.

The point of view then sinks downwards through space, and draws near to the surface of the perturbed countries, where the peoples, distressed by events which they did not cause, are seen writhing, crawling, heaving, and vibrating in their various cities and nationalities.

Spirit of the Years (to the Spirit of the Pities)

As key-scene to the whole, I first lay bare
The Will-webs of thy fearful questioning;
For know that of my antique privileges
This gift to visualize the Mode is one
(Though by exhaustive strain and effort only).
See, then, and learn, ere my power pass again.

A new and penetrating light descends on the spectacle, enduing men and things with a seeming transparency, and exhibiting as one organism the anatomy of life and movement in all humanity and vitalized matter included in the display.

SPIRIT OF THE PITIES (after a pause)

Amid this scene of bodies substantive
Strange waves I sight like winds grown visible,
Which bear men's forms on their innumerous coils,
Twining and serpentining round and through.
Also retracting threads like gossamers—
Except in being irresistible—
Which complicate with some, and balance all.

SPIRIT OF THE YEARS

These are the Prime Volitions,—fibrils, veins,
Will-tissues, nerves, and pulses of the Cause,
That heave throughout the Earth's compositure.
Their sum is like the lobule of a Brain
Evolving always that it wots not of;
A Brain whose whole connotes the Everywhere,
And whose procedure may but be discerned
By phantom eyes like ours; the while unguessed
Of those it stirs, who (even as ye do) dream
Their motions free, their orderings supreme;
Each life apart from each, with power to mete
Its own day's measures; balanced, self complete;
Though they subsist but atoms of the One
Labouring through all, divisible from none;
But this no further now. Deem yet man's deeds self-done.

The anatomy of the Immanent Will disappears.

GENERAL CHORUS OF INTELLIGENCES (aerial music)

We'll close up Time, as a bird its van,
We'll traverse Space, as spirits can,
Link pulses severed by leagues and years,
Bring cradles into touch with biers;
So that the far-off Consequence appears
Prompt at the heel of foregone Cause.—
The PRIME, that willed ere wareness was,
Whose Brain perchance is Space, whose Thought its laws,
Which we as threads and streams discern,
We may but muse on, never learn.

END OF THE FORE SCENE

ACT FIRST

SCENE I

ENGLAND. A RIDGE IN WESSEX

The time is a fine day in March 1805. A highway crosses the ridge, which is near the sea, and the south coast is seen bounding the landscape below, the open Channel extending beyond.

SPIRIT OF THE YEARS

Hark now, and gather how the martial mood
Stirs England's humblest hearts. Anon we'll trace
Its heavings in the upper coteries there.

SPIRIT SINISTER

Ay ; begin small, and so lead up to the greater. It is a sound
dramatic principle. I always aim to follow it in my pestilences,
fires, famines, and other comedies. And though, to be sure, I did
not in my Lisbon earthquake, I did in my French Terror, and my
St. Domingo burlesque.

SPIRIT OF THE YEARS

THY Lisbon earthquake, THY French Terror. Wait.
Thinking thou will'st, thou dost but indicate.

A stage-coach enters, with passengers outside. Their voices after the fore-going sound small and commonplace, as from another medium.

FIRST PASSENGER

There seems to be a deal of traffic over Ridgeway, even at this time o' year.

SECOND PASSENGER

Yes. It is because the King and Court are coming down here later on. They wake up this part rarely ! . . . See, now, how the Channel and coast open out like a chart. That patch of mist below us is the town we are bound for. There's the Isle of Slingers beyond, like a floating snail. That wide bay on the right is where the " Abergavenny," Captain John Wordsworth, was wrecked last month. One can see half across to France up here.

FIRST PASSENGER

Half across. And then another little half, and then all that's behind—the Corsican mischief!

SECOND PASSENGER

Yes. People who live hereabout—I am a native of these parts—feel the nearness of France more than they do inland.

FIRST PASSENGER

That's why we have seen so many of these marching regiments on the road. This year his grandest attempt upon us is to be made, I reckon.

SECOND PASSENGER

May we be ready!

FIRST PASSENGER

Well, we ought to be. We've had alarms enough, God knows.

THIRD PASSENGER

I much doubt his intention to come at all.

Some companies of infantry are seen ahead, and the coach presently overtakes them.

SOLDIERS (singing as they walk)

We be the King's men, hale and hearty,
Marching to meet one Buonaparty;
If he won't sail, lest the wind should blow,
We shall have marched for nothing, O!
          Right fol-lol!

We be the King's men, hale and hearty,
Marching to meet one Buonaparty;
If he be sea-sick, says "No, no!"
We shall have marched for nothing, O!
          Right fol-lol!

The soldiers draw aside, and the coach passes on.

SECOND PASSENGER

Is there truth in it that Bonaparte wrote a letter to the King last month?

First Passenger

Yes, sir. A letter in his own hand, in which he expected the King to reply to him in the same manner.

Soldiers (continuing, as they are left behind)

We be the King's men, hale and hearty,
Marching to meet one Buonaparty ;
Never mind, mates ; we'll be merry, though
We may have marched for nothing, O !
Right fol-lol !

Third Passenger

And was Boney's letter friendly ?

First Passenger

Certainly, sir. He requested peace with the King.

Third Passenger

And why shouldn't the King reply in the same manner ?

First Passenger

What ! Encourage this man in an act of shameless presumption, and give him the pleasure of considering himself the equal of the King of England—whom he actually calls his brother !

Third Passenger

He must be taken for what he is, not for what he was ; and if he calls King George his brother it doesn't speak badly for his friendliness.

First Passenger

Whether or no, the King, rightly enough, did not reply in person, but through Lord Mulgrave our Foreign Minister, to the effect that his Britannic Majesty cannot give a specific answer till he has communicated with the Continental powers.

Third Passenger

Both the manner and the matter of the reply are British ; but a huge mistake.

FIRST PASSENGER

Sir, am I to deem you a friend of Bonaparte, a traitor to your country——

THIRD PASSENGER

Damn my wig, sir, if I'll be called a traitor by you or any Court sycophant at all at all!   [He unpacks a case of pistols.

SECOND PASSENGER

Gentlemen, forbear, forbear! Should such differences be suffered to arise on a spot where we may, in less than three months, be fighting for our very existence? This is foolish, I say. Heaven alone, who reads the secrets of this man's heart, can tell what his meaning and intent may be, and if his letter has been answered wisely or no.

The coach is stopped to skid the wheel for the descent of the hill, and before it starts again a dusty horseman overtakes it.

SEVERAL PASSENGERS

A London messenger! (To horseman) Any news, sir? We are from Bristol only.

HORSEMAN

Yes; much. We have declared war against Spain, an error giving vast delight to France. Bonaparte says he will date his next dispatches from London, and the landing of his army may be daily expected.

[Exit horseman.

THIRD PASSENGER (to First)

Sir, I apologize. He's not to be trusted! War is his name, and aggression is with him!

He repacks the pistols. A silence follows. The coach and passengers move downwards and disappear towards the coast.

SPIRIT OF THE PITIES

Ill chanced it that the English monarch George
Did not respond to the said Emperor!

SPIRIT SINISTER

I saw good sport therein, and pæan'd the Will
To unimpel so stultifying a move!
Which would have marred the European broil,
And sheathed all swords, and silenced every gun
That riddles human flesh.

SPIRIT OF THE PITIES

O say no more;

If aught could gratify the Absolute
'Twould verily be thy censure, not thy praise!

SPIRIT OF THE YEARS

The ruling was that we should witness things
And not dispute them.   To the drama, then.
Emprizes over-Channel are the key
To this land's stir and ferment.—Thither we.

Clouds gather over the scene, and slowly open elsewhere.

SCENE II

PARIS.   OFFICE OF THE MINISTER OF MARINE

ADMIRAL DECRÈS seated at a table.   A knock without.

DECRÈS

Come in !   Good news, I hope !

[An attendant enters.

ATTENDANT

A courier, sir.

DECRÈS

Show him in straightway.

[The attendant goes out.

From the Emperor
As I expected !

A courier is admitted, who delivers a dispatch.

COURIER

Sir, for your own hand
And yours alone.

DECRÈS

Thanks.   Be in waiting near.

[The courier withdraws

DECRÈS *reads :*

" I am resolved that no wild dream of Ind,
And what we there might win ; or of the West,

And bold re-conquest there of Surinam
And other Dutch retreats along those coasts,
Or British islands nigh, shall draw me now
From piercing into England through Boulogne
As lined in my first plan.   If I do strike,
I strike effectively ; to forge which feat
There's but one way—planting a mortal wound
In England's heart—the very English land—
Whose insolent and cynical reply
To my well-based complaint on breach of faith
Concerning Malta, as at Amiens pledged,
Has lighted up anew such flames of ire
As may involve the world.—Now to the case :
Our naval forces can be all assembled
Without the foe's foreknowledge or surmise,
By these rules following ; to whose text I ask
Your gravest application ; and, when conned,
That steadfastly you stand by word and word,
Making no question of one jot therein.

    " First, then, let Villeneuve wait a favouring wind
For process westward swift to Martinique,
Coaxing the English after.   Join him there
Gravina, Missiessy, and Ganteaume ;
Which junction once effected all our keels—
Now nigh to sixty sail—regain the Manche,
While the pursuers linger in the West
At hopeless fault.—Having hoodwinked them thus,
Our boats skim over, disembark the army,
And in the twinkling of a patriot's eye
All London will be ours.

    " In strictest secrecy carve this to shape—
Let never an admiral or captain scent
Save Villeneuve and Ganteaume ; and pen each charge
With your own quill.   The surelier to outwit them
I start for Italy ; and there, as 'twere
Engrossed in fêtes and Coronation rites,
Abide till, at the need, I reach Boulogne,
And head the enterprize.—NAPOLÉON."

      DECRÈS reflects, and turns to write.

SPIRIT OF THE PITIES

More ills?   How is Decrès ordained to move?

SPIRIT OF THE YEARS

He buckles to the work.   First to Villeneuve,
His onetime comrade and his boyhood's friend,
Now lingering at Toulon, he jots swift lines,
Then duly to Ganteaume.—They are sealed forthwith,
And superscribed: "Break not till on the main."

Boisterous singing is heard in the street.

SPIRIT OF THE PITIES

I hear confused and simmering sounds without,
Like those which thrill the hives at evenfall
When swarming pends.

SPIRIT OF THE YEARS

                They but proclaim the crowd,
Which sings and shouts its hot enthusiasms
For this dead-ripe design on England's shore,
Till the persuasion of its own plump words,
Acting upon mercurial temperaments,
Makes hope as prophecy. "Our Emperor
Will show himself (say they) in this exploit
Unwavering, keen, and irresistible
As is the lightning-prong. Our vast flotillas
Have been embodied as by sorcery;
Soldiers made seamen, and the ports transformed
To rocking cities casemented with guns.
Against these valiants balance England's means:
Raw merchant-fellows from the counting-house,
Raw labourers from the fields, who thumb for arms
Clumsy untempered pikes forged hurriedly,
And cry them full-equipt. Their batteries,
Their flying carriages, their catamarans,
Shall profit not, and in one summer night
We'll find us there!"

RECORDING ANGEL

          And is this prophecy true?

SPIRIT OF THE YEARS
Occasion will reveal.

SHADE OF THE EARTH
                 What boots it, Sire,
To down this dynasty, set that one up,
Goad panting peoples to the throes thereof,
Make wither here my fruit, maintain it there,
And hold me travailling through fineless years
In vain and objectless monotony,
When all such tedious conjuring could be shunned
By uncreation?   Howsoever wise
The governance of these massed mortalities,
A juster wisdom his who should have ruled
They had not been.

SPIRIT OF THE YEARS
               Nay, something hidden urged
The giving matter motion; and these coils
Are, maybe, good as any.

SPIRIT OF THE PITIES
                   But why any?

SPIRIT OF THE YEARS
Sprite of Compassions, ask the Immanent!
I am but an accessory of Its works,
Whom the Ages render conscious; and at most
Figure as bounden witness of Its laws.

SPIRIT OF THE PITIES
How ask the aim of unrelaxing Will
Tranced in Its purpose to unknowingness?
(If thy words, Ancient Phantom, token true).

SPIRIT OF THE YEARS
Thou answerest well.   But cease to ask of me.
Meanwhile the mime proceeds.—We turn herefrom,
Change our homuncules, and observe forthwith
How the High Influence sways the English realm,
And how the jacks lip out their reasonings there.

       The Cloud-curtain draws.

SCENE III

LONDON.   THE OLD HOUSE OF COMMONS

A long chamber with a gallery on each side supported by thin columns having gilt Ionic capitals.   Three round-headed windows are at the further end, above the Speaker's chair, which is backed by a huge pedimented structure in white and gilt, surmounted by the lion and the unicorn.   The windows are uncurtained, one being open, through which some boughs are seen waving in the midnight gloom without.   Wax candles, burnt low, wave and gutter in a brass chandelier which hangs from the middle of the ceiling, and in branches projecting from the galleries.

The House is sitting, the benches, which extend round to the Speaker's elbows, being closely packed, and the galleries likewise full.   Among the members present on the Government side are PITT and other ministers with their supporters, including CANNING, CASTLEREAGH, LORD C. SOMERSET, ERSKINE, W. DUNDAS, HUSKISSON, ROSE, BEST, ELLIOT, DALLAS, and the general body of the party.   On the opposite side are noticeable FOX, SHERIDAN, WINDHAM, WHITBREAD, GREY, T. GRENVILLE, TIERNEY, EARL TEMPLE, PONSONBY, G. and H. WALPOLE, DUDLEY NORTH, and TIMOTHY SHELLEY.   Speaker ABBOT occupies the Chair.

SPIRIT OF THE YEARS (to two Recording Angels)

As prelude to the scene, as means to aid
Our younger comrades in its construing,
Pray spread your scripture, and rehearse in brief
The reasonings here of late—to whose effects
Words of to-night form sequence.

The Recording Angels chant from their books, antiphonally, in a minor recitative.

ANGEL I (aerial music)

Feeble-framed dull unresolve, unresourcefulness,
Sat in the halls of the Kingdom's high Councillors,
Whence the grey glooms of a ghost-eyed despondency
Wanned as with winter the national mind.

ANGEL II

England stands forth to the sword of Napoléon
Nakedly—not an ally in support of her;
Men and munitions dispersed inexpediently;
Projects of range and scope poorly defined.

ANGEL I

Once more doth Pitt deem the land crying loud to him.—
Frail though and spent, and an-hungered for restfulness
Once more responds he, dead fervours to energize,
Aims to concentre, slack efforts to bind.

ANGEL II

Ere the first fruit thereof voices grow audible,
Holding as hapless his dream of good guardianship,
Jestingly, earnestly, shouting it serviceless,
Tardy, inept, and uncouthly designed.

ANGELS I AND II

So now, to-night, in the slashing old sentences,
Hear them speak,—gravely these, those with gay-
    heartedness,—
Midst their admonishments little conceiving how
Scarlet the scroll that the years will unwind!

SPIRIT OF THE PITIES (to the Spirit of the Years)

Let us put on and suffer for the nonce
The feverish fleshings of Humanity,
And join the pale debaters here convened.
So may thy soul be won to sympathy
By donning their poor mould.

SPIRIT OF THE YEARS

                I'll humour thee,
Though my unpassioned essence could not change
Did I incarn in moulds of all mankind!

SPIRIT IRONIC

'Tis enough to make every little dog in England run to mixen
to hear this Pitt sung so strenuously! I'll be the third of the
incarnate, on the chance of hearing the tune played the other way.

SPIRIT SINISTER

And I the fourth. There's sure to be something in my line
toward, where politicians are gathered together!

The four Phantoms enter the Gallery of the House in the disguise of
ordinary strangers.

SHERIDAN (rising)

The Bill I would have leave to introduce
Is framed, sir, to repeal last Session's Act,
By party-scribes intituled a Provision
For England's Proper Guard ; but elsewhere known
As Mr. Pitt's new Patent Parish Pill.   (Laughter.)
   The ministerial countenances, I mark,
Congeal to dazed surprise at my straight motion—
Why, passes sane conjecture.   It may be
That, with a haughty and unwavering faith
In their own battering-rams of argument,
They deemed our buoyance whelmed, and sapped, and
     sunk
To hope's sheer bottom, whence a miracle
Was all could friend and float us ; or, maybe,
They are amazed at our rude disrespect
In making mockery of an English Law
Sprung sacred from the King's own Premier's brain !
—I hear them snort ; but let them wince at will,
My duty must be done ; shall be done quickly
By citing some few facts.
                    An Act for our defence !
It weakens, not defends ; and oversea
Swoln France's despot and his myrmidons
This moment know it, and can scoff thereat.
Our people know it too—those who can peer
Behind the scenes of this poor painted show
Called soldiering !—The Act has failed, must fail,
As my right honourable friend well proved
When speaking t'other night, whose silencing
By his right honourable *vis-à-vis*
Was of the genuine Governmental sort,
And like the catamarans their sapience shaped
All fizzle and no harm.   (Laughter.)   The Act, in brief,
Effects this much : that the whole force of England
Is strengthened by—eleven thousand men !
So sorted that the British infantry
Are now eight hundred less than heretofore !
   In Ireland, where the glamouring influence
Of the right honourable gentleman
Prevails with magic might, *eleven* men

Have been amassed.   And in the Cinque-Port towns,
Where he is held in absolute veneration,
His method has so quickened martial fire
As to bring in——one man.   O would that man
Might meet my sight!   (Laughter.)   A Hercules, no doubt,
A god-like emanation from this Act,
Who with his single arm will overthrow
All Buonaparté's legions ere their keels
Have scraped one pebble of our fortless shores! . . .
Such is my motion, sir, and such my mind.

                              [He sits down amid cheers.

    The candle-snuffers go round, and PITT rises.   During the momentary
pause before he speaks the House assumes an attentive stillness, in which can
be heard the rustling of the trees without, a horn from an early coach, and
the voice of the watch crying the hour.

                              PITT

Not one on this side but appreciates
Those mental gems and airy pleasantries
Flashed by the honourable gentleman,
Who shines in them by birthright.   Each device
Of drollery he has laboured to outshape,
(Or treasured up from others who have shaped it,)
Displays that are the conjurings of the moment,
(Or mellowed and matured by sleeping on)——
Dry hoardings in his book of commonplace,
Stored without stint of toil through days and months——
He heaps into one mass, and lights and fans
As fuel for his flaming eloquence,
Mouthed and maintained without a thought or care
If germane to the theme, or not at all.
    Now vain indeed it were should I assay
To match him in such sort.   For, sir, alas,
To use imagination as the ground
Of chronicle, take myth and merry tale
As texts for prophecy, is not my gift
Being but a person primed with simple fact,
Unprinked by jewelled art.——But to the thing.
    The preparations of the enemy,
Doggedly bent to desolate our land,
Advance with a sustained activity.
They are seen, they are known, by you and by us all.

But they evince no clear-eyed tentative
In furtherance of the threat, whose coming off,
Ay, years may yet postpone ; whereby the Act
Will far outstrip him, and the thousands called
Duly to join the ranks by its provisions,
In process sure, if slow, will ratch the lines
Of English regiments—seasoned, cool, resolved—
To glorious length and firm prepotency.
And why, then, should we dream of its repeal
Ere profiting by its advantages ?
Must the House listen to such wilding words
As this proposal, at the very hour
When the Act's gearing finds its ordered grooves
And circles into full utility ?
The motion of the honourable gentleman
Reminds me aptly of a publican
Who should, when malting, mixing, mashing's past,
Fermenting, barrelling, and spigoting,
Quick taste the brew, and shake his sapient head,
And cry in acid voice : The ale is new !
Brew old, you varlets ; cast this slop away !   (Cheers.)
     But gravely, sir, I would conclude to-night,
And, as a serious man on serious things,
I now speak here. . . . I pledge myself to this :
Unprecedented and magnificent
As were our strivings in the previous war,
Our efforts in the present shall transcend them,
As men will learn.   Such efforts are not sized
By this light measuring-rule my critic here
Whips from his pocket like a clerk-o'-works ! . .
Tasking and toilsome war's details must be,
And toilsome, too, must be their criticism,—
Not in a moment's stroke extemporized.
     The strange fatality that haunts the times
Wherein our lot is cast, has no example.
Times are they fraught with peril, trouble, gloom ;
We have to mark their lourings, and to face them.
Sir, reading thus the full significance
Of these big days, large though my lackings be,
Can any hold of those who know my past
That I, of all men, slight our safeguarding ?
No : by all honour no !—Were I convinced

That such could be the mind of members here,
My sorrowing thereat would doubly shade
The shade on England now!   So I do trust
All in the House will take my tendered word,
And credit my deliverance here to-night,
That in this vital point of watch and ward
Against the threatenings from yonder coast
We stand prepared ; and under Providence
Shall fend whatever hid or open stroke
A foe may deal.

*He sits down amid loud ministerial cheers, with symptoms of great
exhaustion.*

WINDHAM

The question that compels the House to-night
Is not of differences in wit and wit,
But if for England it be well or no
To null the new-fledged Act, as one inept
For setting up with speed and hot effect
The red machinery of desperate war.—
Whatever it may do, or not, it stands,
A statesman's raw experiment.   If ill,
Shall more experiments and more be tried
In stress of jeopardy that stirs demand
For sureness of proceeding?   Must this House
Exchange safe action based on practised lines
For yet more ventures into risks unknown
To gratify a quaint projector's whim,
While enemies hang grinning round our gates
To profit by mistake?
                          My friend who spoke
Found comedy in the matter.   Comical
As it may be in parentage and feature,
Most grave and tragic in its consequence
This Act may prove.   We are moving thoughtlessly,
We squander precious, brief, life-saving time
On idle guess-games.   Fail the measure must,
Nay, failed it has already ; and should rouse
Resolve in its progenitor himself
To move for its repeal!   (Cheers.)

WHITBREAD

I rise but to subjoin a phrase or two
To those of my right honourable friend.
I, too, am one who reads the present pinch
As passing all our risks of heretofore.
For why?   Our bold and reckless enemy,
Relaxing not his plans, has treasured time
To mass his monstrous force on all the coigns
From which our coast is close assailable.
Ay, even afloat his concentrations work:
Two vast united squadrons of his sail
Move at this moment viewless on the seas.——
Their whereabouts, untraced, unguessable,
Will not be known to us till some black blow
Be dealt by them in some undreamt-of quarter
To knell our rule.
That we are reasonably enfenced therefrom
By such an Act is but a madman's dream. . . .
A commonwealth so situate cries aloud
For more, far mightier, measures!   End an Act
In Heaven's name, then, which only can obstruct
The fabrication of more trusty tackle
For building up an army!   (Cheers.)

BATHURST

                Sir, the point
To any sober mind is bright as noon;
Whether the Act should have befitting trial
Or be blasphemed at sight.   I firmly hold
The latter loud iniquity.——One task
Is theirs who would inter this corpse-cold Act—
(So said)——to bring to birth a substitute!
Sir, they have none; they have given no thought to one,
And thus their deeds incautiously disclose
Their cloaked intention and most secret aim!
With them the question is not how to frame
A finer trick to trounce intrusive foes,
But who shall be the future ministers
To whom such trick against intrusive foes,
Whatever it may prove, shall be entrusted!
They even ask the country gentlemen

To join them in this job. But, God be praised,
Those gentlemen are sound, and of repute ;
Their names, their property, their character,
Their numbers, their attainments, and their blood,
                                    (Ironical Opposition cheers.)
Safeguard them from an onslaught on an Act
For ends so sinister and palpable ! (Cheers and jeerings.)

FULLER

I disapprove of censures of this Act.—
All who can entertain such hostile thought
Would swear that black is white, that night is day.
No honest man will join a reckless crew
Who'd overthrow their country for their gain ! (Laughter.)

TIERNEY

It is incumbent on me to declare
In the last speaker's face my censure, based
On grounds most clear and constitutional.—
An Act it is that studies to create
A standing army, large and permanent ;
Which kind of force has ever been beheld
With jealous-eyed disfavour in this House.
It makes for sure oppression, binding men
To serve for less than service proves it worth
Conditioned by no hampering penalty.
For these and late-spoke reasons, then, I say,
Let not the Act deface the statute-book,
But blot it out forthwith. (Hear, hear.)

FOX (rising amid cheers)

                        At this late hour,
After the riddling fire the Act has drawn on't,
My words shall hold the House the briefest while.
Too obvious to the most unwilling mind
It grows that the existence of this law
Experience and reflection have condemned.
Professing to do much, it makes for nothing ;
Vouched as assuring all, it comforts none.
Not only so ; while feeble in effect
It shows it vicious in its principle.
Engaging to raise men for the common weal,

It sets a harmful and unequal tax
Capriciously on our communities.——
The annals of a century fail to show
More flagrant cases of oppressiveness
Than those this statute works to perpetrate,
Which (like all Bills this favoured statesman frames,
And clothes with tapestries of rhetoric
Disguising their real web of commonplace)
Though held as shaped for English bulwarking,
Breathes in its heart perversities of party,
And instincts toward oligarchic power,
Galling the many to relieve the few!   (Cheers.)
        Whatever breadth and sense of equity
Inform the methods of this minister,
Those mitigants nearly always trace their root
To measures that his predecessors wrought.
And ere his Government can dare assert
Superior claims to England's confidence,
They owe it to their honour and good name
To furnish better proof of such a claim
Than is revealed by the abortiveness
Of this thing called an Act for our Defence.
    To the great gifts of its artificer
No member of this House is more disposed
To yield full recognition than am I.
No man has found more reason so to do
Through the long roll of disputatious years
Wherein we have stood opposed. . . .
But if one single fact could counsel me
To entertain a doubt of those great gifts,
And cancel faith in his capacity,
That fact would be the vast imprudence shown
In staking recklessly repute like his
On such an Act as he has offered us——
So false in principle, so poor in fruit.
Sir, the achievements and effects thereof
Have furnished not one fragile argument
Which all the partiality of friendship
Can kindle to consider as the mark
Of a clear, vigorous, freedom-fostering mind!

He sits down amid lengthy cheering from the Opposition.

SHERIDAN

My summary shall be brief, and to the point.—
The said right honourable Prime Minister
Has thought it proper to declare my speech
The jesting of an irresponsible ;—
Words from a person who has never read
The Act he claims him urgent to repeal.
Such quips and quizzings (as he reckons them)
He implicates as gathered from long hoards
Stored up with cruel care, to be discharged
With sudden blaze of pyrotechnic art
On the devoted, gentle, shrinking head
O' the right incomparable gentleman !   (Laughter.)
But were my humble, solemn, sad oration   (Laughter.)
Indeed such rattle as he rated it,
Is it not strange, and passing precedent,
That the illustrious chief of Government
Should have uprisen with such indecent speed
And strenuously replied ?   He, sir, knows well
That vast and luminous talents like his own
Could not have been demanded to choke off
A witcraft marked by nothing more of weight
Than ignorant irregularity !
Nec Deus intersit—and so-and-so—
Is a well-worn citation whose close fit
None will perceive more clearly in this Fane
Than its presiding Deity opposite.   (Laughter.)
His thunderous answer thus perforce condemns him !
    Moreover, to top all, the while replying,
He still thought best to leave intact the reasons
On which my blame was founded !

                    Thus, then, stands
My motion unimpaired, convicting clearly
Of dire perversion that capacity
We formerly admired.—   (Cries of " Oh, oh.")
                    This minister
Whose circumventions never circumvent,
Whose coalitions fail to coalesce ;
This dab at secret treaties known to all,
This darling of the aristocracy—

(Laughter, " Oh, oh," cheers, and cries of " Divide.")

Has brought the millions to the verge of ruin,
By pledging them to Continental quarrels
Of which we see no end!   (Cheers.)

The members rise to divide.

SPIRIT OF THE PITIES

It irks me that they thus should Yea and Nay
As though a power lay in their oraclings,
If each decision work unconsciously,
And would be operant though unloosened were
A single lip!

SPIRIT OF RUMOUR

There may react on things
Some influence from these, indefinitely,
And even on That, whose outcome we all are.

SPIRIT OF THE YEARS

Hypotheses!—More boots it to remind
The younger here of our ethereal band
And hierarchy of Intelligences,
That this thwart Parliament whose moods we watch—
So insular, empiric, un-ideal—
May figure forth in sharp and salient lines
To retrospective eyes of afterdays,
And print its legend large on History.
For one cause—if I read the signs aright—
To-night's appearance of its Minister
In the assembly of his long-time sway
Is near his last, and themes to-night launched forth
Will take a tincture from that memory,
When men recall the scene and circumstance
That hung about his pleadings.—But no more;
The ritual of each party is rehearsed,
Dislodging not one vote or prejudice;
The ministers their ministries retain,
And Ins as Ins, and Outs as Outs, remain.

SPIRIT OF THE PITIES

Meanwhile what of the Foeman's vast array
That wakes these tones?

SPIRIT OF THE YEARS

> *Abide the event, young Shade:*
> *Soon stars will shut and show a spring-eyed dawn,*
> *And sunbeams fountain forth, that will arouse*
> *Those forming bands to full activity.*

An honourable member reports that he spies strangers.

> *A timely token that we dally here!*
> *We now cast off these mortal manacles,*
> *And speed us seaward.*

The Phantoms vanish from the Gallery. The members file out to the lobbies. The House and Westminster recede into the films of night, and the point of observation shifts rapidly across the Channel.

SCENE IV

THE HARBOUR OF BOULOGNE

The morning breaks, radiant with early sunlight. The French Army of Invasion is disclosed. On the hills on either side of the town and behind appear large military camps formed of timber huts. Lower down are other camps of more or less permanent kind, the whole affording accommodation for one hundred and fifty thousand men.

South of the town is an extensive basin surrounded by quays, the heaps of fresh soil around showing it to be a recent excavation from the banks of the Liane. The basin is crowded with the flotilla, consisting of hundreds of vessels of sundry kinds : flat-bottomed brigs with guns and two masts ; boats of one mast, carrying each an artillery waggon, two guns, and a two-stalled horse-box ; transports with three low masts ; and long narrow pinnaces arranged for many oars.

Timber, saw-mills, and new-cut planks spread in profusion around, and many of the town residences are seen to be adapted for warehouses and infirmaries.

DUMB SHOW

Moving in this scene are countless companies of soldiery, engaged in a drill-practice of embarking and disembarking, and of hoisting horses into the vessels and landing them again. Vehicles bearing provisions of many sorts load and unload before the temporary warehouses. Further off, on the open land, bodies of troops are at field-drill. Other bodies of soldiers, half stripped and encrusted with mud, are labouring as navvies in repairing the excavations.

An English squadron of about twenty sail, comprising a ship or two of the line, frigates, brigs, and luggers, confronts the busy spectacle from the sea.

The Show presently dims and becomes broken, till only its flashes and gleams are visible. Anon a curtain of cloud closes over it.

SCENE V

LONDON.　THE HOUSE OF A LADY OF QUALITY

A fashionable crowd is present at an evening party, which includes the DUKES of BEAUFORT and RUTLAND, LORDS MALMESBURY, HARROWBY, ELDON, GRENVILLE, CASTLEREAGH, SIDMOUTH, and MULGRAVE, with their ladies; also CANNING, PERCEVAL, TOWNSHEND, LADY ANNE HAMILTON, MRS. DAMER, LADY CAROLINE LAMB, and many other notables.

A GENTLEMAN (offering his snuff-box)

So, then, the Treaty anxiously concerted
Between ourselves and frosty Muscovy
Is duly signed?

A CABINET MINISTER

　　　　　　Was signed a few days back,
And is in force.　And we do firmly hope
The loud pretensions and the stunning dins
From new aggressiveness by France's chief,
Now daily heard, these laudable exertions
May keep in curb; that ere our greening land
Darken its leaves beneath the Dogday suns,
The independence of the Continent
May be assured, and all the rumpled flags
Of famous dynasties so foully mauled,
Extend their honoured hues as heretofore.

GENTLEMAN

So be it.　Yet this man is a volcano;
And proven 'tis, by God, volcanoes choked
Have ere now turned to earthquakes!

A lady comes up and playfully taps his arm.

LADY

　　　　　　What's the news?—
The chequerboard of diplomatic moves
Is London, all the world knows: here are born
All inspirations of the Continent—
So tell!

GENTLEMAN

　　Ay.　Inspirations now abound!

LADY

Nay, but your looks are grave ! That measured speech
Betokened matter that will waken us.—
Is it some piquant cruelty of his ?
Or other tickling horror from abroad
The packet has brought in ?

GENTLEMAN

The treaty's signed !

MINISTER

Whereby the parties mutually agree
To knit in union and in general league
All outraged Europe.

LADY

So to knit sounds well ;
But how ensure its not unravelling ?

MINISTER

Well ; by the terms. There are among them these:
Five hundred thousand active men in arms
Shall strike (supported by Britannic aid
In vessels, men, and money subsidies)
To free North Germany and Hanover
From trampling foes ; deliver Switzerland,
Unbind the galled republic of the Dutch,
Rethrone in Piedmont the Sardinian King,
Make Naples sword-proof, un-French Italy
From shore to shore ; and thoroughly guarantee
A settled order to the divers states ;
Thus rearing breachless barriers in each realm
Against the thrust of his usurping hand.

SPIRIT OF THE YEARS

They trow not what is shaping otherwhere
The while they talk thus stoutly !

SPIRIT OF RUMOUR

Bid me go
And join them, and all blandly kindle them
By bringing, ere material transit can,
A new surprise !

SPIRIT OF THE YEARS

Yea, for a moment, wouldst.

The Spirit of Rumour enters the apartment in the form of a personage of fashion, newly arrived. He advances and addresses the group.

SPIRIT

The Treaty moves all tongues to-night.—Ha, well—
So much on paper!

GENTLEMAN

What on land and sea?
You look, old friend, full primed with latest thence.

SPIRIT

Yea, this. The Italy our mighty pact
Delivers from the French and Bonaparte
Makes haste to crown him!—Turning from Boulogne
He speeds toward Milan, there to glory him
In second coronation by the Pope,
And set upon his irrepressible brow
Lombardy's iron crown.

The Spirit of Rumour mingles with the throng, moves away, and disappears.

LADY

Fair Italy,
Alas, alas!

LORD

Yet thereby English folk
Are freed him.—Faith, as ancient people say,
It's an ill wind that blows good luck to none!

MINISTER

Who is your friend that drops so airily
This precious pinch of salt on our raw skin?

GENTLEMAN

Why, Norton. You know Norton well enough?

MINISTER

Nay, 'twas not he. Norton of course I know.
I thought him Stewart for a moment, but——

LADY

But I well scanned him—'twas Lord Abercorn ;
For, said I to myself, " O quaint old beau,
To sleep in black silk sheets so funnily "—
That is, if the town rumour on't be true.

LORD

My wig, ma'am, no ! 'Twas a much younger man.

GENTLEMAN

But let me call him !   Monstrous silly this,
That I don't know my friends !

They look around. The gentleman goes among the surging and babbling guests, makes inquiries, and returns with a perplexed look.

GENTLEMAN

          They tell me, sure,
That he's not here to-night !

MINISTER

          I can well swear
It was not Norton.—'Twas some lively buck,
Who chose to put himself in masquerade
And enter for a whim.   I'll tell our host.
—Meantime the absurdity of his report
Is more than manifested.   How knows he
The plans of Bonaparte by lightning-flight,
Before another man in England knows ?

LADY

Something uncanny's in it all, if true.
Good Lord, the thought gives me a sudden sweat,
That fairly makes my linen stick to me !

MINISTER

Ha-ha ! 'Tis excellent.   But we'll find out
Who this impostor was.

They disperse, look furtively for the stranger, and speak of the incident to others of the crowded company.

Spirit of the Years

Now let us vision onward, till we sight
Famed Milan's aisles of marble, sun-alight,
And there behold, unbid, the Coronation-rite.

The confused tongues of the assembly waste away into distance, till they are heard but as the babblings of the sea from a high cliff, the scene becoming small and indistinct therewith. This passes into silence, and the whole disappears.

SCENE VI

MILAN.   THE CATHEDRAL

The interior of the building on a sunny May day.

The walls, arches, and columns are draped in silk fringed with gold. A gilded throne stands in front of the High Altar. A closely packed assemblage, attired in every variety of rich fabric and fashion, waits in breathless expectation.

DUMB SHOW

From a private corridor leading to a door in the aisle the EMPRESS JOSÉPHINE enters, in a shining costume, and diamonds that collect rainbow-colours from the sunlight piercing the clerestory windows. She is preceded by PRINCESS ELIZA, and surrounded by her ladies. A pause follows, and then comes the procession of the EMPEROR, consisting of hussars, heralds, pages, aides-de-camp, presidents of institutions, officers of state bearing the insignia of the Empire and of Italy, and seven ladies with offerings. The EMPEROR himself is in royal robes, wearing the Imperial crown, and carrying the sceptre. He is followed by ministers and officials of the household. His gait is rather defiant than dignified, and a bluish pallor overspreads his face.

He is met by the Cardinal Archbishop CAPRARA and the clergy, who burn incense before him as he proceeds towards the throne. Rolling notes of music burst forth, and loud applause from the congregation.

Spirit of the Pities

What is the creed that these rich rites disclose?

Spirit of the Years

A local cult, called Christianity,
Which the wild dramas of the wheeling spheres
Include, with divers other such, in dim
Pathetical and brief parentheses,

Beyond whose span, uninfluenced, unconcerned,
The systems of the suns go sweeping on
With all their many-mortaled planet train
In mathematic roll unceasingly.

SPIRIT OF THE PITIES

I did not recognize it here, forsooth ;
Though in its early, lovingkindly days
Of gracious purpose it was much to me.

ARCHBISHOP (addressing BONAPARTE)

Sire, with that clemency and right goodwill
Which beautify Imperial Majesty,
You deigned acceptance of the homages
That we the clergy and the Milanese
Were proud to offer when your entrance here
Streamed radiance on our ancient capital.
Please, then, to consummate the boon to-day
Beneath this holy roof, so soon to thrill
With solemn strains and lifting harmonies
Befitting such a coronation hour ;
And bend a tender fatherly regard
On this assembly, now at one with me
To supplicate the Author of All Good
That He endow your most Imperial person
With every Heavenly gift.

The procession advances, and the EMPEROR seats himself on the throne,
with the banners and regalia of the Empire on his right, and those of Italy
on his left hand.   Shouts and triumphal music accompany the proceedings,
after which Divine service commences.

SPIRIT OF THE PITIES

Thus are the self-styled servants of the Highest
Constrained by earthly duress to embrace
Mighty imperiousness as it were choice,
And hand the Italian sceptre unto one
Who, with a saturnine, sour-humoured grin,
Professed at first to flout antiquity,
Scorn limp conventions, smile at mouldy thrones,
And level dynasts down to journeymen !—
Yet he, advancing swiftly on that track
Whereby his active soul, fair Freedom's child,

Makes strange decline, now labours to achieve
The thing it overthrew.

SPIRIT OF THE YEARS

Thou reasonest ever thuswise—even as if
A self-formed force had urged his loud career.

SPIRIT SINISTER

Do not the prelate's accents falter thin,
His lips with inheld laughter grow deformed,
While blessing one whose aim is but to win
The golden seats that other b——s have warmed?

SPIRIT OF THE YEARS

Soft, jester; scorn not puppetry so skilled,
Even made to feel by one men call the Dame.

SHADE OF THE EARTH

Yea; that they feel, and puppetry remain,
Is an owned flaw in her consistency
Men love to dub Dame Nature—that lay-shape
They use to hang phenomena upon—
Whose deftest mothering in fairest spheres
Is girt about by terms inexorable!

SPIRIT SINISTER

The lady's remark is apposite, and reminds me that I may as
well hold my tongue as desired.   For if my casual scorn, Father
Years, should set thee trying to prove that there is any right or
reason in the Universe, thou wilt not accomplish it by Doomsday!
Small blame to her, however; she must cut her coat according to
her cloth, as they would say below there.

SPIRIT OF THE YEARS

O would that I could move It to enchain thee,
And shut thee up a thousand years !—(to cite
A grim terrestrial tale of one thy like)
Thou Iago of the Incorporeal World,
" As they would say below there."

SPIRIT OF THE PITIES

Would thou couldst!
But move That scoped above percipience, Sire,
It cannot be!

SHADE OF THE EARTH

The spectacle proceeds.

SPIRIT SINISTER

And we may as well give all attention thereto, for the evils at
work in other continents are not worth eyesight by comparison.

The ceremonial in the Cathedral continues.   NAPOLÉON goes to the front
of the altar, ascends the steps, and, taking up the crown of Lombardy,
places it on his head.

NAPOLÉON

'Tis God has given it to me.   So be it.
Let any who shall touch it now beware!

(Reverberations of applause.)

The Sacrament of the Mass.   NAPOLÉON reads the Coronation Oath in
a loud voice.

HERALDS

Give ear!   Napoléon, Emperor of the French
And King of Italy, is crowned and throned!

CONGREGATION

Long live the Emperor and King.   Huzza!

Music.   The Te Deum.

SPIRIT OF THE PITIES

That vulgar stroke of vauntery he displayed
In planting on his brow the Lombard crown,
Means sheer erasure of the Luneville pacts,
And lets confusion loose on Europe's peace
For many an undawned year!   From this rash hour
Austria but waits her opportunity
By secret swellings of her armaments
To link her to his foes.—I'll speak to him.

He throws a whisper into NAPOLÉON'S ear.

Lieutenant Bonaparte,
Would it not seemlier be to shut thy heart
To these unhealthy splendours?—helmet thee
For her thou swar'st-to first, fair Liberty?

NAPOLÉON

Who spoke to me?

ARCHBISHOP

Not I, Sire. Not a soul.

NAPOLÉON

Dear Joséphine, my queen, didst call my name?

JOSÉPHINE

I spoke not, Sire.

NAPOLÉON

    Thou didst not, tender spouse;
I know it. Such harsh utterance was not thine.
It was aggressive Fancy, working spells
Upon a mind o'erwrought!

The service closes. The clergy advance with the canopy to the foot of the throne, and the procession forms to return to the Palace.

SPIRIT OF THE YEARS

     Officious sprite,
Thou art young, and dost not heed the Cause of things
Which some of us have inkled to thee here;
Else wouldst thou not have hailed the Emperor,
Whose acts do but outshape Its governing.

SPIRIT OF THE PITIES

I feel, Sire, as I must! This tale of Will
And Life's impulsion by Incognizance
I cannot take.

SPIRIT OF THE YEARS

    Let me then once again
Show to thy sceptic eye the very streams
And currents of this all-inhering Power,
And bring conclusion to thy unbelief.

The scene assumes the preternatural transparency before mentioned, and there is again beheld as it were the interior of a brain which seems to manifest the volitions of a Universal Will, of whose tissues the personages of the action form portion.

SPIRIT OF THE PITIES

Enough. And yet for very sorriness
I cannot own the weird phantasma real!

SPIRIT OF THE YEARS

Affection ever was illogical.

SPIRIT IRONIC (aside)

How should the Sprite own to such logic—a mere juvenile—
who only came into being in what the earthlings call their
Tertiary Age!

The scene changes. The exterior of the Cathedral takes the place of the
interior, and the point of view recedes, the whole fabric smalling into distance
and becoming like a rare, delicately carved alabaster ornament. The city
itself sinks to miniature, the Alps show afar as a white corrugation, the
Adriatic and the Gulf of Genoa appear on this and on that hand, with Italy
between them, till clouds cover the panorama.

ACT SECOND

SCENE I

THE DOCKYARD, GIBRALTAR

The Rock is seen rising behind the town and the Alameda Gardens, and
the English fleet rides at anchor in the Bay, across which the Spanish shore
from Algeciras to Carnero Point shuts in the West. Southward over the
Strait is the African coast.

SPIRIT OF THE YEARS

Our migratory Proskenion now presents
An outlook on the storied Kalpe Rock,
As preface to the vision of the Fleets
Spanish and French, linked for fell purposings.

RECORDING ANGEL (reciting)

Their motions and manœuvres, since the fame
Of Bonaparte's enthronement at Milan
Swept swift through Europe's dumbed communities,
Have stretched the English mind to wide surmise.
Many well-based alarms (which strange report
Much aggravates) as to the pondered blow,
Flutter the public pulse; all points in turn—
Malta, Brazil, Wales, Ireland, British Ind—
Being held as feasible for force like theirs,
Of lavish numbers and unrecking aim.

" Where, where is Nelson ?" questions every tongue ;—
" How views he so unparalleled a scheme ?"
Their slow uncertain apprehensions ask.
" When Villeneuve puts to sea with all his force,
What may he not achieve, if swift his course !"

Spirit of the Years

I'll call in Nelson, who has stepped ashore
For the first time these thrice twelvemonths and more,
And with him one whose insight has alone
Pierced the real project of Napoléon.

Enter NELSON and COLLINGWOOD, who pace up and down.

Spirit of the Pities

Note Nelson's worn-out features.   Much has he
Suffered from ghoulish ghast anxiety !

Nelson

In short, dear Coll, the letter which you wrote me
Had so much pith that I was fain to see you ;
For I am sure that you indeed divine
The true intent and compass of a plot
Which I have spelled in vain.

Collingwood

                    I weighed it thus :
Their flight to the Indies being to draw us off,
That and no more, and clear these coasts of us—
The standing obstacle to his device—
He cared not what was done at Martinique,
Or where, provided that the general end
Should not be jeopardized—that is to say,
The full-united squadron's quick return.—
Gravina and Villeneuve, once back to Europe,
Can straight make Ferrol, raise there the blockade,
Then haste to Brest, there to relieve Ganteaume,
And next with four- or five-and-fifty sail
Bear down upon our coast as they see fit.—
I read they aim to strike at Ireland still,
As formerly, and as I wrote to you.

NELSON

So far your thoughtful and sagacious words
Have hit the facts.   But 'tis no Irish bay
The villains aim to drop their anchors in ;
My word for it : they make the Wessex shore,
And this vast squadron handled by Villeneuve
Is meant to cloak the passage of their strength,
Massed in those transports—we being kept elsewhere
By feigning forces.—Good God, Collingwood,
I must be gone !   Yet two more days remain
Ere I can get away.—I must be gone !

COLLINGWOOD

Wherever you may go to, my dear lord,
You carry victory with you.   Let them launch,
Your name will blow them back, as sou'-west gales
The gulls that beat against them from the shore.

NELSON

Good Collingwood, I know you trust in me ;
But ships are ships, and do not kindly come
Out of the slow docks of the Admiralty
Like wharfside pigeons when they are whistled for :—
And there's a damned disparity of force,
Which means tough work awhile for you and me !

       The Spirit of the Years whispers to NELSON.

And I have warnings, warnings, Collingwood,
That my effective hours are shortening here ;
Strange warnings now and then, as 'twere within me,
Which, though I fear them not, I recognize ! . . .
However, by God's help, I'll live to meet
These foreign boasters ; yea, I'll finish them ;
And then—well, Gunner Death may finish me !

COLLINGWOOD

View not your life so gloomily, my lord :
One charmed, a needed purpose to fulfil !

NELSON

Ah, Coll.   Lead bullets are not all that wound. . . .
I have a feeling here of dying fires,

A sense of strong and deep unworded censure,
Which, compassing about my private life,
Makes all my public service lustreless
In my own eyes.—I fear I am much condemned
For those dear Naples and Palermo days,
And her who was the sunshine of them all ! . . .
He who is with himself dissatisfied,
Though all the world find satisfaction in him,
Is like a rainbow-coloured bird gone blind,
That gives delight it shares not.   Happiness ?
It's the philosopher's stone no alchemy
Shall light on in this world I am weary of.—
Smiling I'd pass to my long home to-morrow
Could I with honour, and my country's gain.
—But let's adjourn.   I waste your hours ashore
By such ill-timed confessions !

> They pass out of sight, and the scene closes.

SCENE II

OFF FERROL

The French and Spanish combined squadrons.   On board the French
admiral's flag-ship.   VILLENEUVE is discovered in his cabin, writing a letter.

SPIRIT OF THE PITIES

He pens in fits, with pallid restlessness,
Like one who sees Misfortune walk the wave,
And can nor face nor flee it.

SPIRIT OF THE YEARS

He indites
To his long friend the minister Decrès
Words that go heavily ! . . .

VILLENEUVE (writing)

" I am made the arbiter in vast designs
Whereof I see black outcomes.   Do I this
Or do I that, success, that loves to jilt
Her anxious wooer for some careless blade,
Will not reward me.   For, if I must pen it,

Demoralized past prayer is the marine——
Bad masts, bad sails, bad officers, bad men ;
We cling to naval technics long outworn,
And time and opportunity do not avail me
To take up new.   I have long suspected such,
But till I saw my helps, the Spanish ships,
I hoped somewhat.—Brest is my nominal port ;
Yet if so, Calder will again attack——
Now reinforced by Nelson or Cornwallis——
And shatter my whole fleet. . . . Shall I admit
That my true inclination and desire
Is to make Cadiz straightway, and not Brest ?
Alas ! thereby I fail the Emperor ;
But shame the navy less.——

> Your friend, VILLENEUVE."

GENERAL LAURISTON enters.

LAURISTON

Admiral, my missive to the Emperor,
Which I shall speed by special courier
From Ferrol this near eve, runs thus and thus :——
" Gravina's ships, in Ferrol here at hand,
Embayed but by a temporary wind,
Are all we now await.   Combined with these
We sail herefrom to Brest ; there promptly give
Cornwallis battle, and release Ganteaume ;
Thence, all united, bearing Channelwards :
A step that sets in motion the first wheel
In the proud project of your Majesty
Now to be engined to the very close,
To wit : that a French fleet shall enter in
And hold the Channel four-and-twenty hours."——
Such clear assurance to the Emperor
That our intent is modelled on his will
I hasten to dispatch to him forthwith.[1]

VILLENEUVE

Yes, Lauriston.   I sign to every word.

LAURISTON goes out.   VILLENEUVE remains at his table in reverie.

---

[1] Through this tangle of intentions the writer has in the main followed Thiers, whose access to documents would seem to authenticate his details of the famous scheme for England's ruin.

Spirit of the Years

We may impress him under visible shapes
That seem to shed a silent circling doom;
He's such an one as can be so impressed,
And this much is among our privileges,
Well bounded as they be.—Let us draw near him.

The Spirits of the Years and of the Pities take the form of white sea-birds, which alight on the stern-balcony of VILLENEUVE'S ship, immediately outside his cabin window. VILLENEUVE after a while looks up and sees the birds watching him with large piercing eyes.

VILLENEUVE

My apprehensions even outstep their cause,
As though some influence smote through yonder pane.

He gazes listlessly, and resumes his broodings.

——Why dared I not disclose to him my thought,
As nightly worded by the whistling shrouds,
That Brest will never see our battled hulls
Helming to north in pomp of cannonry
To take the front in this red pilgrimage !
——If so it were, now, that I'd screen my skin
From risks of bloody business in the brunt,
My acts could scarcely wear a difference.
Yet I would die to-morrow—not ungladly—
So far removed is carcase-care from me.
For no self do these apprehensions spring,
But for the cause.—Yes, rotten is our marine,
Which, while I know, the Emperor knows not,
And the pale secret chills !   Though some there be
Would beard contingencies and buffet all,
I'll not command a course so conscienceless.
Rather I'll stand, and face Napoléon's rage
When he shall learn what mean the ambiguous lines
That facts have forced from me.

SPIRIT OF THE PITIES (to the Spirit of the Years)

O Eldest-born of the Unconscious Cause—
If such thou beest, as I can fancy thee—
Why dost thou rack him thus ?   Consistency
Might be preserved, and yet his doom remain.
His olden courage is without reproach ;
Albeit his temper trends toward gaingiving !

SPIRIT OF THE YEARS

I say, as I have said long heretofore,
I know but narrow freedom. Feel'st thou not
We are in Its hand, as he ?—Here, as elsewhere,
We do but as we may ; no further dare.

The birds disappear, and the scene is lost behind sea-mist.

SCENE III

THE CAMP AND HARBOUR OF BOULOGNE

The English coast in the distance. Near the Tour d'Ordre stands a hut, with sentinels and aides outside ; it is NAPOLÉON's temporary lodging when not at his headquarters at the Château of Pont-de-Briques, two miles inland.

DUMB SHOW

A courier arrives with dispatches, and enters the Emperor's quarters, whence he emerges and goes on with other dispatches to the hut of DECRÈS, lower down. Immediately after, NAPOLÉON comes out from his hut with a paper in his hand, and musingly proceeds towards an eminence commanding the Channel.

Along the shore below are forming in a far-reaching line more than a hundred thousand infantry. On the downs in the rear of the camps fifteen thousand cavalry are manœuvring, their accoutrements flashing in the sun like a school of mackerel. The flotilla lies in and around the port, alive with moving figures.

With his head forward and his hands behind him the Emperor surveys these animated proceedings in detail, but more frequently turns his face towards the telegraph on the cliff to the south-west, erected to signal when VILLENEUVE and the combined squadrons shall be visible on the west horizon.

He summons one of the aides, who descends to the hut of DECRÈS. DECRÈS comes out from his hut, and hastens to join the Emperor. Dumb show ends.

NAPOLÉON and DECRÈS advance to the foreground of the scene.

NAPOLÉON

Decrès, this action with Sir Robert Calder
Three weeks ago, whereof we dimly heard,
And clear details of which I have just unsealed,
Is on the whole auspicious for our plan.
It seems that twenty of our ships and Spain's—
None over eighty-gunned, and some far less—
Engaged the English off Cape Finisterre
With fifteen vessels of a hundred each.

We coolly fought and orderly as they,
And, but for mist, we had closed with victory.
Two English were much mauled, some Spanish damaged,
And Calder then drew off with his two wrecks
And Spain's in tow, we giving chase forthwith.
Not overtaking him our admiral,
Having the coast clear for his purposes,
Entered Coruña, and found orders there
To open the port of Brest and come on hither.
Thus hastes the moment when the double fleet
Of Villeneuve and of Ganteaume should appear.

He looks again towards the telegraph.

DECRÈS (with hesitation)

And should they not appear, your Majesty?

NAPOLÉON

Not? But they will; and do it early, too!
There's nothing hinders them. My God, they must,
For I have much before me when this stroke
At England's dealt. I learn from Talleyrand
That Austrian preparations threaten hot,
While Russia's hostile schemes are ripening,
And shortly must be met.—My plan is fixed:
I am prepared for each alternative.
If Villeneuve come, I brave the British coast,
Convulse the land with fear ('tis even now
So far distraught, that generals cast about
To find new modes of warfare; yea, design
Carriages to transport their infantry!).—
Once on the English soil I hold it firm,
Descend on London, and the while my men
Salute the dome of Paul's I cut the knot
Of all Pitt's coalitions; setting free
From bondage to a cold manorial caste
A people who await it.

They stand and regard the chalky cliffs of England, till NAPOLÉON
resumes:

Should it be
Even that my admirals fail to keep the tryst—
A thing scarce thinkable, when all's reviewed—
I strike this seaside camp, cross Germany,

With these two hundred thousand seasoned men,
And pause not till within Vienna's walls
I cry checkmate.   Next, Venice, too, being taken,
And Austria's other holdings down that way,
The Bourbons also driven from Italy,
I strike at Russia—each in turn, you note,
Ere they can act conjoined.
                              Report to me
What has been scanned to-day upon the main,
And on your passage down request them there
To send Daru this way.

DECRÈS (as he withdraws)

The Emperor can be sanguine.   Scarce can I.
His letters are more promising than mine.
Alas, alas, Villeneuve, my dear old friend,
Why do you pen me this at such a time !

[He retires reading VILLENEUVE's letter.

The Emperor walks up and down till DARU, his private secretary, joins him.

NAPOLÉON

Come quick, Daru ; sit down upon the grass,
And write whilst I am in mind.
                              First to Villeneuve :—
" I trust, Vice-Admiral, that before this date
Your fleet has opened Brest, and gone.   If not,
These lines will greet you there.   But pause not, pray :
Waste not a moment dallying.   Sail away :
Once bring my coupled squadrons Channelwards
And England's soil is ours.   All's ready here,
The troops alert, and every store embarked.
Hold the nigh sea but four-and-twenty hours
And our vast end is gained."
                              Now to Ganteaume :—
" My telegraphs will have made known to you
My object and desire to be but this,
That you forbid Villeneuve to lose an hour
In getting fit and putting forth to sea,
To profit by the fifty first-rate craft
Wherewith I now am bettered.   Quickly weigh,
And steer you for the Channel with all your strength.

I count upon your well-known character,
Your enterprize, your vigour, to do this.
Sail hither, then ; and we will be avenged
For centuries of despite and contumely."

DARU

Shall a fair transcript, Sire, be made forthwith ?

NAPOLÉON

This moment.   And the courier will depart
And travel without pause.

DARU goes to his office a little lower down, and the Emperor lingers on the cliffs looking through his glass.

The point of view shifts across the Channel, the Boulogne cliffs sinking behind the water-line.

SCENE IV

SOUTH WESSEX.   A RIDGE-LIKE DOWN NEAR THE COAST

The down commands a wide view over the English Channel in front of it, including the popular Royal watering-place, with the Isle of Slingers and its roadstead, where men-of-war and frigates are anchored.   The hour is ten in the morning, and the July sun glows upon a large military encampment round about the foreground, and warms the stone field-walls that take the place of hedges here.

Artillery, cavalry, and infantry, English and Hanoverian, are drawn up for review under the DUKE OF CUMBERLAND and officers of the staff, forming a vast military array, which extends three miles, and as far as the downs are visible.

In the centre by the Royal Standard appears KING GEORGE on horseback, and his suite.   In a coach drawn by six cream-coloured Hanoverian horses QUEEN CHARLOTTE sits with three Princesses ; in another carriage with four horses are two more Princesses.   There are also present with the Royal Party the LORD CHANCELLOR, LORD MULGRAVE, COUNT MUNSTER, and many other luminaries of fashion and influence.

The Review proceeds in dumb show ; and the din of many bands mingles with the cheers.   The turf behind the saluting-point is crowded with carriages and spectators on foot.

A SPECTATOR

And you've come to see the sight, like the King and myself ? Well, one fool makes many.   What a mampus o' folk it is here to-day !   And what a time we do live in, between wars and wassailings, the goblin o' Boney, and King George in flesh and blood !

Second Spectator

Yes. I wonder King George is let venture down on this
coast, where he might be snapped up in a moment like a minney
by a her'n, so near as we be to the field of Boney's vagaries !
Begad, he's as like to land here as anywhere.   Gloucester Lodge
could be surrounded, and George and Charlotte carried off before he could put on his hat, or she her red cloak and pattens !

Third Spectator

'Twould be no such joke to kidnap 'em as you think.   Look
at the frigates down there.   Every night they are drawn up in a
line across the mouth of the Bay, almost touching each other ;
and ashore a double line of sentinels, well primed with beer and
ammunition, one at the water's edge, and the other on the
Esplanade, stretch along the whole front.   Then close to the
Lodge a guard is mounted after eight o'clock ; there be pickets
on all the hills ; at the Harbour mouth is a battery of twenty four-
pounders ; and over-right 'em a dozen six-pounders, and several
howitzers.   And next look at the size of the camp of horse and
foot up here.

First Spectator

Everybody however was fairly gallied this week when the King
went out yachting, meaning to be back for the theatre ; and the
time passed, and it got dark, and the play couldn't begin, and
eight or nine o'clock came, and never a sign of him.   I don't
know when 'a did land ; but 'twas said by all that it was a fool-
hardy pleasure to take.

Fourth Spectator

He's a very obstinate and comical old gentleman ; and by all
account 'a wouldn't make port when asked to.

Second Spectator

Lard, Lard, if 'a were nabbed, it wouldn't make a deal of
difference ! We should have nobody to zing to, and play single-
stick to, and grin at through horse-collars, that's true.   And
nobody to sign our few documents.   But we should rub along
some way, goodnow.

First Spectator

Step up on this barrow ; you can see better.   The troopers
now passing are the York Hussars—foreigners to a man, except

the officers—the same regiment the two young Germans belonged to who were shot here four years ago. Now come the Light Dragoons; what a time they take to get all past! See, the King turns to speak to one of his notables. Well, well! this day will be recorded in history.

SECOND SPECTATOR

Or another soon to follow it! (He gazes over the Channel.) There's not a speck of an enemy upon that shiny water yet; but the Brest fleet is zaid to have put to sea, to act in concert with the army crossing from Boulogne; and if so the French will soon be here; when God save us all! I've took to drinking neat, for, says I, one may as well have his innerds burnt out as shot out, and 'tis a good deal pleasanter for the man that owns 'em. They say that a cannon-ball knocked poor Jim Popple's maw right up into the futtock-shrouds at the Nile, where 'a hung like a nightcap out to dry. Much good to him his obeying his old mother's wish and refusing his allowance o' rum!

The bands play and the Review continues till past eleven o'clock. Then follows a sham fight. At noon precisely the royal carriages draw off the ground into the highway that leads down to the town and Gloucester Lodge, followed by other equipages in such numbers that the road is blocked. A multitude comes after on foot. Presently the vehicles manage to proceed to the watering-place, and the troops march away to the various camps as a sea-mist cloaks the perspective.

SCENE V

THE SAME. RAINBARROWS' BEACON, EGDON HEATH

Night in mid-August of the same summer. A lofty ridge of heathland reveals itself dimly, terminating in an abrupt slope, at the summit of which are three tumuli. On the sheltered side of the most prominent of these stands a hut of turves with a brick chimney. In front are two ricks of fuel, one of heather and furze for quick ignition, the other of wood, for slow burning. Something in the feel of the darkness and in the personality of the spot imparts a sense of uninterrupted space around, the view by day extending from the cliffs of the Isle of Wight eastward to Blackdon Hill by Deadman's Bay westward, and south across the Valley of the Froom to the ridge that screens the Channel.

Two men with pikes loom up, on duty as beacon-keepers beside the ricks.

OLD MAN

Now, Jems Purchess, once more mark my words. Black'on is the point we've to watch, and not Kingsbere; and I'll tell 'ee for why. If he do land anywhere hereabout 'twill be inside Deadman's Bay, and the signal will straightway come from Black'on. But there thou'st stand, glowering and staring with all thy eyes at Kingsbere! I tell 'ee what 'tis, Jem Purchess, your brain is softening; and you be getting too old for business of state like ours!

YOUNG MAN

You've let your tongue wrack your few rames of good breeding, John.

OLD MAN

The words of my Lord-Lieutenant was, whenever you see Kingsbere-Hill Beacon fired to the eastward, or Black'on to the westward, light up; and keep your second fire burning for two hours. Was that our documents or was it not?

YOUNG MAN

I don't gainsay it. And so I keep my eye on Kingsbere, because that's most likely o' the two, says I.

OLD MAN

That shows the curious depths of your ignorance. However, I'll have patience, and say on. Didst ever larn geography?

YOUNG MAN

No. Nor no other corrupt practices.

OLD MAN

Tcht-tcht!—Well, I'll have patience, and put it to him in another form. Dost know the world is round—eh? I warrant dostn't!

YOUNG MAN

I warrant I do!

OLD MAN

How d'ye make that out, when th'st never been to school?

YOUNG MAN

I larned it at church, thank God.

OLD MAN

Church? What have God A'mighty got to do with profane knowledge? Beware that you baint blaspheming, Jems Purchess!

Young Man

I say I did, whether or no! 'Twas the zingers up in gallery
that I had it from. They busted out that strong with "the
round world and they that dwell therein," that we common fokes
down under could do no less than believe 'em.

Old Man

Canst be sharp enough in the wrong place as usual—I warrant
canst! However, I'll have patience with 'en, and say on!—
Suppose, now, my hat is the world; and there, as might be,
stands the Camp of Belong, where Boney is. The world goes
round, so, and Belong goes round too. Twelve hours pass;
round goes the world still—so. Where's Belong now?

*A pause. Two other figures, a man's and a woman's, rise against the sky
out of the gloom.*

Old Man (shouldering his pike)

Who goes there? Friend or foe, in the King's name!

Woman

Piece o' trumpery! "Who goes" yourself! What d'ye
talk o', John Whiting! Can't your eyes earn their living any
longer, then, that you don't know your own neighbours? 'Tis
Private Cantle of the Locals and his wife Keziar, down at Bloom's-
End—who else should it be!

Old Man (lowering his pike)

A form o' words, Mis'ess Cantle, no more; ordained by his
Majesty's Gover'ment to be spoke by all we on sworn duty for
the defence o' the country. Strict rank-and-file rules is our only
horn of salvation in these times.—But, my dear woman, why
ever have ye come lumpering up to Rainbarrows at this time
o' night?

Woman

We've been troubled with bad dreams, owing to the firing out
at sea yesterday; and at last I could sleep no more, feeling sure
that sommat boded of His coming. And I said to Cantle, I'll
ray myself, and go up to Beacon, and ask if anything have been
heard or seen to-night. And here we be.

Old Man

Not a sign or sound—all's as still as a churchyard. And how is your good man?

Private (advancing)

Clk! I be all right! I was in the ranks, helping to keep the ground at the review by the King this week. We was a wonderful sight—wonderful! The King said so again and again. —Yes, there was he, and there was I, though not daring to move a' eyebrow in the presence of Majesty. I have come home on a night's leave—off there again to-morrow. Boney's expected every day, the Lord be praised! Yes, our hopes are to be fulfilled soon, as we say in the army.

Old Man

There, there, Cantle; don't ye speak quite so large, and stand so over-upright. Your back is as holler as a fire-dog's. Do ye suppose that we on active service here don't know war news? Mind you don't go taking to your heels when the next alarm comes, as you did at last year's.

Private

That had nothing to do with fighting, for I'm as bold as a lion when I'm up, and "Shoulder Fawlocks!" sounds as common as my own name to me. 'Twas—— (Lowering his voice.) Have ye heard?

Old Man

To be sure we have.

Private

Ghastly, isn't it!

Old Man

Ghastly! Frightful!

Young Man (to Private)

He don't know what it is! That's his pride and puffery. What is it that's so ghastly—hey?

Private

Well, there, I can't tell it. 'Twas that that made the whole eighty of our company run away—though we be the bravest of the brave in natural jeopardies, or the little boys wouldn't run after us and call us the "Bang-up-Locals."

WOMAN (in undertones)

I can tell you a word or two on't. It is about His victuals. They say that He lives upon human flesh, and has rashers o' baby every morning for breakfast—for all the world like the Cernel Giant in old ancient times!

YOUNG MAN

Ye can't believe all ye hear.

PRIVATE

I only believe half. And I only own—such is my challengeful character—that perhaps He do eat pagan infants when He's in the desert. But not Christian ones at home. Oh no—'tis too much.

WOMAN

Whether or no, I sometimes—God forgie me!—laugh wi' horror at the queerness o't, till I am that weak I can hardly go round house. He should have the washing of 'em a few times; I warrant 'a wouldn't want to eat babies any more!

A silence, during which they gaze around at the dark dome of starless sky.

YOUNG MAN

There'll be a change in the weather soon, by the look o't. I can hear the cows moo in Froom Valley as if I were close to 'em, and the lantern at Max Turnpike is shining quite plain.

OLD MAN

Well, come in and taste a drop o' sommat we've got here, that will warm the cockles of your heart as ye wamble homealong. We housed eighty tubs last night for them that shan't be named —landed at Lullwind Cove the night afore, though they had a narrow shave with the riding-officers this run.

They make towards the hut, when a light on the west horizon becomes visible, and quickly enlarges.

YOUNG MAN

He's come!

OLD MAN

Come he is, though you do say it! This, then, is the beginning of what England's waited for!

They stand and watch the light awhile.

Young Man

Just what you was praising the Lord for by-now, Private Cantle.

Private

My meaning was——

Woman (simpering)

Oh that I hadn't married a fiery sojer, to make me bring fatherless children into the world, all through his dreadful calling! Why didn't a man of no sprawl content me!

Old Man (shouldering his pike)

We can't heed your innocent pratings any longer, good neighbours, being in the King's service, and a hot invasion on. Fall in, fall in, mate. Straight to the tinder-box. Quick march!

The two men hasten to the hut, and are heard striking a flint and steel. Returning with a lit lantern they ignite a wisp of furze, and with this set the first stack of fuel in a blaze. The private of the Locals and his wife hastily retreat by the light of the flaming beacon, under which the purple rotundities of the heath show like bronze, and the pits like the eye-sockets of a skull.

Spirit Sinister

This is good, and spells blood. (To the Chorus of the Years.) *I assume that It means to let us carry out this invasion with pleasing slaughter, so as not to disappoint my hope?*

Semichorus I of the Years (aerial music)

We carry out? Nay, but should we
Ordain what bloodshed is to be!

Semichorus II

The Immanent, that urgeth all,
Rules what may or may not befall!

Semichorus I

Ere systemed suns were globed and lit
The slaughters of the race were writ,

Semichorus II

And wasting wars, by land and sea,
Fixed, like all else, immutably!

Spirit Sinister

Well; be it so. My argument is that War makes rattling good history; but Peace is poor reading. So I back Bonaparte for the reason that he will give pleasure to posterity.

Spirit of the Pities

Gross hypocrite!

Chorus of the Years

We comprehend him not.

The day breaks over the heathery upland, on which the beacon is still burning. The morning reveals the white surface of a highway which, coming from the royal watering-place beyond the hills, stretches towards the outskirts of the heath and passes away eastward.

DUMB SHOW

Moving figures and vehicles dot the surface of the road, all progressing in one direction, away from the coast. In the foreground the shapes appear as those of civilians, mostly on foot, but many in gigs and tradesmen's carts and on horseback. When they reach an intermediate hill some pause and look back; others enter on the next decline landwards without turning their heads.

From the opposite horizon numerous companies of volunteers, in the local uniform of red with green facings,[1] are moving coastwards in companies; as are also irregular bodies of pikemen without uniform; while on the upper slopes of the downs towards the shore regiments of the line are visible, with cavalry and artillery; all passing over to the coast.

At a signal from the Chief Intelligences two Phantoms of Rumour enter on the highway in the garb of country-men.

First Phantom (to Pedestrians)

Whither so fast, good neighbours, and before breakfast, too? Empty bellies be bad to vamp on.

First Pedestrian (laden with a pack, and speaking breathlessly)

He's landed west'ard, out by Abbot's Beach. And if you have property you'll save it and yourselves, as we are doing!

Second Pedestrian

All yesterday the firing at Boulogne
Was like the seven thunders heard in Heaven

---

[1] These historic facings, which, I believe, won for the local (old 39th) regiment the nickname of "Green Linnets," have been changed for no apparent reason. (They are now restored.—1909.)

When the fierce angel spoke.   So did he draw
Men's eyes that way, the while his thousand boats
Full-manned, flat-bottomed for the shallowest shore,
Dropped down to west, and crossed our frontage here.
Seen from above they specked the water-shine
As will a flight of swallows towards dim eve,
Descending on a smooth and loitering stream
To seek some eyot's sedge.

Second Phantom

We are sent to enlighten you and ease your souls.
Even now a courier canters to the port
To check the baseless scare.

First Pedestrian (to Second Pedestrian)

These be inland men who, I warrant 'ee, don't know a lerret
from a lighter! Let's take no heed of such, comrade ; and
hurry on !

First Phantom

Will you not hear
That what was seen behind the midnight mist,
Their oar-blades tossing twinkles to the moon,
Was but a fleet of fishing-craft belated
By reason of the vastness of their haul?

First Pedestrian

Hey ? And d'ye know it ?—Now I look back to the top o'
Rudgeway the folk do seem as come to a pause there.—Be this
true, never again do I stir my stumps for any alarm short of the
Day of Judgment ! Nine times has my rheumatical rest been
broke in these last three years by hues and cries of Boney
upon us. 'Od rot the feller ; now he's made a fool of me once
more, till my inside is like a wash-tub, what wi' being so gallied,
and running so leery !—But how if you be one of the enemy,
sent to sow these tares, so to speak it, these false tidings,
and coax us into a fancied safety ? Hey, neighbours ? I don't,
after all, care for this story !

SECOND PEDESTRIAN

Onwards again !
If Boney's come, 'tis best to be away ;
And if he's not, why, we've a holiday !

[Exeunt Pedestrians.

The Spirits of Rumour vanish, while the scene seems to become involved
in the smoke from the beacon, and slowly disappears.[1]

ACT THIRD

SCENE I

BOULOGNE.   THE CHÂTEAU AT PONT-DE-BRIQUES

A room in the Château, which is used as the Imperial quarters.   The
EMPEROR NAPOLÉON, and M. GASPARD MONGE, the mathematician and
philosopher, are seated at breakfast.

Enter the officer in attendance.

OFFICER

Monsieur the Admiral Decrès awaits
A moment's audience with your Majesty,
Or now, or later.

NAPOLÉON

Bid him in at once—
At last Villeneuve has raised the Brest blockade !

Enter DECRÈS.

What of the squadrons' movements, good Decrès ?
Brest opened, and all sailing Channelwards,
Like swans into a creek at feeding-time ?

DECRÈS

Such news was what I'd hoped, your Majesty,
To send across this daybreak.   But events
Have proved intractable, it seems, of late ;
And hence I haste in person to report
The featless facts that just have dashed my——

[1] The remains of the lonely hut occupied by the beacon-keepers, consisting of some
half-buried brickbats, and a little mound of peat overgrown with moss, are still visible on
the elevated spot referred to.   The two keepers themselves, and their eccentricities and
sayings, are traditionary, with a slight disguise of names.

NAPOLÉON (darkening)

                     Well?

DECRÈS

Sire, at the very juncture when the fleets
Sailed out from Ferrol, fever raged aboard
"L'Achille" and "l'Algeciras": later on,
Mischief assailed our Spanish comrades' ships;
Several ran foul of neighbours; whose new hurts,
Being added to their innate clumsiness,
Gave hap the upper hand; and in quick course
Demoralized the whole; until Villeneuve,
Judging that Calder now with Nelson rode,
And prescient of unparalleled disaster
If he pushed on in so disjoint a trim,
Bowed to the inevitable; and thus, perforce,
Leaving to other opportunity
Brest and the Channel scheme, with vast regret
Steered southward into Cadiz.

NAPOLÉON (having risen from the table)

                    What!—Is, then,
My scheme of years to be disdained and dashed
By this man's like, a wretched moral coward,
Whom you must needs foist on me as one fit
For full command in pregnant enterprise!

MONGE (aside)

I'm one too many here! Let me step out
Till this black squall blows over. Poor Decrès.
Would that this precious project, disinterred
From naval archives of King Louis' reign,
Had ever lingered fusting where 'twas found![1]

                                [Exit MONGE.

NAPOLÉON

To help a friend you foul a country's fame!—
Decrès, not only chose you this Villeneuve,
But you have nourished secret sour opinions
Akin to his, and thereby helped to scathe

---

[1] "Le projet existe encore aux archives de la marine que Napoléon consultait incessamment : il sentait que cette marine depuis Louis XIV. avait fait de grandes choses : le plan de l'Expédition d'Egypte et de la descente en Angleterre se trouvaient au ministère de la marine."—CAPEFIGUE : *L'Europe pendant le Consulat et l'Empire.*

As stably based a project as this age
Has sunned to ripeness. Ever the French marine
Have you decried, ever contrived to bring
Despair into the fleet! Why, this Villeneuve,
Your man, this rank incompetent, this traitor—
Of whom I asked no more than fight and lose,
Provided he detained the enemy—
A frigate is too great for his command!
What shall be said of one who, at a breath,
When a few casual sailors find them sick,
When falls a broken boom or slitten sail,
When rumour hints that Calder's tubs and Nelson's
May join, and bob about in company,
Is straightway paralyzed, and doubles back
On all his ripened plans!—
Bring him, ay, bodily; hale him out from Cadiz,
Compel him up the Channel by main force,
And, having doffed him his supreme command,
Give the united squadrons to Ganteaume!

DECRÈS

Your Majesty, while umbraged, righteously,
By an event my tongue dragged dry to tell,
Makes my hard situation over-hard
By your ascription to the actors in't
Of motives such and such. 'Tis not for me
To answer these reproaches, Sire, and ask
Why years-long mindfulness of France's fame
In things marine should win no confidence.
I speak; but am unable to convince!
  True is it that this man has been my friend
Since boyhood made us schoolmates; and I say
That he would yield the heel-drops of his heart
With joyful readiness this day, this hour,
To do his country service. Yet no less
Is it his drawback that he sees too far.
And there are times, Sire, when a shorter sight
Charms Fortune more. A certain sort of bravery
Some people have—to wit, this same Lord Nelson—
Which is but fatuous faith in one's own star
Swoln to the very verge of childishness,
(Smugly disguised as putting trust in God,

A habit with these English folk) ; whereby
A headstrong blindness to contingencies
Carries the actor on, and serves him well
In some nice issues clearer sight would mar.
Such eyeless bravery Villeneuve has not ;
But, Sire, he is no coward.

NAPOLÉON

Well, have it so !—What are we going to do ?
My brain has only one wish—to succeed !

DECRÈS

My voice wanes weaker with you, Sire ; is nought !
Yet these few words, as Minister of Marine,
I'll venture now.—My process would be thus :—
Our projects for a junction of the fleets
Being well-discerned and read by every eye
Through long postponement, England is prepared.
I would recast them.   Later in the year
Form sundry squadrons of this massive one,
Harass the English till the winter time,
Then rendezvous at Cadiz ; where leave half
To catch the enemy's eye and call their cruizers,
While, rounding Scotland with the other half,
You make the Channel by the eastern strait,
Cover the passage of our army-boats,
And plant the blow.

NAPOLÉON

                    And what if they perceive
Our Scottish route, and meet us eastwardly ?

DECRÈS

I have thought of it, and planned a countermove ;
I'll write the scheme more clearly and at length,
And send it hither to your Majesty.

NAPOLÉON

Do so forthwith ; and send me in Daru.

Exit DECRÈS.   Re-enter MONGE.

Our breakfast, Monge, to-day has been cut short,
And those discussions on the ancient tongues
Wherein you shine, must yield to modern moils.
Nay, hasten not away ; though feeble wills,

Incompetence, ay, imbecility,
In some who feign to serve the cause of France,
Do make me other than myself just now !—
Ah—here's Daru.

DARU enters. MONGE takes his leave.

Daru, sit down and write. Yes, here, at once,
This room will serve me now. What think you, eh ?
Villeneuve has just turned tail and run to Cadiz,
So quite postponed—perhaps even overthrown—
My long-conned project against yonder shore
As 'twere a juvenile's snow-built device
But made for melting ! Think of it, Daru,—
My God, my God, how can I talk thereon !
A plan well judged, well charted, well upreared,
To end in nothing ! . . . Sit you down and write.

NAPOLÉON *walks up and down, and resumes after a silence :*

Write this.—A volte-face 'tis indeed !—Write, write !

DARU (holding pen to paper)

I wait, your Majesty.

NAPOLÉON

First Bernadotte—
Yes ; " Bernadotte moves out from Hanover
Through Hesse upon Würzburg and the Danube.—
Marmont from Holland bears along the Rhine,
And joins at Mainz and Würzburg Bernadotte . . .
    While these prepare their routes the army here
Will turn its back on Britain's tedious shore,
And, closing up with Augereau at Brest,
Set out full force due eastward. . . .
By the Black Forest feign a straight attack,
The while our purpose is to skirt its left,
Meet in Franconia Bernadotte and Marmont ;
Traverse the Danube somewhat down from Ulm ;
Entrap the Austrian columns by their rear ;
Surround them, cleave them ; roll upon Vienna,
Where, Austria settled, I engage the Tsar,
While Masséna detains in Italy
The Archduke Charles.

Foreseeing such might shape,
Each high- and by-way to the Danube hence
I have of late had measured, mapped, and judged ;
Such spots as suit for depôts chosen and marked ;
Each regiment's daily pace and bivouac
Writ tablewise for ready reference ;
All which itineraries are sent herewith."
  So shall I crush the two gigantic sets
Upon the Empire, now grown imminent.
—Let me reflect.—First Bernadotte——But nay,
The courier to Marmont must go first.
Well, well.—The order of our march from hence
I will advise. . . . My knock at George's door
With bland inquiries why his royal hand
Withheld due answer to my friendly lines,
And tossed the irksome business to his clerks,
Is thus perforce delayed.   But not for long.
Instead of crossing, thitherward I tour
By roundabout contrivance not less sure !

Daru

I'll bring the writing to your Majesty.

NAPOLÉON and DARU go out severally.

Chorus of the Years (aerial music)

Recording Angel, trace
This bold campaign his thought has spun apace—
One that bids fair for immortality
Among the earthlings—if immortal deeds
May be ascribed to so extempory
        And transient a race !
It will be called, in rhetoric and rhyme,
        As son to sire succeeds,
A model for the tactics of all time ;
" The Great Campaign of that so famed year Five,"
By millions of mankind not yet alive.

SCENE II

THE FRONTIERS OF UPPER AUSTRIA AND BAVARIA

A view of the country from mid-air, at a point south of the River Inn, which is seen as a silver thread, winding northward between its junction with the Salza and the Danube, and forming the boundaries of the two countries.

The Danube shows itself as a crinkled satin riband, stretching from left to right in the far background of the picture, the Inn discharging its waters into the larger river.

DUMB SHOW

A vast Austrian army creeps dully along the mid-distance, in the form of detached masses and columns of a whitish cast. The columns insensibly draw nearer to each other, and are seen to be converging from the east upon the banks of the Inn aforesaid.

A RECORDING ANGEL (in recitative)

This movement as of molluscs on a leaf,
Which from our vantage here we scan afar,
Is one manœuvred by the famous Mack
To countercheck Napoléon, still believed
To be intent on England from Boulogne,
And heedless of such rallies in his rear.
Mack's enterprise is now to cross Bavaria—
Beneath us stretched in ripening summer peace
As field unwonted for these ugly jars—
And seize on Ulm, past Swabia leftward there.
  Outraged Bavaria, simmering in disquiet
At Munich down behind us, Isar-fringed,
And torn between his fair wife's hate òf France
And his own itch to gird at Austrian bluff
For riding roughshod through his territory,
Wavers from this to that.   The while Time hastes
The eastward streaming of Napoléon's host,
As soon we see.

The silent insect-creep of the Austrian columns towards the banks of the Inn continues to be seen till the view fades to nebulousness and dissolves.

SCENE III

BOULOGNE.   THE ST. OMER ROAD

It is a morning at the end of August, and the road stretches out of the town eastward.

The divisions of the "Army-for-England" are making preparations to march. Some portions are in marching order. Bands strike up, and the regiments start on their journey towards the Rhine and Danube. Bonaparte and his officers watch the movements from an eminence. The soldiers, as they pace along under their eagles with beaming eyes, sing "Le Chant du Départ," and other martial songs, shout "Vive l'Empereur !" and babble of repeating the days of Italy, Egypt, Marengo, and Hohenlinden.

NAPOLÉON

Anon to England!

CHORUS OF INTELLIGENCES (aerial music)

If Time's weird threads so weave!

The scene as it lingers exhibits the gradual diminishing of the troops along the roads through the undulating August landscape, till each column is seen but as a train of dust; and the disappearance of each marching mass over the eastern horizon.

ACT FOURTH

SCENE I

KING GEORGE'S WATERING-PLACE, SOUTH WESSEX

A sunny day in autumn. A room in the red-brick royal residence known as Gloucester Lodge.[1]

At a front triple-lighted window stands a telescope on a tripod. Through the open middle sash is visible the crescent-curved expanse of the Bay as a sheet of brilliant translucent green, on which ride vessels of war at anchor. On the left hand white cliffs stretch away till they terminate in St. Aldhelm's Head, and form a background to the level water-line on that side. In the centre are the open sea and blue sky. A near headland rises on the right, surmounted by a battery, over which appears the remoter bald grey brow of the Isle of Slingers.

In the foreground yellow sands spread smoothly, whereon there are sundry temporary erections for athletic sports; and closer at hand runs an esplanade on which a fashionable crowd is promenading. Immediately outside the Lodge are companies of soldiers, groups of officers, and sentries.

Within the room the KING and PITT are discovered. The KING's eyes show traces of recent inflammation, and the Minister has a wasted look.

KING

Yes, yes; I grasp your reasons, Mr. Pitt,
And grant you audience gladly. More than that,
Your visit to this shore is apt and timely,
And if it do but yield you needful rest
From fierce debate, and other strains of office
Which you and I in common have to bear,

---

[1] This weather-beaten old building, though now an hotel, is but little altered.

'Twill be well earned.   The bathing is unmatched
Elsewhere in Europe,—see its mark on me !—
The air like liquid life.—But of this matter :
What argue these late movements seen abroad ?
What of the country now the session's past ;
What of the country, eh ? and of the war ?

PITT

The thoughts I have laid before your Majesty
Would make for this, in sum :—
That Mr. Fox, Lord Grenville, and their friends,
Be straightway asked to join.   With Melville gone,
With Sidmouth, and with Buckinghamshire too,
The steerage of affairs has stood of late
Somewhat provisional, as you, sir, know,
With stop-gap functions thrust on offices
Which common weal can tolerate but awhile.
So, for the weighty reasons I have urged,
I do repeat my most respectful hope
To win your Majesty's ungrudged assent
To what I have proposed.

KING

                        But nothing, sure,
Has been more plain to all, dear Mr. Pitt,
Than that your own proved energy and scope
Is ample, without aid, to carry on
Our just crusade against this Corsican.
Why, then, go calling Fox and Grenville in ?
Such helps we need not.   Pray you think upon't,
And speak to me again.—We've had alarms
Making us skip like crackers at our heels,
That Bonaparte had landed close hereby.

PITT

Such rumours come as regularly as harvest.

KING

And now he has left Boulogne with all his host ?
Was it his object to invade at all,
Or was his vast assemblage there a blind ?

PITT

Undoubtedly he meant invasion, sir,
Had fortune favoured.   He may try it yet.
And, as I said, could we but close with Fox——

KING

But, but ;—I ask, what is his object now?
Lord Nelson's Captain—Hardy—whose old home
Stands in a peaceful vale hard by us here——
Who came two weeks ago to see his friends,
I talked to in this room a lengthy while.
He says our navy still is in thick night
As to the aims by sea of Bonaparte
Now the Boulogne attempt has fizzled out,
And what he schemes afloat with Spain combined.
The "Victory" lay that fortnight at Spithead,
And Nelson since has gone aboard and sailed ;
Yes, sailed again.   The "Royal Sovereign" follows,
And others her.   Nelson was hailed and cheered
To huskiness while leaving Southsea shore,
Gentle and simple wildly thronging round.

PITT

Ay, sir.   Young women hung upon his arm,
And old ones blessed, and stroked him with their hands.

KING

Ah—you have heard, of course.   God speed him, Pitt.

PITT

Amen, amen !

KING

              I read it as a thing
Of signal augury, and one which bodes
Heaven's confidence in me and in my line,
That I should rule as King in such an age ! . . .
Well, well.—So this new march of Bonaparte's
Was unexpected, forced perchance on him?

PITT

It may be so, your Majesty ; it may.
Last noon the Austrian ambassador,

Whom I consulted ere I posted down,
Assured me that his latest papers word
How General Mack and eighty thousand men
Have made good speed across Bavaria
To wait the French and give them check at Ulm,
That fortress-frontier-town, entrenched and walled,
A place long chosen as a vantage-point
Whereon to encounter them as they outwind
From the blind shades and baffling green defiles
Of the Black Forest, worn with wayfaring.
Here Mack will intercept his agile foe
Hasting to meet the Russians in Bohemia,
And cripple him, if not annihilate.

    Thus now, sir, opens out this Great Alliance
Of Russia, Austria, England, whereto I
Have lent my earnest efforts through long months,
And the realm gives her money, ships, and men.—
It claps a muffler round this Cock's steel spurs,
And leaves me sanguine on his overthrow.
But then,—this coalition of resources
Demands a strong and active Cabinet
To aid your Majesty's directive hand ;
And thus I urge again the said additions—
These brilliant intellects of the other side
Who stand by Fox.   With us conjoined, they——

KING

What, what, again—in face of my sound reasons !
Believe me, Pitt, you underrate yourself ;
You do not need such aid.   The splendid feat
Of banding Europe in a righteous cause
That you have achieved, so soon to put to shame
This wicked bombardier of dynasties
That rule by right Divine, goes straight to prove
We had best continue as we have begun,
And call no partners to our management.
To fear dilemmas horning up ahead
Is not your wont.   Nay, nay, now, Mr. Pitt,
I must be firm.   And if you love your King
You'll goad him not so rashly to embrace
This Fox-and-Grenville faction and its friends.

Rather than Fox, why, give me civil war!
Hey, what?   But what besides?

PITT

I say besides, sir, . . . nothing!

A silence.

KING (cheerfully)

The Chancellor's here, and many friends of mine: Lady
Winchelsea, Lord and Lady Chesterfield, Lady Bulkeley, General
Garth, and Mr. Phipps the oculist—not the least important to me.
He is a worthy and a skilful man.   My eyes, he says, are as
marvellously improved in durability as I know them to be in
power.   I have arranged to go to-morrow with the Princesses,
and the Dukes of Cumberland, Sussex, and Cambridge (who are
also here) for a ride on the Ridgeway, and through the Camp on
the downs.   You'll accompany us there?

PITT

I am honoured by your Majesty's commands.

PITT looks resignedly out of the window.

What curious structure do I see outside, sir?

KING

It's but a stage, a type of all the world.   The burgesses have
arranged it in my honour.   At six o'clock this evening there are
to be combats at single-stick to amuse the folk; four guineas the
prize for the man who breaks most heads.   Afterwards there is
to be a grinning match through horse-collars—a very humorous
sport which I must stay here and witness; for I am interested in
whatever entertains my subjects.

PITT

Not one in all the land but knows it, sir.

KING

Now, Mr. Pitt, you must require repose;
Consult your own convenience then, I beg,
On when you leave.

PITT

I thank your Majesty.

He departs as one whose purpose has failed, and the scene shuts.

SCENE II

BEFORE THE CITY OF ULM

A prospect of the city from the east, showing in the foreground a low-lying marshy country bounded in mid-distance by the banks of the Danube, which, bordered by poplars and willows, flows across the picture from the left to the Elchingen Bridge near the right of the scene, and is backed by irregular heights and terraces of espaliered vines. Between these and the river stands the city, crowded with old gabled houses and surrounded by walls, bastions, and a ditch, all the edifices being dominated by the nave and tower of the huge Gothic Münster.

On the most prominent of the heights at the back—the Michaelsberg—to the upper-right of the view, is encamped the mass of the Austrian army, amid half-finished entrenchments. Advanced posts of the same are seen south-east of the city, not far from the advanced corps of the French Grand-Army under SOULT, MARMONT, MURAT, LANNES, NEY, and DUPONT, which occupy in a semicircle the whole breadth of the flat landscape in front, and extend across the river to higher ground on the right hand of the panorama.

Heavy mixed drifts of rain and snow are descending impartially on the French and on the Austrians, the downfall nearly blotting out the latter on the hills. A chill October wind wails across the country, and the poplars yield slantingly to the gusts.

DUMB SHOW

Drenched peasants are busily at work, fortifying the heights of the Austrian position in the face of the enemy. Vague companies of Austrians above, and of the French below, hazy and indistinct in the thick atmosphere, come and go without apparent purpose near their respective lines.

Closer at hand NAPOLÉON, in his familiar blue-grey overcoat, rides hither and thither with his marshals, haranguing familiarly the bodies of soldiery as he passes them, and observing and pointing out the disposition of the Austrians to his companions.

Thicker sheets of rain fly across as the murk of evening increases, which at length entirely obscures the prospect, and cloaks its bleared lights and fires.

SCENE III

ULM.   WITHIN THE CITY

The interior of the Austrian headquarters on the following morning. A tempest raging without.

GENERAL MACK, haggard and anxious, the ARCHDUKE FERDINAND, PRINCE SCHWARZENBERG, GENERAL JELLACHICH, GENERALS RIESC, BIBERACH, and other field officers discovered, seated at a table with a map spread out before them. A wood fire blazes between tall andirons in a yawning fireplace. At every more than usually boisterous gust of wind the smoke flaps into the room.

MACK

The accursèd cunning of our adversary
Confounds all codes of honourable war,
Which ever have held as granted that the track
Of armies bearing hither from the Rhine—
Whether in peace or strenuous invasion—
Should pierce the Schwarzwald, and through Memmingen,
And meet us in our front.   But he must wind
And corkscrew meanly round, where foot of man
Can scarce find pathway, stealing up to us
Thiefwise, by our back door!   Nevertheless,
If English war-fleets be abreast Boulogne,
As these deserters tell, and ripe to land there,
It destines Bonaparte to pack him back
Across the Rhine again.   We've but to wait,
And see him go.

ARCHDUKE

But who shall say if these bright tales be true?

MACK

Even then, small matter, your Imperial Highness;
The Russians near us daily, and must soon—
Ay, far within the eight days I have named—
Be operating to untie this knot,
If we hold on.

ARCHDUKE

         Conjectures these—no more;
I stomach not such waiting.   Neither hope
Has kernel in it.   I and my cavalry
With caution, when the shadows fall to-night,
Can bore some hole in this engirdlement;
Outpass the gate north-east; join General Werneck,
And somehow cut our way Bohemia-wards:
Well worth the hazard, in our straitened case!

MACK (firmly)

The body of our force stays here with me.
And I am much surprised, your Highness, much,
You mark not how destructive 'tis to part!
If we wait on, for certain we should wait
In our full strength, compacted, undispersed
By such partition as your Highness plans.

Schwarzenberg

There's truth in urging we should not divide,
But weld more closely.——Yet why stay at all ?
Methinks there's but one sure salvation left,
To wit, that we conjunctly march herefrom,
And with much circumspection, towards the Tyrol.
The subtle often rack their wits in vain——
Assay whole magazines of strategy——
To shun ill loomings deemed insuperable,
When simple souls by stumbling up to them
Find the grim shapes but air.   But let us grant
That the investing French so ring us in
As to leave not a span for such exploit ;
Then go we——throw ourselves upon their steel,
And batter through, or die !——
What say you, Generals ?   Speak your minds, I pray.

Jellachich

I favour marching out——the Tyrol way.

Riesc

Bohemia best !   The route thereto is open.

Archduke

My course is chosen.   O this black campaign,
Which Pitt's alarmed dispatches pricked us to,
All unforeseeing !   Any risk for me
Rather than court humiliation here !

MACK has risen during the latter remarks, walked to the window, and looked out at the rain.   He returns with an air of embarrassment.

Mack (to Archduke)

It is my privilege firmly to submit
That your Imperial Highness undertake
No venturous vaulting into risks unknown.——
Assume that you, Sire, as you have proposed,
With your light regiments and the cavalry,
Detach yourself from us, to scoop a way
By circuits northwards through the Rauhe Alps
And Herdenheim, into Bohemia :
Reports all point that you will be attacked,
Enveloped, borne on to capitulate.

What worse can happen here ?—
Remember, Sire, the Emperor deputes me,
Should such a clash arise as has arisen,
To exercise supreme authority.
The honour of our arms, our race, demands
That none of your Imperial Highness' line
Be pounded prisoner by this vulgar foe,
Who is not France, but an adventurer
Imposing on that country for his gain.

ARCHDUKE

I amply recognize the drear disgrace
Involving Austria if this upstart chief
Should of his cunning seize and hold in pawn
A royal-lineaged son, whose ancestors
Root on the primal rocks of history.

SPIRIT IRONIC

Note that.   Five years, and legal brethren they—
This feudal treasure and the upstart man !

ARCHDUKE

But it seems clear to me that loitering here
Is full as like to compass our surrender
As moving hence.   And ill it therefore suits
The mood of one of my high temperature
To pause inactive while await me means
Of desperate cure for these so desperate ills !

[The ARCHDUKE FERDINAND goes out,
A troubled silence follows, during which the gusts call into the chimney,
and raindrops spit on the fire.

SCHWARZENBERG

The Archduke bears him shrewdly in this course.
We may as well look matters in the face,
And that we are cooped and cornered is most clear ;
Clear is it, too, that but a miracle
Can work to loose us !   I have stoutly held
That this man's three years' ostentatious scheme
To fling his army on the tempting shores
Of our allies the English was a—well—
Scarce other than a trick of thimble-rig
To still us into false security.

Jellachich

Well, I know nothing.   None needs list to me,
But, on the whole, to southward seems the course
For plunging, all in force, immediately.

Another pause.

Spirit Sinister

The Will throws Mack again in agitation:
Ho-ho—what he'll do now!

Spirit of the Pities

    Nay, hard one, nay;
The clouds weep for him!

Spirit Sinister

    If he must he must;
And it's good antic at a vacant time!

Mack goes restlessly to the door, and is heard pacing about the vestibule,
and questioning the aides and other officers gathered there.

A General

He wavers like this smoke-wreath that inclines
Or north, or south, as the storm-currents rule!

Mack (returning)

Bring that deserter hither once again.

A French soldier is brought in, blindfolded and guarded.   The bandage is
removed.

 Well, tell us what he says.

An Officer (after speaking to the prisoner in French)

    He still repeats
That the whole body of the British strength
Is even now descending on Boulogne,
And that self-preservation must, of need,
Clear us from Bonaparte ere many days,
Who momently is moving.

Mack

    Still retain him.

He walks to the fire, and stands looking into it.   The soldier is taken out.

JELLACHICH (bending over the map in argument with RIESC)

I much prefer our self-won information ;
And if we have Marshal Soult at Landsberg here,
(Which seems to be the truth, despite this man,)
And Dupont hard upon us at Albeck,
With Ney not far from Günzburg ; somewhere here,
Or further down the river, lurking Lannes,
Our game's to draw off southward—if we can !

MACK (turning)

I have it.   This we'll do.   You, Jellachich,
Unite with Spangen's troops at Memmingen,
To fend off mischief there.   And you, Riesc,
Will make your utmost haste to occupy
The bridge and upper ground at Elchingen,
And all along the left bank of the stream,
Till you observe whereon to concentrate
And sever their connections.   I couch here,
And hold the city till the Russians come.

A GENERAL (in a low voice)

Disjunction seems of all expedients worst :
If any stay, then stay should every man,
Gather, inlace, and close up hip to hip,
And perk and bristle hedgehog-like with spines !

MACK

The conference is ended, friends, I say,
And orders will be issued here forthwith.

Guns heard.

AN OFFICER

Surely that's from the Michaelsberg above us ?

MACK

Never care.   Here we stay.   In five more days
The Russians hail, and we regain our bays.

[Exeunt severally.

SCENE IV

BEFORE ULM.   THE SAME DAY

A high wind prevails, and rain falls in torrents.   An elevated terrace near Elchingen forms the foreground.

DUMB SHOW

From the terrace BONAPARTE surveys and dictates operations against the entrenched heights of the Michaelsberg that rise in the middle distance on the right above the city.   Through the gauze of descending waters the French soldiery can be discerned climbing to the attack under NEY.

They slowly advance, recede, re-advance, halt.   A time of suspense follows. Then they are seen in a state of irregular movement, even confusion ; but in the end they carry the heights with the bayonet.

Below the spot whereon NAPOLÉON and his staff are gathered, glistening wet and plastered with mud, obtrudes on the left the village of Elchingen, now in the hands of the French.   Its white-walled monastery, its bridge over the Danube, recently broken by the irresistible NEY, wear a desolated look, and the stream, which is swollen by the rainfall and rasped by the storm, seems wanly to sympathize.

Anon shells are dropped by the French from the summits they have gained into the city below.   A bomb from an Austrian battery falls near NAPOLÉON, and in bursting raises a fountain of mud.   The Emperor retreats with his officers to a less conspicuous station.

Meanwhile LANNES advances from a position near NAPOLÉON till his columns reach the top of the Frauenberg hard by.   The united corps of LANNES and NEY descend on the inner slope of the heights towards the city walls, in the rear of the retreating Austrians.   One of the French columns scales a bastion, but NAPOLÉON orders the assault to be discontinued, and with the wane of day the spectacle disappears.

SCENE V

THE SAME.   THE MICHAELSBERG

A chilly but rainless noon three days later.   At the back of the scene, northward, rise the Michaelsberg heights ; below stretches the panorama of the city and the Danube.   On a secondary eminence forming a spur of the upper hill, a fire of logs is burning, the foremost group beside it being NAPOLÉON and his staff, the latter in gorgeous uniform, the former in his shabby greatcoat and plain turned-up hat, walking to and fro with his hands behind him, and occasionally stopping to warm himself.   The French infantry are drawn up in a dense array at the back of these.

The whole Austrian garrison of Ulm marches out of the city gate opposite NAPOLÉON.   GENERAL MACK is at the head, followed by GIULAY, GOTTES-HEIM, KLENAU, LICHTENSTEIN, and many other officers, who advance to BONAPARTE and deliver their swords.

MACK

Behold me, Sire.   Mack the unfortunate !

NAPOLÉON

War, General, ever has its ups and downs,
And you must take the better and the worse
As impish chance or destiny ordains.
Come near and warm you here.   A glowing fire
Is life on these depressing, mired, moist days
Of smitten leaves down-dropping clammily,
And toadstools like the putrid lungs of men.

      (To his lieutenants)

Cause them to stand to right and left of me.

The Austrian officers arrange themselves as directed, and the body of the
Austrians now file past their Conqueror, laying down their arms as they
approach ; some with angry gestures and words, others in moody silence.

Listen, I pray you, Generals gathered here.
I tell you frankly that I know not why
Your master wages this wild war with me.
I know not what he seeks by such injustice,
Unless to give me practice in my trade—
That of a soldier—whereto I was bred :
Deemed he my craft might slip from me, unplied ?
Let him now own me still a dab therein !

MACK

Permit me, your Imperial Majesty,
To speak one word in answer ; which is this,
No war was wished for by my Emperor :
Russia constrained him to it !

NAPOLÉON

          If that be,
You are no more a European power.—
I would point out to him that my resources
Are not confined to these my musters here ;
My prisoners of war, in route for France,
Will see some marks of my resources there !
Two hundred thousand volunteers, right fit,
Will join my standards at a single nod,
And in six weeks prove soldiers to the bone,

Whilst your recruits, compulsion's scavengings,
Scarce weld to warriors after toilsome years.
　　But I want nothing on this Continent:
The English only are my enemies.
Ships, colonies, and commerce I desire,
Yea, therewith to advantage you as me.
Let me then charge your Emperor, my brother,
To turn his feet the shortest way to peace.—
All states must have an end, the weak, the strong;
Ay; even may fall the dynasty of Lorraine!

*The filing past and laying down of arms by the Austrian army continues
with monotonous regularity, as if it would never end.*

NAPOLÉON (in a murmur, after a while)

Well, what cares England! She has won her game;
I have unlearnt to threaten her from Boulogne. . . .
　　Her gold it is that forms the weft of this
Fair tapestry of armies marshalled here!
Likewise of Russia's, drawing steadily nigh.
But they may see what these see, by and by.

SPIRIT OF THE YEARS

*So let him speak, the while we clearly sight him
Moved like a figure on a lantern-slide.
Which, much amazing uninitiate eyes,
The all-compelling crystal pane but drags
Whither the showman wills.*

SPIRIT IRONIC

*　　　　　　And yet, my friend,
The Will Itself might smile at this collapse
Of Austria's men-at-arms, so drolly done;
Even as, in your phantasmagoric show,
The deft manipulator of the slide
Might smile at his own art.*

CHORUS OF THE YEARS (aerial music)

*　　Ah, no: ah, no!
It is impassible as glacial snow.—
　　Within the Great Unshaken
　　These painted shapes awaken*

A lesser thrill than doth the gentle lave
Of yonder bank by Danube's wandering wave
Within the Schwarzwald heights that give it flow !

SPIRIT OF THE PITIES

But O, the intolerable antilogy
Of making figments feel !

SPIRIT IRONIC

             Logic's in that.
IT does not, I must own, quite play the game.

CHORUS OF IRONIC SPIRITS (aerial music)

And this day wins for Ulm a dingy fame,
Which centuries shall not bleach from her old name !

The procession of Austrians continues till the scene is hidden by haze.

SCENE VI

LONDON.   SPRING GARDENS

Before LORD MALMESBURY'S house, on a Sunday morning in the same autumn.   Idlers pause and gather in the background.
PITT enters, and meets LORD MULGRAVE,

MULGRAVE

Good day, Pitt.   Ay, these leaves that skim the ground
With withered voices, hint that sunshine-time
Is well-nigh past.—And so the game's begun
Between him and the Austro-Russian force,
As second movement in the faceabout
From Boulogne shore, with which he has hocussed us ?—
What has been heard on't ?   Have they clashed as yet ?

PITT

The Emperor Francis, partly at my instance,
Has thrown the chief command on General Mack,
A man most capable and far of sight.
He centres by the Danube-bank at Ulm,
A town well-walled, and firm for leaning on
To intercept the French in their advance
From the Black Forest towards the Russian troops

Approaching from the east.   If Bonaparte
Sustain his marches at the break-neck speed
That all report, they must have met ere now.
—There is a rumour . . . quite impossible ! . . .

MULGRAVE

You still have faith in Mack as strategist ?
There have been doubts of his far-sightedness.

PITT (hastily)

I know, I know.—I am calling here at Malmesbury's
At somewhat an unceremonious time
To ask his help to translate this Dutch print
The post has brought.   Malmesbury is great at Dutch,
Learning it long at Leyden, years ago.

He draws a newspaper from his pocket, unfolds it, and glances it down.

There's news here unintelligible to me
Upon the very matter !   You'll come in ?

They call at LORD MALMESBURY'S.   *He meets them in the hall, and*
welcomes them with an apprehensive look of foreknowledge.

PITT

Pardon this early call.   The packet's in,
And wings me this unreadable Dutch paper,
So, as the offices are closed to-day,
I have brought it round to you.

(*Handing the paper.*)

                              What does it say ?
For God's sake, read it out.   You know the tongue.

MALMESBURY (with hesitation)

I have glanced it through already—more than once—
A copy having reached me, too, by now . . .
We are in the presence of a great disaster !
See here.   It says that Mack, enjailed in Ulm
By Bonaparte—from four sides shutting round—
Capitulated, and with all his force
Laid down his arms before his conqueror !

PITT's face changes.   A silence.

MULGRAVE

Outrageous !   Ignominy unparalleled !

PITT

By God, my lord, these statements must be false !
These foreign prints are trustless as Cheap Jack
Dumfounding yokels at a country fair.
I heed no word of it.—Impossible.
What !   Eighty thousand Austrians, nigh in touch
With Russia's levies that Kutúzof leads,
To lay down arms before the war's begun ?
'Tis too much !

MALMESBURY

                  But I fear it is too true !
Note the assevered source of the report—
One beyond thought of minters of mock tales.
The writer adds that military wits
Cry that the Little Corporal now makes war
In a new way, using his soldiers' legs
And not their arms, to bring him victory.
Ha-ha !   The quip must sting the Corporal's foes.

PITT (after a pause)

O vacillating Prussia !   Had she moved,
Had she but planted one foot firmly down,
All this had been averted.—I must go.
'Tis sure, 'tis sure, I labour but in vain !

MALMESBURY accompanies him to the door, and PITT walks away
disquietedly towards Whitehall, the other two regarding him as he goes.

MULGRAVE

Too swiftly he declines to feebleness,
And these things well might shake a stouter frame !

MALMESBURY

Of late the burden of all Europe's cares,
Of hiring and maintaining half her troops,
His single pair of shoulders has upborne,
Thanks to the obstinacy of the King.—
His thin, strained face, his ready irritation,
Are ominous signs.   He may not be for long.

MULGRAVE

He alters fast, indeed,—as do events.

MALMESBURY

His labour's lost ; and all our money gone !
It looks as if this doughty coalition
On which we have lavished so much pay and pains
Would end in wreck.

MULGRAVE

All is not over yet ;
The gathering Russian forces are unbroke.

MALMESBURY

Well ; we shall see.   Should Boney vanquish these,
And silence all resistance on that side,
His move will then be backward to Boulogne,
And so upon us.

MULGRAVE

Nelson to our defence !

MALMESBURY

Ay ; where is Nelson ?   Faith, by this late time
He may be sodden ; churned in Biscay swirls ;
Or blown to polar bears by boreal gales ;
Or sleeping amorously in some calm cave
On the Canaries' or Atlantis' shore
Upon the bosom of his Dido dear,
For all that we know !   Never a sound of him
Since passing Portland one September day—
To make for Cadiz ; so 'twas then believed.

MULGRAVE

He's staunch.   He's watching, or I am much deceived.

MULGRAVE departs.   MALMESBURY goes within.   The scene shuts.

ACT FIFTH

SCENE I

OFF CAPE TRAFALGAR

A bird's-eye view of the sea discloses itself.   It is daybreak, and the broad face of the ocean is fringed on its eastern edge by the Cape and the Spanish shore.   On the rolling surface immediately beneath the eye, ranged more or less in two parallel lines running north and south, one group from the twain standing off somewhat, are the vessels of the combined French and Spanish navies, whose canvases, as the sun edges upward, shine in its rays like satin.

On the western horizon two columns of ships appear in full sail, small as moths to the aerial vision.   They are bearing down towards the combined squadrons.

RECORDING ANGEL I (intoning from his book)

At last Villeneuve accepts the sea and fate,
Despite the Cadiz council called of late,
Whereat his stoutest captains—men the first
          To do all mortals durst—
Willing to sail, and bleed, and bear the worst,
Short of cold suicide, did yet opine
That plunging mid those teeth of treble line
          In jaws of oaken wood
Held open by the English navarchy
With suasive breadth and artful modesty,
Would smack of purposeless foolhardihood.

RECORDING ANGEL II

But word came, writ in mandatory mood,
To put from Cadiz, gain Toulon, and straight
At a said sign on Italy operate.
Moreover that Villeneuve, arrived as planned,
Would find Rosily in supreme command.—
Gloomy Villeneuve grows rash, and, darkly brave,
Leaps to meet war, storm, Nelson—even the grave.

SEMICHORUS I OF THE YEARS (aerial music)

Ere the concussion hurtle, draw abreast
          Of the sea.

SEMICHORUS II

Where Nelson's hulls are rising from the west,
Silently.

SEMICHORUS I

Each linen wing outspread, each man and lad
Sworn to be

SEMICHORUS II

Amid the vanmost, or for Death, or glad
Victory!

The point of sight descends till it is near the deck of the "Bucentaure," the flag-ship of VILLENEUVE. Present thereon are the ADMIRAL, his FLAG-CAPTAIN MAGENDIE, LIEUTENANT DAUDIGNON, other naval officers and seamen.

MAGENDIE

All night we have read their signals in the air,
Whereby the peering frigates of their van
Have told them of our trend.

VILLENEUVE

                The enemy
Makes threat as though to throw him on our stern:
Signal the fleet to wear; bid Gravina
To come in from manœuvring with his twelve,
And range himself in line.

Officers murmur.

                I say again
Bid Gravina draw hither with his twelve,
And signal all to wear!—and come upon
The larboard tack with every bow anorth!—
So we make Cadiz in the worst event,
And patch our rags up there. As we head now
Our only practicable thoroughfare
Is through Gibraltar Strait—a fatal door!
   Signal to close the line and leave no gaps.
Remember, too, what I have already told:
Remind them of it now. They must not pause
For signallings from me amid a strife
Whose chaos may prevent my clear discernment,
Or may forbid my signalling at all.

The voice of honour then becomes the chief's ;
Listen they thereto, and set every stitch
To heave them on into the fiercest fight.
Now I will sum up all : heed well the charge ;
EACH CAPTAIN, PETTY OFFICER, AND MAN
IS ONLY AT HIS POST WHEN UNDER FIRE.

The ships of the whole fleet turn their bows from south to north as
directed, and close up in two parallel curved columns, the concave side of
each column being towards the enemy, and the interspaces of the first column
being, in general, opposite the hulls of the second.

AN OFFICER (straining his eyes towards the English fleet)

How they skip on ! Their overcrowded sails
Bulge like blown bladders in a tripeman's shop
The market-morning after slaughterday !

PETTY OFFICER (aside)

It's morning before slaughterday with us,
I make so bold to bode !

The English Admiral is seen to be signalling to his fleet. The signal is :
" ENGLAND EXPECTS EVERY MAN WILL DO HIS DUTY." A loud cheering
from all the English ships comes undulating on the wind when the signal
is read.

VILLENEUVE

They are signalling too.—Well, business soon begins !
You will reserve your fire. And be it known
That we display no admirals' flags at all
Until the action's past. 'Twill puzzle them,
And work to our advantage when we close.—
Yes, they are double-ranked, I think, like us ;
But we shall see anon.

MAGENDIE

                    The foremost one
Makes for the " Santa Ana." In such case
The " Fougueux " might assist her.

VILLENEUVE

                    Be it so—
There's time enough.—Our ships will be in place,
And ready to speak back in iron words
When theirs cry Hail ! in the same sort of voice.

They prepare to receive the northernmost column of the enemy's ships
headed by the " Victory," trying the distance by an occasional single shot.

During their suspense a discharge is heard southward, and turning they behold COLLINGWOOD at the head of his column in the "Royal Sovereign," just engaging with the Spanish "Santa Ana." Meanwhile the "Victory" draws still nearer, preserving silence with brazen sang-froid. At a concerted moment full broadsides are discharged into her simultaneously from the "Bucentaure," the "Santísima Trinidad," and the "Redoutable."

When the smoke clears the "Victory's" mizzen-topmast, with spars and a quantity of rigging, is seen to have fallen, her wheel to be shot away, and her deck encumbered with dead and wounded men.

VILLENEUVE

'Tis well! But see; their course is undelayed,
And still they near in clenched audacity!

DAUDIGNON

This northmost column bears upon our beam.
Their prows will pierce us thwartwise. That's the aim.

MAGENDIE

Which aim deft Lucas o' the "Redoutable"
Most gallantly bestirs him to outscheme.——
See, how he strains, that on his timbers fall
Blows that were destined for his Admiral!

During this the French ship "Redoutable" is moving forward to interpose itself between the approaching "Victory" and the "Bucentaure."

VILLENEUVE

Now comes it! The "Santísima Trinidad,"
The old "Redoutable's" hard sides, and ours,
Will take the touse of this bombastic blow.
Your grapnels and your boarding-hatchets—ready!
We'll dash our eagle on the English deck,
And swear to fetch it!

CREW

Aye! We swear. Huzza!
Long live the Emperor!

But the "Victory" suddenly swerves to the rear of the "Bucentaure," and crossing her stern-waters, discharges a broadside into her and the "Redoutable" endwise, wrapping the scene in folds of smoke.

The point of view changes.

SCENE II

THE SAME.   THE QUARTER-DECK OF THE "VICTORY"

The van of each division of the English fleet has drawn to the windward side of the combined fleets of the enemy, and broken their order, the "Victory" being now parallel to and alongside the "Redoutable," the "Téméraire" taking up a station on the other side of that ship. The "Bucentaure" and the "Santísima Trinidad" become jammed together a little way ahead. A smoke and din of cannonading prevail, amid which the studding-sail booms are shot away.

NELSON, HARDY, BLACKWOOD, SECRETARY SCOTT, LIEUTENANT PASCO, BURKE the Purser, CAPTAIN ADAIR of the Marines, and other officers are on or near the quarter-deck.

NELSON

See, there, that noble fellow Collingwood,
How straight he helms his ship into the fire !—
Now you'll haste back to yours (to Blackwood).
    —We must henceforth
Trust to the Great Disposer of events,
And justice of our cause ! . . .

[BLACKWOOD leaves.

The battle grows hotter. A double-headed shot cuts down seven or eight marines on the "Victory's" poop.

Captain Adair, part those marines of yours,
And hasten to disperse them round the ship.—
Your place is down below, Burke, not up here ;
Ah, yes ; like David you would see the battle !

A heavy discharge of musket-shot comes from the tops of the "Santísima Trinidad." ADAIR and PASCO fall. Another swathe of marines is mowed down by chain-shot.

SCOTT

My lord, I use to you the utmost prayers
That I have privilege to shape in words :
Remove your stars and orders, I would beg ;
That shot was aimed at you.

NELSON

They were awarded to me as an honour,
And shall I do despite to those who prize me,
And slight their gifts ? No, I will die with them,
If die I must.

He walks up and down with HARDY.

HARDY

At least let's put you on
Your old greatcoat, my lord—(the air is keen).—
'Twill cover all.   So while you still retain
Your dignities, you baulk these deadly aims.

NELSON

Thank 'ee, good friend.   But no,—I haven't time,
I do assure you—not a trice to spare,
As you well see.

A few minutes later SCOTT falls dead, a bullet having pierced his skull.
Immediately after a shot passes between the Admiral and the Captain,
tearing the instep of HARDY's shoe, and striking away the buckle.   They
shake off the dust and splinters it has scattered over them.   NELSON glances
round, and perceives what has happened to his secretary.

NELSON

Poor Scott, too, carried off!   Warm work this, Hardy ;
Too warm to go on long.

HARDY

I think so, too ;
Their lower ports are blocked against our hull,
And our charge now is less.   Each knock so near
Sets their old wood on fire.

NELSON

Ay, rotten as peat.
What's that ?   I think she has struck, or pretty nigh !

A cracking of musketry.

HARDY

Not yet.—Those small-arm men there, in her tops,
Thin our crew fearfully.   Now, too, our guns
Have to be dipped full down, or they would rake
The "Téméraire" there on the other side.

NELSON

True.—While you deal good measure out to these,
Keep slapping at those giants over here—
The "Trinidad," I mean, and the "Bucentaure,"
To win'ard—swelling up so pompously.

HARDY

I'll see no slackness shall be shown that way.

They part and go in their respective directions. Gunners, naked to the
waist and reeking with sweat, are now in swift action on the several decks,
and firemen carry buckets of water hither and thither. The killed and
wounded thicken around, and are being lifted and examined by the surgeons.
NELSON and HARDY meet again.

NELSON

Bid still the firemen bring more bucketfuls,
And dash the water into each new hole
Our guns have gouged in the " Redoutable,"
Or we shall all be set ablaze together.

HARDY

Let me once more advise, entreat, my lord,
That you do not expose yourself so clearly.
Those fellows in the mizzen-top up there
Are peppering round you quite perceptibly.

NELSON

Now, Hardy, don't offend me. They can't aim;
They only set their own rent sails on fire.—
But if they could, I would not hide a button
To save ten lives like mine. I have no cause
To prize it, I assure 'ee.—Ah, look there,
One of the women hit,—and badly, too.
Poor wench! Let some one shift her quickly down.

HARDY

My lord, each humblest sojourner on the seas,
Dock-labourer, lame longshore-man, bowed bargee,
Sees it as policy to shield his life
For those dependent on him. Much more, then,
Should one upon whose priceless presence here
Such issues hang, so many strivers lean,
Use average circumspection at an hour
So critical for us all.

NELSON

          Ay, ay. Yes, yes;
I know your meaning, Hardy; and I know
That you disguise as frigid policy
What really is your honest love of me.

But, faith, I have had my day.   My work's nigh done ;
I serve all interests best by chancing it
Here with the commonest.—Ah, their heavy guns
Are silenced every one !   Thank God for that.

HARDY

'Tis so.   They only use their small arms now.

He goes to larboard to see what is progressing on that side between his ship and the " Santísima Trinidad."

OFFICER (to a seaman)

Swab down these stairs.   The mess of blood about
Makes 'em so slippery that one's like to fall
In carrying the wounded men below.

While CAPTAIN HARDY *is still a little way off,* LORD NELSON *turns to walk aft, when a ball from one of the muskets in the mizzen-top of the " Redoutable " enters his left shoulder.   He falls upon his face on the deck.* HARDY *looks round, and sees what has happened.*

HARDY (hastily)

Ah—what I feared, and strove to hide I feared ! . . .

He goes towards NELSON, *who in the meantime has been lifted by* SERGEANT-MAJOR SECKER *and two seamen.*

NELSON

Hardy, I think they've done for me at last !

HARDY

I hope not !

NELSON

Yes.   My backbone is shot through.
I have not long to live.

The men proceed to carry him below.

Those tiller ropes
They've torn away, get instantly repaired !

At sight of him borne along wounded there is great agitation among the crew.

Cover my face.   There will no good be done
By drawing their attention off to me.
Bear me along, good fellows ; I am but one
Among the many darkened here to-day !

He is carried on to the cockpit over the crowd of dead and wounded.
(To the Chaplain)

Doctor, I'm gone.   I am waste o' time to you.

HARDY (remaining behind)

Hills, go to Collingwood and let him know
That we've no Admiral here.

He passes on.

A LIEUTENANT

Now quick and pick him off who did the deed—
That white-bloused man there in the mizzen-top.

POLLARD, a midshipman (shooting)

No sooner said than done.   A pretty aim!

The Frenchman falls dead upon the poop.

The spectacle seems now to become enveloped in smoke, and the point of view changes.

SCENE III

THE SAME.   ON BOARD THE "BUCENTAURE"

The bowsprit of the French Admiral's ship is stuck fast in the stern-gallery of the "Santísima Trinidad," the starboard side of the "Bucentaure" being shattered by shots from two English three-deckers which are pounding her on that hand.   The poop is also reduced to ruin by two other English ships that are attacking her from behind.

On the quarter-deck are ADMIRAL VILLENEUVE, the FLAG-CAPTAIN MAGENDIE, LIEUTENANTS DAUDIGNON, FOURNIER, and others, anxiously occupied.   The whole crew is in desperate action of battle and stumbling among the dead and dying, who have fallen too rapidly to be carried below.

VILLENEUVE

We shall be crushed if matters go on thus.—
Direct the "Trinidad" to let her drive,
That this foul tangle may be loosened clear!

DAUDIGNON

It has been tried, sir ; but she cannot move.

VILLENEUVE

Then signal to the "Hero" that she strive
Once more to drop this way.

MAGENDIE

            We may make signs,
But in the thickened air what signal's marked ?—
'Tis done, however.

VILLENEUVE

                   The " Redoutable "
And " Victory " there,—they grip in dying throes !
Something's amiss on board the English ship.
Surely the Admiral's fallen ?

A PETTY OFFICER

                        Sir, they say
That he was shot some hour, or half, ago.—
With dandyism raised to godlike pitch
He stalked the deck in all his jewellery,
And so was hit.

MAGENDIE

            Then Fortune shows her face !
We have scotched England in dispatching him.
                                    (He watches.)
Yes ! He commands no more ; and Lucas, joying,
Has taken steps to board.   Look, spars are laid,
And his best men are mounting at his heels.

                    A crash is heard.

VILLENEUVE

Ah, God—he is too late !   Whence came that hurl
Of heavy grape ?   The smoke prevents my seeing
But at brief whiles.—The boarding band has fallen,
Fallen almost to a man.—'Twas well assayed !

MAGENDIE

That's from their " Téméraire," whose vicious broadside
Has cleared poor Lucas' decks.

VILLENEUVE

                    And Lucas, too.
I see him no more there.   His red planks show
Three hundred dead if one.   Now for ourselves !

Four of the English three-deckers have gradually closed round the
" Bucentaure," whose bowsprit still sticks fast in the gallery of the " Santísima
Trinidad."   A broadside comes from one of the English, resulting in worse
havoc on the " Bucentaure."   The main and mizzen masts of the latter fall,
and the boats are beaten to pieces.   A raking fire of musketry follows from
the attacking ships, to which the " Bucentaure " heroically continues still to
keep up a reply.

CAPTAIN MAGENDIE falls wounded.   His place is taken by LIEUTENANT
DAUDIGNON.

VILLENEUVE

Now that the fume has lessened, code my biddance
Upon our only mast, and tell the van
At once to wear, and come into the fire.
(Aside) If it be true that, as *he* sneers, success
Demands of me but cool audacity,
To-day shall leave him nothing to desire !

Musketry continues. DAUDIGNON falls. He is removed, his post being
taken by LIEUTENANT FOURNIER. Another crash comes, and the deck is
suddenly encumbered with rigging.

FOURNIER

There goes our foremast ! How for signalling now ?

VILLENEUVE

To try that longer, Fournier, is in vain
Upon this haggard, scorched, and ravaged hulk,
Her decks all reeking with such gory shows,
Her starboard side in rents, her stern nigh gone !
How does she keep afloat ?—
" Bucentaure," O unlucky good old ship !
My part in you is played. Ay—I must go ;
I must tempt Fate elsewhere,—if but a boat
Can bear me through this wreckage to the van.

FOURNIER

Our boats are stove in, or as full of holes
As the cook's skimmer, from their cursèd balls !

Musketry. VILLENEUVE'S Head-of-Staff, DE PRIGNY, falls wounded,
and many additional men. VILLENEUVE glances troublously from ship to
ship of his fleet.

VILLENEUVE

How hideous are the waves, so pure this dawn !—
Red-frothed ; and friends and foes all mixed therein.—
Can we in some way hail the " Trinidad "
And get a boat from her ?

They attempt to attract the attention of the " Santísima Trinidad " by
shouting.

                              Impossible ;
Amid the loud combustion of this strife
As well try holloing to the antipodes ! . . .

So here I am.   The bliss of Nelson's end
Will not be mine ; his full refulgent eve
Becomes my midnight !   Well ; the fleets shall see
That I can yield my cause with dignity.

The " Bucentaure " strikes her flag.

A boat then puts off from the English ship " Conqueror," and VILLENEUVE, having surrendered his sword, is taken out from the " Bucentaure." But being unable to regain her own ship, the boat is picked up by the " Mars," and the French Admiral is received aboard her.

The point of view changes.

SCENE IV

THE SAME.   THE COCKPIT OF THE " VICTORY "

A din of trampling and dragging overhead, which is accompanied by a continuous ground-bass roar from the guns of the warring fleets, culminating at times in loud concussions.   The wounded are lying around in rows for treatment, some groaning, some silently dying, some dead.   The gloomy atmosphere of the low-beamed deck is pervaded by a thick haze of smoke, powdered wood, and other dust, and is heavy with the fumes of gunpowder and candle-grease, the odour of drugs and cordials, and the smell from abdominal wounds.

NELSON, his face now pinched and wan with suffering, is lying undressed in a midshipman's berth, dimly lit by a lantern.   Dr. BEATTY, Dr. MAGRATH, the Rev. Dr. SCOTT the Chaplain, BURKE the Purser, the Steward, and a few others stand around.

MAGRATH (in a low voice)

Poor Ram, and poor Tom Whipple, have just gone.

BEATTY

There was no hope for them.

NELSON (brokenly)

Who have just died ?

BEATTY

Two who were badly hit by now, my lord;
Lieutenant Ram and Mr. Whipple.

NELSON

Ah !—
So many lives—in such a glorious cause. . . ,
I join them soon, soon, soon !—O where is Hardy ?

Will nobody bring Hardy to me—none?
He must be killed, too.　Surely Hardy's dead?

A MIDSHIPMAN

He's coming soon, my lord.　The constant call
On his full heed of this most mortal fight
Keeps him from hastening hither as he would.

NELSON

I'll wait, I'll wait.　I should have thought of it.

Presently HARDY comes down.　NELSON and he grasp hands.

Hardy, how goes the day with us and England?

HARDY

Well; very well, thank God for't, my dear lord.
Villeneuve their Admiral has this moment struck,
And put himself aboard the "Conqueror."
Some fourteen of their first-rates, or about,
Thus far we've got.　The said "Bucentaure" chief:
The "Santa Ana," the "Redoutable,"
The "Fougueux," the "Santísima Trinidad,"
"San Augustino," "San Francisco," "Aigle";
And our old "Swiftsure," too, we've grappled back,
To every seaman's joy.　But now their van
Has tacked to bear round on the "Victory"
And crush her by sheer weight of wood and brass:
Three of our best I am therefore calling up,
And make no doubt of worsting theirs, and France.

NELSON

That's well.　I swore for twenty.—But it's well.

HARDY

We'll have 'em yet!　But without you, my lord,
We have to make slow plodding do the deeds
That sprung by inspiration ere you fell;
And on this ship the more particularly.

NELSON

No, Hardy.—Ever 'twas your settled fault
So modestly to whittle down your worth.

But I saw stuff in you which admirals need
When, taking thought, I chose the "Victory's" keel
To do my business with these braggarts in.
A business finished now, for me!—Good friend,
Slow shades are creeping on me. . . . I scarce see you.

HARDY

The smoke from ships upon our win'ard side,
And the dust raised by their worm-eaten hulks,
When our balls touch 'em, blind the eyes, in truth.

NELSON

No; it is not that dust; 'tis dust of death
That darkens me.

A shock overhead. HARDY *goes up. One or two other officers go up,
and by and by return.*

What was that extra noise?

OFFICER

The "Formidable" passed us by, my lord,
And thumped a stunning broadside into us.—
But, on their side, the "Hero's" captain's fallen;
The "Algeciras" has been boarded, too,
By Captain Tyler, and the captain shot:
Admiral Gravina desperately holds out;
They say he's lost an arm.

NELSON

And we ourselves—
Who have we lost on board here? Nay, but tell me!

BEATTY

Besides poor Scott, my lord, and Charles Adair,
Lieutenant Ram, and Whipple, captain's clerk,
There's Smith, and Palmer, midshipmen, just killed,
And fifty odd of seamen and marines.

NELSON

Poor youngsters! Scarred old Nelson joins you soon.

BEATTY

And wounded : Bligh, lieutenant ; Pasco, too,
And Reeves, and Peake, lieutenants of marines,
And Rivers, Westphall, Bulkeley, midshipmen,
With, of the crew, a hundred odd just now,
Unreckoning those late fallen not brought below.

BURKE

That fellow in the mizzen-top, my lord,
Who made it his affair to wing you thus,
We took good care to settle ; and he fell
Like an old rook, smack from his perch, stone dead.

NELSON

'Twas not worth while !—He was, no doubt, a man
Who in simplicity and sheer good faith
Strove but to serve his country. Rest be to him !
And may his wife, his friends, his little ones,
If such he had, be tided through their loss,
And soothed amid the sorrow brought by me.

HARDY re-enters.

Who's that ? Ah—here you come ! How, Hardy, now ?

HARDY

The Spanish Admiral's rumoured to be wounded,
We know not with what truth. But, be as 'twill,
He sheers away with all he could call round,
And some few frigates, straight to Cadiz port.

A violent explosion is heard above the confused noises on deck. A midshipman goes above and returns.

MIDSHIPMAN (in the background)

It is the enemy's first-rate, the " Achille,"
Blown to a thousand atoms !—While on fire,
Before she burst, the captain's woman there,
Desperate for life, climbed from the gunroom port
Upon the rudder-chains ; stripped herself stark,
And swam for the Pickle's boat. Our men in charge,
Seeing her great breasts bulging on the brine,
Sang out, " A mermaid 'tis, by God ! "—then rowed
And hauled her in.—

BURKE

           Such unbid sights obtrude
On death's dyed stage !

MIDSHIPMAN

      Meantime the " Achille " fought on,
Even while the ship was blazing, knowing well
The fire must reach their powder ; which it did.
The spot is covered now with floating men,
Some whole, the main in parts ; arms, legs, trunks, heads,
Bobbing with tons of timber on the waves,
And splinters looped with entrails of the crew.

NELSON (arousing)

Our course will be to anchor.   Let them know.

HARDY

But let me ask, my lord, as needs I must,
Seeing your state, and that our work's not done,
Shall I, from you, bid Admiral Collingwood
Take full on him the conduct of affairs ?

NELSON (trying to raise himself)

Not while I live, I hope !   No, Hardy ; no.
Give Collingwood my order.   Anchor all !

HARDY (hesitating)

You mean the signal's to be made forthwith ?

NELSON

I do !—By God, if but our carpenter
Could rig me up a jury-backbone now,
To last one hour—until the battle's done,
I'd see to it !   But here I am—stove in—
Broken—all logged and done for !   Done, ay done !

BEATTY (returning from the other wounded)

My lord, I must implore you to lie calm !
You shorten what at best may not be long.

NELSON (exhausted)

I know, I know, good Beatty!   Thank you well
Hardy, I was impatient.   Now I am still.
Sit here a moment, if you have time to spare?

BEATTY and the others retire, and the two abide in silence, except for the trampling overhead and the moans from adjoining berths.   NELSON is apparently in less pain, seeming to doze.

NELSON (suddenly)

What are you thinking, that you speak no word?

HARDY (waking from a short reverie)

Thoughts all confused, my lord :——their needs on deck,
Your own sad state, and your unrivalled past ;
Mixed up with flashes of old things afar——
Old childish things at home, down Wessex way,
In the snug village under Blackdon Hill
Where I was born.   The tumbling stream, the garden,
The placid look of the grey dial there,
Marking unconsciously this bloody hour,
And the red apples on my father's trees,
Just now full ripe.

NELSON

                    Ay, thus do little things
Steal into my mind, too.   But ah, my heart
Knows not your calm philosophy !——There's one——
Come nearer to me, Hardy.——One of all,
As you well guess, pervades my memory now ;
She, and my daughter——I speak freely to you.
'Twas good I made that codicil this morning
That you and Blackwood witnessed.   Now she rests
Safe on the nation's honour. . . . Let her have
My hair, and the small treasured things I owned,
And take care of her, as you care for me !

HARDY promises.

NELSON (resuming in a murmur)

Does love die with our frame's decease, I wonder,
Or does it live on ever? . . .

A silence.   BEATTY reapproaches.

E

HARDY

       Now I'll leave,
See if your order's gone, and then return.

NELSON (symptoms of death beginning to change his face)

Yes, Hardy; yes; I know it. You must go.—
Here we shall meet no more; since Heaven forfend
That care for me should keep you idle now,
When all the ship demands you. Beatty, too,
Go to the others who lie bleeding there;
Them you can aid. Me you can render none!
My time here is the briefest.—If I live
But long enough I'll anchor. . . . But—too late—
My anchoring's elsewhere ordered! . . . Kiss me, Hardy:

    HARDY bends over him.

I'm satisfied. Thank God, I have done my duty!

 HARDY brushes his eyes with his hand, and withdraws to go above, pausing to look back before he finally disappears.

BEATTY (watching Nelson)

Ah!—Hush around! . . .
He's sinking. It is but a trifle now
Of minutes with him. Stand you, please, aside,
And give him air.

 BEATTY, the Chaplain, MAGRATH, the Steward, and attendants continue to regard NELSON. BEATTY looks at his watch.

BEATTY

Two hours and fifty minutes since he fell,
And now he's going.

    They wait. NELSON dies.

CHAPLAIN

      Yes. . . . He has homed to where
There's no more sea.

      BEATTY

       We'll let the Captain know,
Who will confer with Collingwood at once.
I must now turn to these.

 He goes to another part of the cockpit, a midshipman ascends to the deck, and the scene overclouds.

Chorus of the Pities (aerial music)

His thread was cut too slowly!   When he fell,
*   And bade his fame farewell,*
He might have passed, and shunned his long-drawn pain,
*   Endured in vain, in vain!*

Spirit of the Years

Young Spirits, be not critical of That
Which was before, and shall be after you!

Spirit of the Pities

But out of tune the Mode and meritless
That quickens sense in shapes whom, thou hast said,
Necessitation sways!   A life there was
Among these self-same frail ones—Sophocles—
Who visioned it too clearly, even the while
He dubbed the Will "the gods."   Truly said he,
"Such gross injustice to their own creation
Burdens the time with mournfulness for us,
And for themselves with shame." [1]—Things mechanized
By coils and pivots set to foreframed codes
Would, in a thorough-sphered melodic rule,
And governance of sweet consistency,
Be cessed no pain, whose burnings would abide
With That Which holds responsibility,
Or inexist.

Chorus of the Pities (aerial music)

*   Yea, yea, yea!*
*   Thus would the Mover pay*
*   The score each puppet owes,*
The Reaper reap what his contrivance sows!
Why make Life debtor when it did not buy?
Why wound so keenly Right that it would die?

Spirit of the Years

Nay, blame not!   For what judgment can ye blame?—
In that immense unweeting Mind is shown
One far above forethinking; processive,
Yet superconscious; a Clairvoyancy
That knows not what It knows, yet works therewith.—

[1] Soph. *Trach.* 1266-72.

The cognizance ye mourn, Life's doom to feel,
If I report it meetly, came unmeant,
Emerging with blind gropes from impercipience
By listless sequence—luckless, tragic Chance,
In your more human tongue.

Spirit of the Pities

And hence unneeded

In the economy of Vitality,
Which might have ever kept a sealed cognition
As doth the Will Itself.

Chorus of the Years (aerial music)

Nay, nay, nay;
Your hasty judgments stay,
Until the topmost cyme
Have crowned the last entablature of Time.
O heap not blame on that in-brooding Will;
O pause, till all things all their days fulfil!

SCENE V

LONDON.   THE GUILDHALL

A crowd of citizens has gathered outside to watch the carriages as they drive up and deposit guests invited to the Lord Mayor's banquet, for which event the Hall is brilliantly lit within.   A cheer rises when the equipage of any popular personage arrives at the door.

First Citizen

Well, well! Nelson is the man who ought to have been banqueted to-night. But he is coming to Town in a coach different from these!

Second Citizen

Will they bring his poor splintered body home?

First Citizen

Yes.   They say he's to be tombed in marble, at St. Paul's or Westminster.   We shall see him if he lays in state.   It will make a patriotic spectacle for a fine day.

BOY

How can you see a dead man, father, after so long?

FIRST CITIZEN

They'll embalm him, my boy, as they did all the great Egyptian admirals.

BOY

His lady will be handy for that, won't she?

FIRST CITIZEN

Don't ye ask awkward questions.

SECOND CITIZEN

Here's another coming!

FIRST CITIZEN

That's my Lord Chancellor Eldon. Wot he'll say, and wot he'll look!—Mr. Pitt will be here soon.

BOY

I don't like Billy. He killed Uncle John's parrot.

SECOND CITIZEN

How may ye make that out, youngster?

BOY

Mr. Pitt made the war, and the war made us want sailors; and Uncle John went for a walk down Wapping High Street to talk to the pretty ladies one evening; and there was a press all along the river that night—a regular hot one—and Uncle John was carried on board a man-of-war to fight under Nelson; and nobody minded Uncle John's parrot, and it talked itself to death. So Mr. Pitt killed Uncle John's parrot; see it, sir?

SECOND CITIZEN

You had better have a care of this boy, friend. His brain is too precious for the common risks of Cheapside. Not but what he might as well have said Boney killed the parrot when he was about it. And as for Nelson—who's now sailing shinier seas than ours, if they've rubbed Her off his slate where he's gone to,

—the French papers say that our loss in him is greater than our gain in ships ; so that logically the victory is theirs. Gad, sir, it's almost true !

A hurrahing is heard from Cheapside, and the crowd in that direction begins to hustle and show excitement.

FIRST CITIZEN

He's coming, he's coming ! Here, let me lift you up, my boy. —Why, they have taken out the horses, as I am man alive !

SECOND CITIZEN

Pitt for ever !—Why, here's a blade opening and shutting his mouth like the rest, but never a sound does he raise !

THIRD CITIZEN

I've not too much breath to carry me through my day's work, so I can't afford to waste it in such luxuries as crying Hurrah to aristocrats. If ye was ten yards off y'd think I was shouting as loud as any.

SECOND CITIZEN

It's a very mean practice of ye to husband yourself at such a time, and gape in dumbshow like a frog in Plaistow Marshes.

THIRD CITIZEN

No, sir ; it's economy ; a very necessary instinct in these days of ghastly taxations to pay half the armies in Europe ! In short, in the words of the Ancients, it is scarcely compass-mentas to do otherwise ! Somebody must save something, or the country will be as bankrupt as Mr. Pitt himself is, by all account ; though he don't look it just now.

PITT's coach passes, drawn by a troop of running men and boys. The Prime Minister is seen within, a thin, erect, up-nosed figure, with a flush of excitement on his usually pale face. The vehicle reaches the doorway to the Guildhall and halts with a jolt. PITT gets out shakily, and amid cheers enters the building.

FOURTH CITIZEN

Quite a triumphal entry. Such is power ;
Now worshipped, now accursed ! The overthrow
Of all Pitt's European policy
When his hired army and his chosen general
Surrendered them at Ulm a month ago,
Is now forgotten ! Ay ; this Trafalgár

Will botch up many a ragged old repute,
Make Nelson figure as domestic saint
No less than country's saviour, Pitt exalt
As zenith-star of England's firmament,
And uncurse all the bogglers of her weal
At this adventurous time.

Third Citizen

Talk of Pitt being ill.　He looks hearty as a buck.

First Citizen

It's the news—no more.　His spirits are up like a rocket for
the moment.

Boy

Is it because Trafalgar is near Portingal that he loves Port
wine ?

Second Citizen •

Ah, as I said, friend ; this boy must go home and be care-
fully put to bed !

First Citizen

Well, whatever William's faults, it is a triumph for his virtues
to-night !

Pitt having disappeared, the Guildhall doors are closed, and the crowd
slowly disperses, till in the course of an hour the street shows itself empty
and dark, only a few oil lamps burning.

The Scene Opens, revealing the interior of the Guildhall, and the
brilliant assembly of City magnates, Lords, and Ministers seated there, Mr.
Pitt occupying a chair of honour by the Lord Mayor.　His health has been
proposed as that of the Saviour of England, and drunk with acclamations.

Pitt (standing up after repeated calls)

My lords and gentlemen :—You have toasted me
As one who has saved England and her cause.
I thank you, gentlemen, unfeignedly.
But—no man has saved England, let me say :
England has saved herself, by her exertions :
She will, I trust, save Europe by her example !

Loud applause, during which he sits down, rises, and sits down again.
The scene then shuts, and the night without has place.

SPIRIT OF THE YEARS

Those words of this man Pitt—his last large words,
As I may prophesy—that ring to-night
In their first mintage to the feasters here,
Will spread with ageing, lodge, and crystallize,
And stand embedded in the English tongue
Till it grow thin, outworn, and cease to be.—
So is't ordained by That Which all ordains;
For words were never winged with after grace.
Or blent with happier choice of time and place,
To hold the imagination of this strenuous race.

SCENE VI [1]

AN INN AT RENNES

Night.   A sleeping-chamber.   Two candles are burning near a bed in an alcove, and writing-materials are on the table.

The French admiral, VILLENEUVE, partly undressed, is pacing up and down the room.

VILLENEUVE

These hauntings have at last nigh proved to me
That this thing must be done.   Illustrious foe
And teacher, Nelson: blest and over blest
In thy outgoing at the noon of strife
When glory clasped thee round ; while wayward Death
Refused my coaxings for the like-timed call! !
Yet I did press where thickest missiles fell,
And both by precept and example showed
Where lay the line of duty, patriotism,
And honour, in that combat of despair.

He sees himself in the glass as he passes.

Unfortunate Villeneuve !—whom fate has marked
To suffer for too firm a faithfulness.—
An Emperor's chide is a command to die.—
By him accursed, forsaken by my friend,
Awhile stern England's prisoner, then unloosed
Like some poor dolt unworth captivity,
Time serves me now for ceasing.   Why not cease ? . . .
When, as Shades whisper in the chasmal night,

---

[1] This scene is a little antedated, to include it in the Act to which it essentially belongs.

" Better, far better, no percipience here."—
O happy lack, that I should have no child
To come into my hideous heritage,
And groan beneath the burden of my name ! [1]

SPIRIT OF THE YEARS

I'll speak.   His mood is ripe for such a parle.

(Sending a voice into VILLENEUVE'S ear.)

Thou dost divine the hour !

VILLENEUVE

                                    But those stern Nays,
That heretofore were audible to me
At each unhappy time I strove to pass ?

SPIRIT OF THE YEARS

Have been annulled.   The Will grants exit freely ;
Yea, It says " Now."   Therefore make now thy time.

SPIRIT OF THE PITIES

May his sad sunken soul merge into nought
Meekly and gently as a breeze at eve !

VILLENEUVE

From skies above me and the air around
Those callings which so long have circled me
At last do whisper " Now."   Now it shall be !

He seals a letter, and addresses it to his wife ; then takes a dagger from his accoutrements that are hanging alongside, and, lying down upon his back on the bed, stabs himself determinedly in many places, leaving the weapon in the last wound.

Ungrateful master ; generous foes ; Farewell !

VILLENEUVE *dies ; and the scene darkens.*

---

[1] "Quel bonheur que je n'aie aucun enfant pour recueillir mon horrible héritage et qui soit chargé du poids de mon nom !"—(Extract from the poignant letter to his **wife** written on this night.—See Lanfrey iii. 374.)

SCENE VII

KING GEORGE'S WATERING-PLACE, SOUTH WESSEX

The interior of the "Old Rooms" Inn. Boatmen and burghers are sitting on settles round the fire, smoking and drinking.

FIRST BURGHER

So they've brought him home at last, hey? And he's to be solemnized with a roaring funeral?

FIRST BOATMAN

Yes, thank God. . . . 'Tis better to lie dry than wet, if canst do it without stinking on the road gravewards. And they took care that he shouldn't.

SECOND BOATMAN

'Tis to be at Paul's; so they say that know. And the crew of the "Victory" have to walk in front, and Captain Hardy is to carry his stars and garters on a great velvet pincushion.

FIRST BURGHER

Where's the Captain now?

SECOND BOATMAN (nodding in the direction of
Captain Hardy's house)

Down at home here biding with his own folk a bit. I zid en walking with them on the Esplanade yesterday. He looks ten years older than he did when he went. Ay—he brought the galliant hero home!

SECOND BURGHER

Now how did they bring him home so that he could lie in state afterwards to the naked eye!

FIRST BOATMAN

Well, as they always do,—in a cask of sperrits.

SECOND BURGHER

Really, now!

FIRST BOATMAN (lowering his voice)

But what happened was this. They were a long time coming, owing to contrary winds, and the "Victory" being little more than a wreck. And grog ran short, because they'd used near all they had to peckle his body in. So—they broached the Adm'l!

SECOND BURGHER

How?

FIRST BOATMAN

Well; the plain calendar of it is, that when he came to be unhooped, it was found that the crew had drunk him dry. What was the men to do? Broke down by the battle, and hardly able to keep afloat, 'twas a most defendable thing, and it fairly saved their lives. So he was their salvation after death as he had been in the fight. If he could have knowed it, 'twould have pleased him down to the ground! How 'a would have laughed through the spigot-hole: "Draw on, my hearties! Better I shrivel than you famish." Ha-ha!

SECOND BURGHER

It may be defendable afloat; but it seems queer ashore.

FIRST BOATMAN

Well, that's as I had it from one that knows—Bob Loveday of Overcombe—one of the "Victory" men that's going to walk in the funeral. However, let's touch a livelier string. Peter Green, strike up that new ballet that they've lately had prented here, and were hawking about town last market-day.

SECOND BOATMAN

With all my heart. Though my wyndpipe's a bit clogged since the wars have made beer so mortal small!

SONG

THE NIGHT OF TRAFALGÁR

I

In the wild October night-time, when the wind raved round the
    land,
And the Back-sea [1] met the Front-sea, and our doors were
    blocked with sand,

---

[1] In those days the hind-part of the harbour adjoining this scene was so named, and at high tides the waves washed across the isthmus at a point called "The Narrows."

And we heard the drub of Dead-man's Bay, where bones of
  thousands are,
We knew not what the day had done for us at Trafalgár.
   (All) Had done,
      Had done,
    For us at Trafalgár!

II

"Pull hard, and make the Nothe, or down we go!" one says,
  says he.
We pulled; and bedtime brought the storm; but snug at home
  slept we.
Yet all the while our gallants after fighting through the day,
Were beating up and down the dark, sou'-west of Cadiz Bay.
    The dark,
    The dark,
   Sou'-west of Cadiz Bay!

III

The victors and the vanquished then the storm it tossed and
  tore,
As hard they strove, those worn-out men, upon that surly shore;
Dead Nelson and his half-dead crew, his foes from near and far,
Were rolled together on the deep that night at Trafalgár!
    The deep
    The deep,
   That night at Trafalgár!

   The Cloud-curtain draws.

CHORUS OF THE YEARS (aerial music)

Meanwhile the month moves on to counter-deeds
  Vast as the vainest needs,
And fiercely the predestined plot proceeds.

ACT SIXTH

SCENE I

THE FIELD OF AUSTERLITZ.   THE FRENCH POSITION

The night is the 1st of December following, and the eve of the battle.   The view is from the elevated position of the Emperor's bivouac.   The air cuts keen and the sky glistens with stars, but the lower levels are covered with a white fog stretching like a sea, from which the heights protrude as dusky rocks.

To the left are discernible high and wooded hills.   In the front mid-distance the plateau of Pratzen outstands, declining suddenly on the right to a low flat country covered with marshes and pools now mostly obscured. On the plateau itself are seen innumerable and varying lights, marking the bivouac of the centre divisions of the Austro-Russian army.   Close to the foreground the fires of the French are burning, surrounded by soldiery.   The invisible presence of the countless thousands of massed humanity that compose the two armies makes itself felt indefinably.

The tent of NAPOLÉON rises nearest at hand, with sentinel and other military figures looming around, and saddled horses held by attendants.   The accents of the Emperor are audible, through the canvas from inside, dictating a proclamation.

VOICE OF NAPOLÉON

" Soldiers, the hordes of Muscovy now face you,
To mend the Austrian overthrow at Ulm !
But how so ?   Are not these the self-same bands
You met and swept aside at Hollabrünn,
And whose retreating forms, dismayed to flight,
Your feet pursued along the trackways here ?
   " Our own position, massed and menacing,
Is rich in chance for opportune attack ;
For, say they march to cross and turn our right—
A course almost their need—their stretching flank
Will offer us, from points now prearranged——"

VOICE OF A MARSHAL

Shows it, your Majesty, the wariness
That marks your usual far-eyed policy,
To openly announce your tactics thus
Some twelve hours ere their form can actualize ?

Voice of Napoléon

The zest such knowledge will impart to all
Is worth the risk of leakages.   (To Secretary)
       Write on.

(Dictation resumed)

" Soldiers, your sections I myself shall lead ;
But ease your minds who would expostulate
Against my undue rashness.   If your zeal
Sow hot confusion in the hostile files
As your old manner is, and in our rush
We mingle with our foes, I'll use fit care.
Nevertheless, should issues stand at pause
But for a wink-while, that time you will eye
Your Emperor the foremost in the shock,
Taking his risk with every ranksman here.
For victory, men, must be no thing surmised,
As that which may or may not beam on us,
Like noontide sunshine on a dubious morn ;
It must be sure !—The honour and the fame
Of France's gay and gallant infantry—
So dear, so cherished all the Empire through—
Binds us to compass it !
                         Maintain the ranks ;
Let none be thinned by impulse or excuse
Of bearing back the wounded : and, in fine,
Be every one in this conviction firm :—
That 'tis our sacred bond to overthrow
These hirelings of a country not their own :
Yea, England's hirelings, they !—a realm stiff-steeled
In deathless hatred of our land and lives.
   " The campaign closes with this victory ;
And we return to find our standards joined
By vast young armies forming now in France.
Forthwith resistless, Peace establish we,
Worthy of you, the nation, and of me !
                              " Napoléon.'

(To his Marshals)

So shall we prostrate these paid slaves of hers—
England's, I mean—the root of all the war.

Voice of Murat

The further details sent of Trafalgár
Are not assuring

Voice of Lannes

What may the details be?

Voice of Napoléon (moodily)

We learn that six-and-twenty ships of war,
During the fight and after, struck their flags,
And that the tigerish gale throughout the night
Gave fearful finish to the English rage.
By luck their Nelson's gone, but gone withal
Are twenty thousand prisoners, taken off
To gnaw their finger-nails in British hulks.
Of our vast squadrons of the summer-time
But rags and splintered remnants now remain.—
Thuswise Villeneuve, poor craven, quitted him!
Thus are my projects for the navy damned,
And England puffed to yet more bombastry.
—Well, well; I can't be everywhere.   No matter;
A victory's brewing here as counterpoise!
These water-rats may paddle in their salt slush,
And welcome.   'Tis not long they'll have the lead.
Ships can be wrecked by land!

Another Voice

                                And how by land,
Your Majesty, if one may query such?

Voice of Napoléon (sardonically)

I'll bid all states of Europe shut their ports
To England's arrogant bottoms, slowly starve
Her bloated revenues and monstrous trade,
Till all her hulls lie sodden in their docks,
And her grey island eyes in vain shall seek
One jack of hers upon the ocean plains!

Voice of Soult

A few more master-strokes, your Majesty,
Must be dealt hereabout to compass such!

VOICE OF NAPOLÉON

God, yes!—Even here Pitt's guineas are the foes:
'Tis all a duel 'twixt this Pitt and me;
And, more than Russia's host, and Austria's flower,
I everywhere to-night around me feel
As from an unseen monster haunting nigh
His country's hostile breath!—But come: to choke it
By our to-morrow's feats, which now, in brief,
I recapitulate.—First Soult will move
To forward the grand project of the day:
Namely: ascend in échelon, right to front,
With Vandamme's men, and those of Saint Hilaire:
Legrand's division somewhere further back—
Nearly whereat I place my finger here—
To be there reinforced by tirailleurs:
Lannes to the left here, on the Olmütz road,
Supported by Murat's whole cavalry.
While in reserve, here, are the grenadiers
Of Oudinot, the corps of Bernadotte,
Rivaud, Drouet, and the Imperial Guard.

MARSHALS' VOICES

Even as we understood, Sire, and have ordered.
Nought lags but day, to light our victory!

VOICE OF NAPOLÉON

Now let us up and ride the bivouacs round,
And note positions ere the soldiers sleep.
—Omit not from to-morrow's home dispatch
Direction that this blow of Trafalgár
Be hushed in all the news-sheets sold in France,
Or, if reported, let it be portrayed
As a rash fight whereout we came not worst,
But were so broken by the boisterous eve
That England claims to be the conqueror.

There emerge from the tent NAPOLÉON and the Marshals, who all mount
the horses that are led up, and proceed through the frost and rime towards
the bivouacs. At the Emperor's approach to the nearest soldiery they
spring up.

SOLDIERS

The Emperor!   He's here!   The Emperor's here!

AN OLD GRENADIER (approaching Napoléon familiarly)

We'll bring thee Russian guns and flags galore
To celebrate thy coronation-day !

They gather into wisps the straw, hay, and other litter on which they have been lying, and kindling these at the dying fires, wave them as torches. This is repeated as each fire is reached, till the whole French position is one wide illumination. The most enthusiastic of the soldiers follow the Emperor in a throng as he progresses, and his whereabouts in the vast field is denoted by their cries.

CHORUS OF THE PITIES (aerial music)

Strange suasive pull of personality !

CHORUS OF IRONIC SPIRITS

His projects they unknow, his grin unsee !

CHORUS OF THE PITIES

Their loyal luckless hearts say blindly—He !

The night-shades close over.

SCENE II

THE SAME. THE RUSSIAN POSITION

Midnight at the quarters of FIELD-MARSHAL PRINCE KUTÚZOF at Kresnowitz. An inner apartment is discovered, roughly adapted as a council-room. On a table with candles is unfolded a large map of Austerlitz and its environs.

The Generals are assembled in consultation round the table, WEIROTHER pointing to the map, LANGERON, BUXHÖVDEN, and MILORÁDOVICH standing by, DOKHTÓROF bending over the map, PRSCHEBISZEWSKY [1] indifferently walking up and down. KUTÚZOF, old and weary, with a scarred face and only one eye, is seated in a chair at the head of the table, nodding, waking, and nodding again. Some officers of lower grade are in the background, and horses in waiting are heard hoofing and champing outside.

WEIROTHER speaks, referring to memoranda, snuffing the nearest candle, and moving it from place to place on the map as he proceeds importantly.

WEIROTHER

Now here, our right, along the Olmütz Road
Will march and oust our counterfacers there,
Dislodge them from the Sainton Hill, and thence
Advance direct to Brünn.—You heed me, sirs ?—

---

[1] This General's name should, it is said, be pronounced in three syllables, nearly PRESH-EV'-SKY.

The cavalry will occupy the plain :
Our centre and main strength,—you follow me ?—
Count Langeron, Dokhtórof, with Prschebiszewsky
And Kollowrath—now on the Pratzen heights—
Will down and cross the Goldbach rivulet,
Seize Tilnitz, Kobelnitz, and hamlets nigh,
Turn the French right, move onward in their rear,
Cross Schwarsa, hold the great Vienna road :—
So, with the nightfall, centre, right, and left,
Will rendezvous beneath the walls of Brünn.

> LANGERON (taking a pinch of snuff)

Good, General ; very good !—if Bonaparte
Will kindly stand and let you have your way.
But what if he do not !—if he forestall
These sound slow movements, mount the Pratzen hills
When we descend, fall on *our* rear forthwith,
While we go crying for *his* rear in vain ?

> KUTÚZOF (waking up)

Ay, ay, Weirother ; that's the question—eh ?

> WEIROTHER (impatiently)

If Bonaparte had meant to climb up there,
Being one so spry and so determinate,
He would have set about it ere this eve !
He has not troops to do so, sirs, I say :
His utmost strength is forty thousand men.

> LANGERON

Then if so weak, how can so wise a brain
Court ruin by abiding calmly here
The impact of a force so large as ours ?
He may be mounting up this very hour !
What think you, General Milorádovich ?

> MILORÁDOVICH

I ?   What's the use of thinking, when to-morrow
Will tell us, with no need to think at all !

WEIROTHER

Pah! At this moment he retires apace.
His fires are dark; all sounds have ceased that way
Save voice of owl or mongrel wintering there.
But, were he nigh, these movements I detail
Would knock the bottom from his enterprize.

KUTÚZOF (rising)

Well, well.   Now this being ordered, set it going.
One here shall make fair copies of the notes,
And send them round.   Colonel von Toll I ask
To translate part.—Generals, it grows full late,
And half-a-dozen hours of needed sleep
Will aid us more than maps.   We now disperse,
And luck attend us all.   Good-night.   Good-night.

The Generals and other officers go out severally.

Such plans are—paper!   Only to-morrow's light
Reveals the true manœuvre to my sight!

He flaps out with his hand all the candles but one or two, slowly walks
outside the house, and listens. On the high ground in the direction of the
French lines are heard shouts, and a wide illumination grows and strengthens;
but the hollows are still mantled in fog.

Are these the signs of regiments out of heart,
And beating backward from an enemy!

                                      [He remains pondering.

On the Pratzen heights immediately in front there begins a movement
among the Russians, signifying that the plan which involves desertion of that
vantage-ground is about to be put in force. Noises of drunken singing arise
from the Russian lines at various points elsewhere.

KUTÚZOF re-enters his quarters with a face of misgiving.
           The night shades involve the whole.[1]

SCENE III

THE SAME.   THE FRENCH POSITION

Shortly before dawn on the morning of the 2nd of December. A white
frost and fog still prevail in the low-lying areas; but overhead the sky is
clear. A dead silence reigns.

NAPOLÉON, on a grey horse, closely attended by BERTHIER, and
surrounded by MARSHALS SOULT, LANNES, MURAT, and their aides-de-

---

[1] In depicting this scene, the writer, like others, has followed without question the
MS. of Count Langeron quoted by M. Thiers. But the singular soundness of the
Count's own opinion in the consultation, as recorded, suggests that it may have been
somewhat strengthened on paper at the expense of that of his companions.

camp, all cloaked, is discernible in the gloom riding down from the high ground before Bellowitz, on which they have bivouacked, to the village of Puntowitz on the Goldbach stream, quite near the front of the Russian position of the day before on the Pratzen crest. The Emperor and his companions come to a pause, look around and upward to the hills, and listen.

NAPOLÉON

Their bivouac fires, that lit the top last night,
Are all extinct.

LANNES

          And hark you, Sire ; I catch
A sound which, if I err not, means the thing
We have hoped, and hoping, feared fate would not yield !

NAPOLÉON

My God, it surely is the tramp of horse
And jolt of cannon downward from the hill
Towards our right here, by the swampy lakes
That face Davout ?   Thus, as I sketched, they work !

MURAT

Yes !   They already move upon Tilnitz.

NAPOLÉON

Leave them alone !   Nor stick nor stone we'll stir
To interrupt them.   Nought that we can scheme
Will help us like their own stark sightlessness !—
Let them get down to those white lowlands there,
And so far plunge in the level that no skill,
When sudden vision flashes on their fault,
Can help them, though despair-stung, to regain
The key to mastery held at yestereve !
     Meantime move onward these divisions here
Under the fog's kind shroud ; descend the slope,
And cross the stream below the Russian lines :
There halt concealed, till I send down the word.

NAPOLÉON and his staff retire to the hill south-east of Bellowitz as the day dawns pallidly.

'Tis good to get above that rimy cloak
And into cleaner air.   It chilled me through.

When they reach the summit they are over the fog : and suddenly the sun breaks forth radiantly to the left of the Pratzen upland, illuminating the

ash-hued face of NAPOLÉON and the faces of those around him.   All eyes are
turned first to the sun, and thence to look for the dense masses of men that
had occupied the upland the night before.

MURAT

I see them not.   The plateau seems deserted!

NAPOLÉON (exultantly)

Gone ; verily !—Ah, how much will you bid,
An hour hence, for the coign abandoned now !
The battle's ours.—It was, then, their rash march
Downwards to Tilnitz and the Goldbach swamps
Before dawn, that we heard.—No hurry, Lannes !
Enjoy this sun, that rests its chubby jowl
Upon the plain, and thrusts its bristling beard
Across the lowlands' fleecy counterpane,
Peering beneath our broadest hat-brims' shade. . . .
Soult, how long hence to win the Pratzen top ?

SOULT

Some twenty minutes or less, your Majesty :
Our troops down there, still mantled by the mist,
Are half upon the way.

NAPOLÉON

                        Good !   Set forthwith
Vandamme and Saint Hilaire to mount the slopes——

Firing begins in the marsh to the right by Tilnitz and the pools, though
the thick air yet hides the operations.

O, there you are, blind boozy Buxhövden !
Achieve your worst.   Davout will hold you firm.

The head of an aide-de-camp rises through the fog on that side, and he
hastens up to NAPOLÉON and his companions, to whom the officer announces
what has happened.   DAVOUT rides off, disappearing legs first into the
white stratum that covers the attack.

Lannes and Murat, you have concern enough
Here on the left, with Prince Bagration
And all the Austro-Russian cavalry.
Haste off.   The victory promising to-day
Will, like a thunder-clap, conclude the war !

The Marshals with their aides gallop away towards their respective
divisions.   Soon the two divisions under SOULT are seen ascending in close
column the inclines of the Pratzen height.   Thereupon the heads of the

Russian centre columns disclose themselves, breaking the sky-line of the summit from the other side, in a desperate attempt to regain the position vacated by the Russian left. A fierce struggle develops there between SOULT'S divisions and these, who, despite their tardy attempt to recover the lost post of dominance, are pressed by the French off the slopes into the lowland.

SEMICHORUS I OF THE PITIES (aerial music)

O Great Necessitator, heed us now !
*   If it indeed must be*
That this day Austria smoke with slaughtery,
Quicken the issue as Thou knowest how ;
And dull to suffering those whom it befalls
To quit their lodgment in a flesh that galls !

SEMICHORUS II

If it be in the future human story
To lift this man to yet intenser glory,
*   Let the exploit be done*
*   With the least sting, or none,*
To those, his kind, at whose expense such pitch is won !

SPIRIT OF THE YEARS

Again ye deprecate the World-Soul's way
That I so long have told ?   Then note anew
(Since ye forget) the ordered potencies,
Nerves, sinews, trajects, eddies, ducts of It
The Eternal Urger, pressing change on change.

At once, as earlier, a preternatural clearness possesses the atmosphere of the battle-field, in which the scene becomes anatomized and the living masses of humanity transparent. The controlling Immanent Will appears therein, as a brain-like network of currents and ejections, twitching, inter-penetrating, entangling, and thrusting hither and thither the human forms.

SEMICHORUS I OF IRONIC SPIRITS (aerial music)

O Innocents, can ye forget
That things to be were shaped and set
Ere mortals and this planet met ?

SEMICHORUS II

Stand ye apostrophizing That
Which, working all, works but thereat
Like some sublime fermenting-vat

SEMICHORUS I

*Heaving throughout its vast content
With strenuously transmutive bent
Though of its aim unsentient ?—*

SEMICHORUS II

*Could ye have seen Its early deeds
Ye would not cry, as one who pleads
For quarter, when a Europe bleeds!*

SEMICHORUS I

*Ere ye, young Pities, had upgrown
From out the deeps where mortals moan
Against a ruling not their own,*

SEMICHORUS II

*He of the Years beheld, and we,
Creation's prentice artistry
Express in forms that now unbe*

SEMICHORUS I

*Tentative dreams from day to day;
Mangle its types, re-knead the clay
In some more palpitating way;*

SEMICHORUS II

*Beheld the rarest wrecked amain,
Whole nigh-perfected species slain
By those that scarce could boast a brain;*

SEMICHORUS I

*Saw ravage, growth, diminish, add,
Here peoples sane, there peoples mad,
In choiceless throws of good and bad;*

SEMICHORUS II

*Heard laughters at the ruthless dooms
Which tortured to the eternal glooms
Quick, quivering hearts in hecatombs.*

CHORUS

Us Ancients, then, it ill befits
To quake when Slaughter's spectre flits
Athwart this field of Austerlitz!

SHADE OF THE EARTH

Pain not their young compassions by such lore,
But hold you mute, and read the battle yonder:
The moment marks the day's catastrophe.

SCENE IV

THE SAME.   THE RUSSIAN POSITION

It is about noon, and the vital spectacle is now near the village of Tilnitz. The fog has dispersed, and the sun shines clearly, though without warmth, the ice on the pools gleaming under its radiance.

GENERAL BUXHÖVDEN and his aides-de-camp have reined up, and remain at pause on a hillock.   The General watches through a glass his battalions, which are still disputing the village.   Suddenly approach down the track from the upland of Pratzen large companies of Russian infantry helter-skelter. COUNT LANGERON is beheld to be retreating with them; and soon, pale and agitated, he hastens up to GENERAL BUXHÖVDEN, whose face is flushed.

LANGERON

While they are upon us you stay idle here!
Prschebiszewsky's column is distraught and rent,
And more than half my own made captive!   Yea,
Kreznówitz carried, and Sokólnitz hemmed:
The enemy's whole strength will stound you soon!

BUXHÖVDEN

You seem to see the enemy everywhere.

LANGERON

You cannot see them, be they here or no!

BUXHÖVDEN

I only wait Prschebiszewsky's nearing corps
To join Dokhtórof's to them.   Here they come.

SOULT, supported by BERNADOTTE and OUDINOT, having cleared and secured the Pratzen height, his battalions are perceived descending from it on this side, behind DOKHTÓROF'S division, so placing the latter between themselves and the pools.

LANGERON

You cannot tell the Frenchmen from ourselves !
These are the victors.——Ah——Dokhtórof——lost !

DOKHTÓROF'S troops are seen to be retreating towards the water. The watchers stand in painful tenseness.

BUXHÖVDEN

Dokhtórof tell to save him as he may !
We, Count, must gather up our shaken flesh
And hurry them by the road through Austerlitz.

BUXHÖVDEN'S regiments and the remains of LANGERON'S are rallied and collected, and they retreat by way of the hamlet of Aujezd. As they go over the summit of a hill BUXHÖVDEN looks back. LANGERON'S columns, which were behind his own, have been cut off by VANDAMME'S division coming down from the Pratzen plateau. This and some detachments from DOKHTÓROF'S column rush towards the Satschan lake and endeavour to cross it on the ice. It cracks beneath their weight. At the same moment NAPOLÉON and his brilliant staff appear on the top of the Pratzen.

The Emperor watches the scene with a vulpine smile ; and directs a battery near at hand to fire down upon the ice on which the Russians are crossing. A ghastly crash and splashing follows the discharge, the shining surface breaking into pieces like a mirror, which fly in all directions. Two thousand fugitives are engulfed, and their groans of despair reach the ears of the watchers like ironical huzzas.

A general flight of the Russian army from wing to wing is now disclosed, involving in its current the EMPEROR ALEXANDER and the EMPEROR FRANCIS, with the reserve, who are seen towards Austerlitz endeavouring to rally their troops in vain. They are swept along by the disordered soldiery.

SCENE V

THE SAME. NEAR THE WINDMILL OF PALENY

The mill is about seven miles to the southward, between the French advanced posts and the Austrians.

A bivouac fire is burning. NAPOLÉON, in grey overcoat and beaver hat turned up front and back, rides to the spot with BERTHIER, SAVARY, and his aides, and alights. He walks to and fro complacently, meditating or talking to BERTHIER. Two groups of officers, one from each army, stand in the background on their respective sides.

NAPOLÉON

What's this of Alexander ? Weep, did he,
Like his old namesake, but for meaner cause ?
Ha, ha !

BERTHIER

Word goes, your Majesty, that Colonel Toll,
One of Field-Marshal Prince Kutúzof's staff,
In the retreating swirl of overthrow,
Found Alexander seated on a stone
Beneath a leafless roadside apple-tree,
Out here by Göding on the Holitsch way ;
His coal-black uniform and snowy plume
Unmarked, his face disconsolate, his grey eyes
Mourning in tears the fate of his brave array—
All flying southward, save the steadfast slain.

NAPOLÉON

Poor devil !—But he'll soon get over it—
Sooner than his employers oversea !—
Ha !—this will make friend Pitt and England writhe,
And cloud somewhat their lustrous Trafalgár.

An open carriage approaches from the direction of Holitsch, accompanied
by a small escort of Hungarian guards.   NAPOLÉON walks forward to
meet it as it draws up, and welcomes the Austrian Emperor, who alights.
He is wearing a grey cloak over a white uniform, carries a light walking-cane,
and is attended by PRINCE JOHN OF LICHTENSTEIN, SWARZENBERG, and
others.   His fresh-coloured face contrasts strangely with the bluish pallor of
NAPOLÉON'S ; but it is now thin and anxious.

They formally embrace.   BERTHIER, PRINCE JOHN, and the rest retire,
and the two Emperors are left by themselves before the fire.

NAPOLÉON

Here on the roofless ground do I receive you—
My only mansion for these two months past !

FRANCIS

Your tenancy thereof has brought such fame
That it must needs be one which charms you, Sire.

NAPOLÉON

Good !   Now this war.   It has been forced on me
Just at a crisis most inopportune,
When all my energies and arms were bent
On teaching England that her watery walls
Are no defence against the wrath of France
Aroused by breach of solemn covenants.

FRANCIS

I had no zeal for violating peace
Till ominous events in Italy
Revealed the gloomy truth that France aspires
To conquest there, and undue sovereignty.
Since when mine eyes have seen no sign outheld
To signify a change of purposings.

NAPOLÉON

Yet there were terms distinctly specified
To General Giulay in November past,
Whereon I'd gladly fling the sword aside.
To wit : that hot armigerent jealousy
Stir us no further on transalpine rule,
I'd take the Isonzo River as our bounds.

FRANCIS

Roundly, that I cede all !—And how may stand
Your views as to the Russian forces here ?

NAPOLÉON

You have all to lose by that alliance, Sire.
Leave Russia.   Let the Emperor Alexander
Make his own terms ; whereof the first must be
That he retire from Austrian territory.
I'll grant an armistice therefor.   Anon
I'll treat with him to weld a lasting peace,
Based on some simple understandings ; chief,
That Russian armies keep to Russian soil,
And that, moreover, every English keel
Be locked from out the ports of his domain.
Meanwhile to you I'll tender this good word :
Keep Austria to herself.   To Russia bound,
You pay your own costs with your provinces,
And Alexander's likewise therewithal.

FRANCIS

I see as much, and long have seen it, Sire ;
And standing here the vanquished, let me own
What happier issues might have left unsaid :

Long, long I have lost the wish to bind myself
To Russia's purposings and Russia's risks ;
Little do I count these alliances
With Powers that have no substance seizable !

As they converse they walk away.

An Austrian Officer

O strangest scene of an eventful life,
This junction that I witness here to-day !
An Emperor—in whose majestic veins
Aeneas and the proud Caesarian line
Claim yet to live ; and those scarce less renowned,
The dauntless Hawks'-Hold Counts, of gallantry
So great in fame one thousand years ago—
To bend with deference and manners mild
In talk with this adventuring campaigner,
Raised but by pikes above the common herd !

Another Austrian Officer

Ay !   There be Satschan swamps and Pratzen heights
In royal lines, as here at Austerlitz.

The Emperors again draw near.

Francis

Then, to this armistice, which shall be called
Immediately at all points, I agree ;
And pledge my word that my august ally
Accept it likewise, and withdraw his force
By daily measured march to his own realm.

Napoléon

For him I take your word.   And pray believe
That rank ambitions are your own, not mine ;
That though I have postured as your enemy,
And likewise Alexander's, we are one
In interests, have in all things common cause.
    One country sows these mischiefs Europe through
By her insidious chink of luring ore—
False-featured England, who, to aggrandize
Her name, her influence, and her revenues,
Schemes to impropriate the whole world's trade,
And starves and bleeds the folk of other lands.

Her rock-rimmed situation walls her off
Like a slim selfish mollusk in its shell
From the wide views and fair fraternities
Which on the mainland we reciprocate,
And quicks her quest for profit in our woes!

FRANCIS

I am not competent, your Majesty,
To estimate that country's conscience now,
Nor to engage on my ally's behalf
That English ships be shut from Russian trade.
But joyful am I that in all things else
My promise can be made ; and that this day
Our conference ends in friendship and esteem.

NAPOLÉON

I will send Savary at to-morrow's blink
And make all lucid to the Emperor.
For us, I wholly can avow as mine
The cordial spirit of your Majesty.

They retire towards the carriage of FRANCIS. BERTHIER, SAVARY, LICHTENSTEIN, and the suite of officers advance from the background, and with mutual gestures of courtesy and amicable leave-takings the two Emperors part company.

CHORUS OF THE PITIES (aerial music)

Each for himself, his family, his heirs ;
For the wan weltering nations who concerns, who cares ?

CHORUS OF IRONIC SPIRITS

A pertinent query, in truth !—
But spoil not the sport by your ruth :
*   'Tis enough to make half*
*   Yonder zodiac laugh*
When rulers begin to allude
*   To their lack of ambition,*
*   And strong opposition*
To all but the general good !

SPIRIT OF THE YEARS

Hush levities. Events press : turn ye westward.

A nebulous curtain draws slowly across.

SCENE VI

SHOCKERWICK HOUSE, NEAR BATH

The interior of the Picture Gallery. Enter WILTSHIRE the owner, and PITT, who looks emaciated and walks feebly.

WILTSHIRE (pointing to a portrait)

Now here you have the lady we discussed :
A fine example of his manner, sir ?

PITT

It is a fine example, sir, indeed,—
With that transparency amid the shades,
And those thin blue-green-greyish leafages
Behind the pillar in the background there,
Which seem the leaves themselves.—Ah, this is Quin.

(Moving to another picture.)

WILTSHIRE

Yes, Quin.   A man of varied parts, though rough
And choleric at times.   Yet, at his best,
As Falstaff, never matched, they say.   But I
Had not the fate to see him in the flesh.

PITT

Churchill well carves him in his " Characters " :—
" His eyes, in gloomy socket taught to roll,
Proclaimed the sullen habit of his soul.
In fancied scenes, as in Life's real plan,
He could not for a moment sink the man :
Nature, in spite of all his skill, crept in ;
Horatio, Dorax, Falstaff—still 'twas Quin."
—He was at Bath when Gainsborough settled there
In that house in the Circus which we know.—
I like the portrait much.—The brilliancy
Of Gainsborough lies in this his double sway :
Sovereign of landscape he ; of portraiture
Joint monarch with Sir Joshua. . . . Ah ?—that's—hark !
Is that the patter of a horse's hoofs .
Along the road ?

WILTSHIRE

I notice nothing, sir.

PITT

It is a gallop, growing quite distinct.
And—can it be a messenger for me!

WILTSHIRE

I hope no ugly European news
To stop the honour of this visit, sir!

They listen.   The gallop of the horse grows louder, and is checked at the door of the house.   There is a hasty knocking, and a courier, splashed with mud from hard riding, is shown into the gallery.   He presents a dispatch to PITT, who sits down and hurriedly opens it.

PITT (to himself)

O heavy news indeed! . . . Disastrous; dire!

He appears overcome as he sits, and covers his forehead with his hand.

WILTSHIRE

I trust you are not ill, sir?

PITT (after some moments)

Could I have
A little brandy, sir, quick brought to me?

WILTSHIRE

In one brief minute.

Brandy is brought in, and PITT takes it.

PITT

Now leave me, please, alone.   I'll call anon.
Is there a map of Europe handy here?

WILTSHIRE fetches a map from the library, and spreads it before the minister.   WILTSHIRE, courier, and servant go out.

O God that I should live to see this day!

He remains awhile in a profound reverie; then resumes the reading of the dispatch.

" Defeated—the Allies—quite overthrown
At Austerlitz—last week."—Where's Austerlitz?
—But what avails it where the place is now;
What corpse is curious on the longitude

And situation of his cemetery ! . . .
The Austrians and the Russians overcome,
That vast adventuring army is set free
To bend unhindered strength against our strand. . . .
So do my plans through all these plodding years
Announce them built in vain !
His heel on Europe, monarchies in chains
To France, I am as though I had never been !

He gloomily ponders the dispatch and the map some minutes longer.   At
last he rises with difficulty, and rings the bell.

A servant enters.

Call up my carriage, please you, now at once ;
And tell your master I return to Bath
This moment—I may want a little help
In getting to the door here.

SERVANT

Sir, I will,
And summon you my master instantly.

He goes out and re-enters with WILTSHIRE.   PITT is assisted from the
room.

PITT

Roll up that map.   'Twill not be needed now
These ten years !   Realms, laws, peoples, dynasties,
Are churning to a pulp within the maw
Of empire-making Lust and personal Gain !

[Exeunt PITT, WILTSHIRE, and servant ; and in a few minutes
the carriage is heard driving off, and the scene closes.

SCENE VII

PARIS.   A STREET LEADING TO THE TUILERIES

It is night, and the dim oil lamps reveal a vast concourse of citizens of
both sexes around the Palace gates and in the neighbouring thoroughfares.

SPIRIT OF THE YEARS (to the Spirit of Rumour)

Thou may'st descend and join this crowd awhile,
And speak what things shall come into thy mouth.

SPIRIT SINISTER

I'll harken! I wouldn't miss it for the groans of another Austerlitz!

The Spirit of Rumour enters on the scene in the disguise of a young foreigner.

SPIRIT (to a street-woman)

Lady, a late hour this to be afoot!

WOMAN

But such is meet in gallant dames like me,
For now He nears!—after a three months' whirl
Of victories won on fields whose homely names
Had never swept the ear of mortal man
Beyond the haunts of neighbour peasantry;
But, cymballed now by deathless deeds, become
Familiar rhythms in remotest homes!

SPIRIT

Rare! To it again. I could give heed all night.

WOMAN

Poor profit, then, to me from my true trade,
Wherein hot competition is so rife
Already, since these victories brought to town
So many foreign jobbers in my line,
That I'd best hold my tongue from praise of fame!
However, one is caught by popular zeal,
And though five midnights have not brought a sou,
I, too, chant *Jubilate* like the rest.—
    In courtesies have haughty monarchs vied
Towards the Conqueror! who, with men-at-arms
One quarter theirs, has vanquished by his nerve
Vast musterings four-hundred-thousand strong,
And given new tactics to the art of war
Unparalleled in Europe's history!

SPIRIT

What man is this, whose might thou blazonest so—
Who makes the earth to tremble, shakes old thrones,
And turns the plains to wilderness?

F

WOMAN

Dost ask

As ignorant, yet asking can define?
What mean you, traveller?

SPIRIT

I am a stranger here,
A wandering wight, whose life has not been spent
This side the globe, though I can speak the tongue.

WOMAN

Your air has truth in't; but your state is strange!
Had I a husband he should tackle thee.

SPIRIT

Dozens thou hast had—batches more than she
Samaria knew, if now thou hast not one!

WOMAN

Wilt take the situation from this hour?

SPIRIT

Thou know'st not what thy frailty asks, good dame!

WOMAN

Well, learn in small the Emperor's chronicle,
As gleaned from what my soldier-husbands say:—
Some five-and-forty standards of his foes
Are brought to Paris, borne triumphantly
In proud procession through the surging streets,
Ever as brands of fame to shine aloft
In dim-lit senate-halls and city aisles.

SPIRIT

Fair Munich sparkled with festivity
As there awhile he tarried, and was met
By the gay Joséphine your Empress here.—
There, too, Eugène—

WOMAN

Napoléon's stepson he——

SPIRIT

Received for gift the hand of fair Princess
Augusta (daughter of Bavaria's crown,
Forced from her plighted troth to Baden's heir),
And, to complete his honouring, was hailed
Successor to the throne of Italy.

WOMAN

How know you, ere this news has got abroad?

SPIRIT

Channels have I the common people lack.—
There, on the nonce, the forenamed Baden prince
Was joined to Stéphanie Beauharnais, her
Who stands as daughter to the man we wait,
Some say as more.

WOMAN

          They do?   Then such not I.
Can revolution's dregs so soil thy soul
That thou shouldst doubt the eldest son thereof?
'Tis dangerous to insinuate nowadays!

SPIRIT

Right!   Lady many-spoused, more charity
Upbrims in thee than in some loftier ones
Who would not name thee with their white-washed
     tongues.—
Enough.   I am one whom, didst thou know my name,
Thou would'st not grudge a claim to speak his mind.

WOMAN

A thousand pardons, sir.

SPIRIT

           Resume thy tale
If so thou wishest.

WOMAN

      Nay, but you know best——

SPIRIT

How laurelled progress through applauding crowds
Have marked his journey home.   How Strasburg town,
Stuttgart, Carlsruhe, acclaimed him like the rest:

How pageantry would here have welcomed him,
Had not his speed outstript intelligence.
—Now will a glimpse of him repay thee.   Hark!

Shouts arise and increase in the distance, announcing BONAPARTE'S
approach.

Well, Buonaparté has revived by land,
But not by sea.   On that thwart element
Never will he incorporate his dream,
And float as master!

WOMAN

What shall hinder him?

SPIRIT

That which has hereto.   England, so to say.

WOMAN

But she's in straits.   She's lost her Nelson now,
(A worthy man : he loved a woman well !)
George drools and babbles in a darkened room ;
Her heaven-born Minister declines apace ;
All smooths the Emperor's sway.

SPIRIT

Tales have two sides,
Sweet lady.   Vamped-up versions reach thee here.—
That Austerlitz was lustrous none ignores,
But would it shock thy garrulousness to know
That the true measure of this Trafalgár—
Utter defeat, ay, France's naval death—
Your Emperor bade be hid?

WOMAN

The seer's gift
Has never plenteously endowed me, sir,
As in appearance you.   But to plain sense
Things seem as stated.

SPIRIT

We'll let seemings be.—
But know, these English take to liquid life
Right patly—nursed therefor in infancy

By rimes and rains which creep into their blood,
Till like seeks like.   The sea is their dry land,
And, as on cobbles you, they wayfare there.

WOMAN

Heaven prosper, then, their watery wayfarings
If they'll leave us the land !—(The Imperial carriage appears.)
        The Emperor !—
Long live the Emperor !—He's the best by land.

BONAPARTE'S carriage arrives, without an escort.   The street lamps shine
in, and reveal the EMPRESS JOSÉPHINE seated beside him.   The plaudits of
the people grow boisterous as they hail him Victor of Austerlitz.   The more
active run after the carriage, which turns in from the Rue St. Honoré to the
Carrousel, and thence vanishes into the Court of the Tuileries.

WOMAN

May all success attend his next exploit !

SPIRIT

Namely : to put the knife in England's trade,
And teach her treaty-manners—if he can !

WOMAN

I like not your queer knowledge, creepy man.
There's weirdness in your air.   I'd call you ghost
Had not the Goddess Reason laid all such
Past Mother Church's cunning to restore.
—Adieu.   I'll not be yours to-night.   I'd starve first !

She withdraws.   The crowd wastes away, and the Spirit vanishes.

SCENE VIII

PUTNEY.   BOWLING GREEN HOUSE

PITT'S bedchamber, from the landing without.   It is afternoon.   At the
back of the room as seen through the doorway is a curtained bed, beside
which a woman sits, the LADY HESTER STANHOPE.   Bending over a table
at the front of the room is SIR WALTER FARQUHAR, the physician.
PARSLOW the footman and another servant are near the door.

TOMLINE, Bishop of Lincoln, enters.

FARQUHAR (in a subdued voice)

I grieve to call your lordship up again,
But symptoms lately have disclosed themselves
That mean the knell to the frail life in him.

And whatsoever things of gravity
It may be needful to communicate,
Let them be spoken now.   Time may not serve
If they be much delayed.

TOMLINE

                    Ah, stands it thus ? . . .
The name of his disease is—Austerlitz !
His brow's inscription has been Austerlitz
From that dire morning in the month just past
When tongues of rumour twanged the word across
From its hid nook on the Moravian plains.

FARQUHAR

And yet he might have borne it, had the weight
Of governmental shackles been unclasped,
Even partly, from his limbs last Lammastide,
When that despairing journey to the King
At Gloucester Lodge by Wessex shore was made
To beg such.   But relief the King refused.
"Why want you Fox ?   What — Grenville and his
        friends ? "
He harped.   "You are sufficient without these—
Rather than Fox, why, give me civil war ! "
And fibre that would rather snap than shrink
Held out no longer.   Now the upshot nears.

LADY HESTER STANHOPE turns her head and comes forward.

LADY HESTER

I am grateful you are here again, good friend !
He's sleeping some light seconds ; but once more
Has asked for tidings of Lord Harrowby,
And murmured of his mission to Berlin
As Europe's haggard hope ; if, sure, it be
That any hope remain !

TOMLINE

                    There's no news yet.—
These several days while I have been sitting by him
He has inquired the quarter of the wind,
And where that moment beaked the stable-cock.
When I said "East," he answered "That is well !
Those are the breezes that will speed him home ! "
So cling his heart-strings to his country's cause.

FARQUHAR

I fear that Wellesley's visit here by now
Strung him to tensest strain. He quite broke down,
And has fast faded since.

LADY HESTER

      Ah! now he wakes.
Please come and speak to him as you would wish
        (to TOMLINE).

LADY HESTER, TOMLINE, and FARQUHAR retire behind the bed, where
in a short time voices are heard in prayer. Afterwards the Bishop goes to a
writing-table, and LADY HESTER comes to the doorway. Steps are heard
on the stairs, and PITT's friend ROSE, the President of the Board of Trade,
appears on the landing and makes inquiries.

LADY HESTER (whispering)

He wills the wardenry of his affairs
To his old friend the Bishop. But his words
Bespeak too much anxiety for me,
And underrate his services so far
That he has doubts if his high deeds deserve
Such size of recognition by the State
As would award slim pensions to his kin.
He had been fain to write down his intents,
But the quill dropped from his unmuscled hand.—
Now his friend Tomline pens what he dictates
And gleans the lippings of his last desires.

ROSE and LADY HESTER turn. They see the Bishop bending over the
bed with a sheet of paper on which he has previously been writing. A little
later he dips a quill and holds it within the bed-curtain, spreading the paper
beneath. A thin white hand emerges from behind the curtain and signs the
paper. The Bishop beckons forward the two servants, who also sign.
FARQUHAR on one side of the bed, and TOMLINE on the other, are
spoken to by the dying man. The Bishop afterwards withdraws from the
bed and comes to the landing where the others are.

TOMLINE

A list of his directions has been drawn,
And feeling somewhat more at mental ease
He asks Sir Walter if he has long to live.
Farquhar just answered, in a soothing tone,

That hope still frailly breathed recovery.
At this my dear friend smiled and shook his head,
As if to say : "I can translate your words,
But I reproach not friendship's lullabies."

ROSE

Rest he required ; and rest was not for him.

FARQUHAR comes forward as they wait.

FARQUHAR

His spell of concentration on these things,
Determined now, that long have wasted him,
Have left him in a numbing lethargy,
From which I fear he may not rouse to strength
For speech with earth again.

ROSE

But hark.   He does.

They listen.

PITT

My country !   How I leave my country ! . . .

TOMLINE

Ah,—
Immense the matter those poor words contain !

ROSE

Still does his soul stay wrestling with that theme,
And still it will, even semi-consciously,
Until the drama's done.

They continue to converse by the doorway in whispers.   PITT sinks
slowly into a stupor, from which he never awakens.

SPIRIT OF THE PITIES (to the Spirit of the Years)

Do you intend to speak to him ere the close?

SPIRIT OF THE YEARS

Nay, I have spoke too often !   Time and time,
When all Earth's light has lain on the nether side,
And yapping midnight winds have leapt on roofs,
And raised for him an evil harlequinade
Of national disasters in long train,

That tortured him with harrowing grimace,
Have I communed with that intelligence.
Now I would leave him to pass out in peace,
And seek the silence unperturbedly.

SPIRIT SINISTER

Even ITS official Spirit can show ruth
At man's fag end, when his destruction's sure!

SPIRIT OF THE YEARS

It suits us ill to cavil each with each.
I might retort.   I only say to thee
ITS slaves we are: ITS slaves must ever be!

CHORUS (aerial music)

Yea, from the Void we fetch, like these,
  And tarry till That please
To null us by Whose stress we emanate.—
  Our incorporeal sense,
Our overseeings, our supernal state,
  Our readings Why and Whence,
Are but the flower of Man's intelligence;
And that but an unreckoned incident
Of the all-urging Will, raptly magnipotent.

A gauze of shadow overdraws.

PART SECOND

CHARACTERS

I. Phantom Intelligences

{ The Ancient Spirit of the Years.
Chorus of the Years.

{ The Spirit of the Pities.
Chorus of the Pities.

{ Spirits Sinister and Ironic.
Choruses of Sinister and Ironic Spirits.

{ The Spirit of Rumour.
Chorus of Rumours.

The Shade of the Earth.

Spirit-Messengers.

Recording Angels.

II. Persons

The names printed in italics are those of mute figures.

MEN

George the Third.
The Prince of Wales, afterwards Prince Regent.
The Royal Dukes.
Fox.
Perceval.
Castlereagh.
An Under-Secretary of State.
Sheridan.
The Duke of Bedford.
Lord Moira.
Two Young Lords.
Lords Yarmouth and Keith.
Another Lord.
Other Peers, Ambassadors, Ministers, ex-Ministers, Members of Parlia-

ment, and Persons of Quality and Office.

———

Sir Arthur Wellesley, afterwards Lord Wellington.
Sir John Moore.
Sir John Hope.
Sir David Baird.
General Beresford.
Colonel Anderson.
Colonel Graham.
Major Colborne, principal Aide-de-Camp to Moore.
Captain Hardinge.
Paget, Fraser, Hill, Napier.

139

A Captain of Hussars and Others.
Other English Generals, Colonels, Aides, Couriers, and Military Officers.
Two Spies.
Two Army Surgeons.
An Army Chaplain.
A Sergeant of the Waggon-Train.
A Sergeant of the Forty-Third.
Two Soldiers of the Ninth.
English Forces.
Deserters and Stragglers.

———

Dr. Willis.
Sir Henry Halford.
Dr. Heberden.
Dr. Baillie.
The King's Apothecary.
A Gentleman.
Two Attendants on the King.

———

Members of a London Club.
An Englishman in Vienna.
Trotter, Secretary to Fox.
Mr. Bagot.
Mr. Forth, Master of Ceremonies.
Servants.
A Beau, A Constable, etc.

———

Napoléon Bonaparte.
Joseph Bonaparte.
Louis and Jérôme Bonaparte, and other Members of Napoléon's Family.
Cambacérès, Arch-Chancellor.
Talleyrand.
President of the Senate.
Caulaincourt.
Lebrun, Duroc, Prince of Neufchâtel, Grand-Duke of Berg.
Eugène de Beauharnais.
Champagny, Foreign Minister.
De Bausset, Chamberlain.

———

Murat.
Soult.
Masséna.
Berthier.
Junot.
Foy.
Loison.
Ney, Lannes, and other French Marshals, general and regimental Officers, Aides, and Couriers.
Two French Subalterns.
Another French Officer.
French Forces.

———

Grand Marshal, Grand Almoners, Heralds, and other Officials at Napoléon's marriage.
Abbé de Pradt, Chapel-Master.
Corvisart, First Physician. ⎫
Bourdier, Second Physician. ⎬ To Marie Louise.
Dubois, Accoucheur. ⎭
Maskers at a Ball.
Two Servants at the Tuileries.
A Parisian Crowd.
Guillet de Gevrillière, a Conspirator.
Louis XVIII. of France.
French Princes in England.

———

The King of Prussia.
Prince Henry of Prussia.
Prince Royal of Bavaria.
Prince Hohenlohe.
Generals Ruchel, Tauenzien, and Attendant Officers.
Prussian Forces.
Prussian Stragglers.
Berlin Citizens.

———

Carlos IV., King of Spain.
Fernando, Prince of Asturias, Son to the King.
Godoy, "Prince of Peace," Lover of the Queen.
Count of Montijo.

VISCOUNT MATEROSA
DON DIEGO DE LA
 VEGA.
} Spanish Deputies.

Godoy's Guards and other Soldiery.
SPANISH CITIZENS.
A LIFE-GUARDSMAN OF ARANJUEZ.
A SERVANT TO GODOY.
Spanish Forces.
Camp-Followers.
Muleteers.

————

FRANCIS, EMPEROR OF AUSTRIA.
METTERNICH.
ANOTHER AUSTRIAN MINISTER.
SCHWARZENBERG.

D'AUDENARDE, AN EQUERRY.
AUSTRIAN OFFICERS.
AIDES-DE-CAMP.
Austrian Forces.
Couriers and Secretaries.
VIENNESE CITIZENS.

————

THE EMPEROR ALEXANDER.
The Grand-Duke Constantine.
Prince Labanoff.
Count Lieven.
Generals Bennigsen, Ouwaroff, and others.
Officers in attendance on Alexander.

WOMEN

CAROLINE, PRINCESS OF WALES.
DUCHESS OF YORK.
DUCHESS OF RUTLAND.
MARCHIONESS OF SALISBURY.
MARCHIONESS OF HERTFORD.
Other Peeresses.
MRS. FITZHERBERT.
Ambassadors' Wives, Wives of Ministers and Members of Parliament, and other Ladies of Note.

————

THE EMPRESS JOSÉPHINE.
HORTENSE, QUEEN OF HOLLAND.
The Mother of Napoléon.
Princess Pauline, and others of Napoléon's Family.
DUCHESS OF MONTEBELLO.
MADAME DE MONTESQUIOU.
MADAME BLAISE, NURSE TO MARIE LOUISE.
Wives of French Ministers, and of other Officials.
Other Ladies of the French Court.
DUCHESS OF ANGOULÊME.

————

LOUISA, QUEEN OF PRUSSIA.
The Countess Voss, Lady-in-Waiting.
BERLIN LADIES.

————

MARÍA LUISA, QUEEN OF SPAIN.
THEREZA OF BOURBON, WIFE OF GODOY.
DOÑA JOSEFA TUDO, MISTRESS OF GODOY.
Lady-in-Waiting to the Queen.
A Servant.

————

M. LOUISA BEATRIX, EMPRESS OF AUSTRIA.
THE ARCHDUCHESS MARIA LOUISA, afterwards the EMPRESS MARIE LOUISE.
MADAME METTERNICH.
LADIES OF THE AUSTRIAN COURT.

————

THE EMPRESS-MOTHER OF RUSSIA.
GRAND-DUCHESS ANNE OF RUSSIA.

ACT FIRST

SCENE I

LONDON. FOX'S LODGINGS, ARLINGTON STREET

Fox, the Foreign Secretary in the new Ministry of All-the-Talents, sits at a table writing. He is a stout, swarthy man, with shaggy eyebrows, and his breathing is somewhat obstructed. His clothes look as though they had been slept in. TROTTER, his private secretary, is writing at another table near.

A servant enters.

SERVANT

Another stranger presses to see you, sir.

FOX *(without raising his eyes)*

Oh; another. What's he like?

SERVANT

A foreigner, sir; though not so out-at-elbows as might be thought from the denomination. He says he's from Gravesend, having lately left Paris, and that you sent him a passport. He comes with a police-officer.

FOX

Ah, to be sure. I remember. Bring him in, and tell the officer to wait outside. *(Servant goes out.)* Trotter, will you leave us for a few minutes? But be within hail.

The secretary retires, and the servant shows in a man who calls himself GUILLET DE GEVRILLIÈRE—a tall, thin figure of thirty, with restless dark eyes. The door being shut behind him, he is left alone with the minister. Fox points to a seat, leans back, and surveys his visitor.

GEVRILLIÈRE

Thanks to you, sir, for this high privilege
Of hailing England, and of entering here.
Without a fore-extended confidence
Like this of yours, my plans would not have sped.
(A pause.)
Europe, alas! sir, has her waiting foot
Upon the sill of further slaughter-scenes!

FOX

I fear it is so!—In your lines you wrote,
I think, that you are a true Frenchman born?

GEVRILLIÈRE

I did, sir.
FOX
          How contrived you, then, to cross?

GEVRILLIÈRE

It was from Embden that I shipped for Gravesend,
In a small sailer called the "Toby," sir,
Masked under Prussian colours.   Embden I reached
On foot, on horseback, and by sundry shifts,
From Paris over Holland, secretly.

FOX

And you are stored with tidings of much pith,
Whose tenour would be priceless to the state?

GEVRILLIÈRE

I am.   It is, in brief, no more nor less
Than means to mitigate and even end
These welfare-wasting wars; ay, usher in
A painless spell of peace.

FOX

                    Prithee speak on.
No statesman can desire it more than I.

GEVRILLIÈRE (looking to see that the door is shut)
No nation, sir, can live its natural life,
Or think its thoughts in these days unassailed,
No crown-capt head enjoy tranquillity.

The fount of such high spring-tide of disorder,
Fevered disquietude, and forceful death,
Is One,—a single man.   He—need I name?—
The ruler is of France.

Fox

             Well, in the past
I fear that it has looked so.   But we see
Good reason still to hope that broadening views,
Politer wisdom, now is helping him
To saner guidance of his arrogant car.

Gevrillière

The generous hope will never be fulfilled!
Ceasing to bluff, then ceases he to be.
None sees that written largelier than himself.

Fox

Then what may be the valued revelation
That you can unlock in such circumstance?
Sir, I incline to spell you as a spy,
And not the honest help for honest men
You gave you out to be!

Gevrillière

             I beg you, sir,
To spare me that suspicion.   Never a thought
Could be more groundless.   Solemnly I vow
That notwithstanding what his signals show
The Emperor of France is as I say.—
Yet bring I good assurance, and declare
A medicine for all bruised Europe's sores!

Fox (impatiently)

Well, parley to the point, for I confess
No new negotiation do I note
That you can open up to work such cure.

Gevrillière

To speak then to the point permit me, sir :—
The sovereign remedy for an ill effect
Is the extinction of its evil cause.

Safely and surely how to compass this
I have the weighty honour to disclose,
Certain immunities being guaranteed
By those your power can influence, and yourself.

FOX (astonished)

Assassination ?

GEVRILLIÈRE

I care not for names !
A deed's true name is as its purpose is.
The lexicon of Liberty and Peace
Defines not this deed as assassination ;
Though maybe it is writ so in the tongue
Of courts and universal tyranny.

FOX

Why brought you this proposal here to me ?

GEVRILLIÈRE

My knowledge of your love of things humane,
Things free, things fair, of truth, of tolerance,
Right, justice, national felicity,
Prompted belief and hope in such a man !—
The matter is by now well forwarded,
A house at Plassy hired as pivot-point
From which the sanct intention can be worked.
And soon made certain.   To our good allies
No risk attaches ; merely to ourselves.

FOX (touching a private bell)

Sir, your unconscienced hardihood confounds me,
And your mind's measure of my character
Insults it sorely.   By your late-sent lines
Of specious import, by your bland address,
I have been led to prattle hopefully
With a cut-throat confessed !

The head constable and the secretary enter at the same moment.

Ere worse befall,
Sir, up and get you gone most dexterously !
Conduct this man ; lose never sight of him   (to the officer)
Till haled aboard some anchor-weighing craft
Bound to remotest coasts from us and France.

GEVRILLIÈRE (unmoved)

How you may handle me concerns me little.
The project will as roundly ripe itself
Without as with me.   Trusty souls remain,
Though my far bones bleach white on austral shores !—
I thank you for the audience.   Long ere this
I might have reft your life !   Ay, notice here—

(He produces a dagger; which is snatched from him.)

They need not have done that !   Even had you risen
To wrestle with, insult, strike, pinion me,
It would have lain unused.   In hands like mine
And my allies', the man of peace is safe,
Treat as he may our corporal tenement
In his misreading of a moral code.

[Exeunt GEVRILLIÈRE and the constable.

FOX

Trotter, indeed you well may stare at me !
I look warm, eh ?—and I am windless, too ;
I have sufficient reason to be so.
That dignified and pensive gentleman
Was a bold bravo, waiting for his chance.
He sketched a scheme for murdering Bonaparte,
Either—as in my haste I understood—
By shooting from a window as he passed,
Or by some other wry and stealthy means
That haunt sad brains which brood on despotism,
But lack the tools to justly cope therewith ! . . .
On later thoughts I feel not fully sure
If, in my ferment, I did right in this.
No ; hail at once the man in charge of him,
And give the word that he is to be detained.

The secretary goes out.   FOX walks to the window in deep reflection till
the secretary returns.

SECRETARY

I was in time, sir.   He has been detained.

FOX

Now what does strict state-honour ask of me ?—
No less than that I bare this poppling plot
To the French ruler and our fiercest foe !—

Maybe 'twas but a hoax to pocket pay ;
And yet it can mean more . . .
The man's indifference to his own vague doom
Beamed out as one exalted trait in him,
And showed the altitude of his rash dream !—
Well, now I'll get me on to Downing Street,
There to draw up a note to Talleyrand
Retailing him the facts.—What signature
Subscribed this desperate fellow when he wrote ?

SECRETARY

" Guillet de la Gevrillière."   Here it stands.

FOX

Doubtless it was a false one.   Come along.

(Looking out of the window.)

Ah—here's Sir Francis Vincent : he'll go with us.
Ugh, what a twinge !   Time signals that he draws
Towards the twelfth stroke of my working-day !
I fear old England soon must voice her speech
With Europe through another mouth than mine !

SECRETARY

I trust not, sir.   Though you should rest awhile.
The very servants half are invalid
From the unceasing labours of your post,
And these cloaked visitors of every clime
That market on your magnanimity
To gain an audience morning, night, and noon,
Leaving you no respite.

FOX

                         'Tis true ; 'tis true.—
How I shall love my summer holiday
At pleasant Saint-Ann's Hill !

        He leans on the secretary's arm, and they go out.

SCENE II

THE ROUTE BETWEEN LONDON AND PARIS

A view now nocturnal, now diurnal, from on high over the Straits of Dover, and stretching from city to city. By night Paris and London seem each as a little swarm of lights surrounded by a halo; by day as a confused glitter of white and grey. The Channel between them is as a mirror reflecting the sky, brightly or faintly, as the hour may be.

SPIRIT OF THE PITIES

What mean these couriers shooting shuttlewise
To Paris and to London, turn and turn?

RUMOURS (chanting in antiphons)

I

The aforesaid tidings from the minister, spokesman in England's
*   cause to states afar;*

II

Traverse the waters borne by one of such; and thereto Bonaparte's
*   responses are:*

I

" The principles of honour and of truth which ever actuate the
*   sender's mind*

II

" Herein are written largely! Take our thanks: we read that
*   this conjuncture undesigned*

I

" Unfolds felicitous means of showing you that still our eyes are
*   set, as yours, on peace,*

II

" To which great end the Treaty of Amiens must be the ground-
*   work of our amities."*

I

From London then: " The path to amity the King of England
*   studies to pursue;*

II

" With Russia hand in hand he is yours to close the long con-
vulsions thrilling Europe through."

I

Still fare the shadowy missioners across, by Dover-road and
Calais Channel-track,

II

From Thames-side towers to Paris palace-gates; from Paris
leisurely to London back.

I

Till thus speaks France: " Much grief it gives us that, being
pledged to treat, one Emperor with one King,

II

" You yet have struck a jarring counternote and tone that keys
not with such promising.

I

" In these last words, then, of this pregnant parle; I trust I may
persuade your Excellency

II

" That in no circumstance, on no pretence, a party to our pact can
Russia be."

SPIRIT SINISTER

Fortunately for the manufacture of corpses by machinery
Napoléon sticks to this veto, and so wards off the awkward
catastrophe of a general peace descending upon Europe. Now
England.

RUMOURS (continuing)

I

Thereon speeds down through Kent and Picardy, evenly as some
southing sky-bird's shade:

II

" We gather not from your Imperial lines a reason why our
words should be reweighed.

I

"*We hold to Russia not as our ally that is to be: she stands full-plighted so;*

II

"*Thus trembles peace upon this balance-point: will you that Russia be let in or no?*"

I

Then France rolls out rough words across the strait: "*To treat with you confederate with the Tsar,*

II

"*Presumes us sunk in sloughs of shamefulness from which we yet stand gloriously afar!*

I

"*The English army must be Flanders-fed, and entering Picardy with pompous prance,*

II

"*To warrant such! Enough. Our comfort is, the crime of further strife lies not with France.*"

SPIRIT OF THE PITIES

Alas! what prayer will save the struggling lands,
Whose lives are ninepins to these bowling hands?

CHORUS OF RUMOURS

France secretly with—Russia plights her troth!
Britain, that lonely isle, is slurred by both.

SPIRIT SINISTER

It is as neat as an uncovered check at chess! You may now mark Fox's blank countenance at finding himself thus rewarded for the good turn done to Bonaparte, and at the extraordinary conduct of his chilly friend the Muscovite.

SPIRIT OF THE PITIES

His hand so trembles it can scarce retain
The quill wherewith he lets Lord Yarmouth know
Reserve is no more needed!

SPIRIT IRONIC

Now enters another character of this remarkable little piece—
Lord Lauderdale—and again the messengers fly!

SPIRIT OF THE PITIES

> *But what strange figure, pale and noiseless, comes,*
> *By us perceived, unrecognized by those,*
> *Into the very closet and retreat*
> *Of England's Minister?*

SPIRIT OF THE YEARS

>   *The Tipstaff he*
> *Of the Will, the Many-masked, my good friend Death.—*
> *The statesman's feeble form you may perceive*
> *Now hustled into the Invisible,*
> *And the unfinished game of Dynasties*
> *Left to proceed without him!*

SPIRIT OF THE PITIES

>   *Here, then, ends*
> *My hope for Europe's reason-wrought repose!*
> *He was the friend of peace—did his great best*
> *To shed her balms upon humanity;*
> *And now he's gone!   No substitute remains.*

SPIRIT IRONIC

Ay; the remainder of the episode is frankly farcical.   Negotia-
tions are again affected; but finally you discern Lauderdale
applying for passports; and the English Parliament declares to
the nation that peace with France cannot be made.

RUMOURS (concluding)

I

The smouldering dudgeon of the Prussian king, meanwhile, upon
*   the horizon's rim afar*

II

Bursts into running flame, that all his signs of friendliness were
*   met by moves for war.*

I

Attend and hear, for hear ye faintly may, his manifesto made at
*   Erfurt town,*

II

That to arms only dares he now confide the safety and the honour
    of his crown !

SPIRIT OF THE YEARS

Draw down the curtain, then, and overscreen
This too-protracted verbal fencing-scene ;
And let us turn to clanging foot and horse,
Ordnance, and all the enginry of Force !

Clouds close over the perspective.

SCENE III

THE STREETS OF BERLIN

It is afternoon, and the thoroughfares are crowded with citizens in an excited and anxious mood. A central path is left open for some expected arrival.

There enters on horseback a fair woman, whose rich brown curls stream flutteringly in the breeze, and whose long blue habit flaps against the flank of her curvetting white mare. She is the renowned LOUISA, QUEEN OF PRUSSIA, riding at the head of a regiment of hussars and wearing their uniform. As she prances along the thronging citizens acclaim her enthusiastically.

SPIRIT OF THE PITIES

Who is this fragile Fair, in fighting trim ?

SPIRIT OF THE YEARS

She is the pride of Prussia, whose resolve
Gives ballast to the purpose of her spouse,
And holds him to what men call governing.

SPIRIT OF THE PITIES

Queens have engaged in war ; but war's loud trade
Rings with a roar unnatural, fitful, forced,
Practised by woman's hands !

SPIRIT OF THE YEARS

           Of her we view
The enterprise is that of scores of men,
The strength but half-a-one's.

Spirit of the Pities

Would fate had ruled
The valour had been his, hers but the charm!

Spirit of Rumour

But he has nothing on't, and she has all.
The shameless satires of the bulletins
Dispatched to Paris, thence the wide world through,
Disturb the dreams of her by those who love her,
And thus her brave adventures for the realm
Have blurred her picture, soiled her gentleness,
And wrought her credit harm.

First Citizen (vociferously)

Yes, by God: send an ultimatum to Paris, by God; that's
what we'll do, by God. This Confederation of the Rhine was
the evil thought of an evil man bent on ruining us!

Second Citizen

This country double-faced and double-tongued,
This France, or rather say, indeed, this Man—
(Peoples are honest dealers in the mass)—
This man, to sign a stealthy scroll with Russia
That shuts us off from all indemnities,
While swearing faithful friendship with our King,
And, still professing our safe wardenry,
To fatten other kingdoms at our cost,
Insults us grossly, and makes Europe clang
With echoes of our wrongs. The little states
Of this antique and homely German land
Are severed from their blood-allies and kin—
Hereto of one tradition, interest, hope—
In calling lord this rank adventurer,
Who'll thrust them as a sword against ourselves.—
Surely Great Frederick sweats within his tomb!

Third Citizen

Well, we awake, though we have slumbered long,
And She is sent by Heaven to kindle us.

The Queen approaches to pass back again with her suite. The vociferous
applause is repeated. They regard her as she nears.

To cry her Amazon, a blusterer,
A brazen comrade of the bold dragoons
Whose uniform she dons !   Her, whose each act
Shows but a mettled modest woman's zeal,
Without a hazard of her dignity
Or moment's sacrifice of seemliness,
To fend off ill from home !

FOURTH CITIZEN (entering)

The tidings fly that Russian Alexander
Declines with emphasis to ratify
The pact of his ambassador with France,
And that the offer made the English King
To compensate the latter at our cost
Has not been taken.

THIRD CITIZEN

     And it never will be !
Thus evil does not always flourish, faith.
Throw down the gage while God is fair to us ;
He may be foul anon !   (A pause.)

FIFTH CITIZEN (entering)

Our ambassador Lucchesini is already leaving Paris. He
could stand the Emperor no longer, so the Emperor said he
could not stand Lucchesini. Knobelsdorf, who takes his place,
has decided to order his snuff by the ounce and his candles by
the pound, lest he should not be there long enough to use more.

The QUEEN goes by, and they gaze at her and at the escort of soldiers.

Haven't we soldiers ?   Haven't we the Duke of Brunswick to
command 'em ?   Haven't we provisions, hey ?   Haven't we
fortresses and an Elbe, to bar the bounce of an invader ?

The cavalcade passes out of sight and the crowd draws off.

FIRST CITIZEN

By God, I must to beer and 'bacco, to soften my rage !

[Exeunt citizens.

SPIRIT OF THE YEARS

So doth the Will objectify Itself
In likeness of a sturdy people's wrath,

Which takes no count of the new trends of time,
Trusting ebbed glory in a present need.—
What if their strength should equal not their fire,
And their devotion dull their vigilance?—
Uncertainly, by fits, the Will doth work
In Brunswick's blood, their chief, as in themselves;
It ramifies in streams that intermit
And make their movement vague, old-fashioned, slow
To foil the modern methods counterposed!

Evening descends on the city, and it grows dusk. The soldiers being dismissed from duty, some young officers in a frolic of defiance halt, draw their swords and whet them on the steps of the FRENCH AMBASSADOR'S residence as they pass. The noise of whetting is audible through the street.

CHORUS OF THE PITIES (aerial music)

The soul of a nation distrest
Is aflame,
And heaving with eager unrest
In its aim
To assert its old prowess, and stouten its chronicled fame!

SEMICHORUS I

It boils in a boisterous thrill
Through the mart,
Unconscious well-nigh as the Will
Of its part:
Would it wholly might be so, and feel not the forthcoming smart!

SEMICHORUS II

In conclaves no voice of reflection
Is heard,
King, Councillors, grudge circumspection
A word,
And victory is visioned, and seemings as facts are averred.

CHORUS

Yea, the soul of a nation distrest
Is aflame,
And heaving with eager unrest
In its aim
At supreme desperations to blazon the national name!

Midnight strikes, lights are extinguished one by one, and the scene disappears.

SCENE IV

THE FIELD OF JENA

Day has just dawned through a grey October haze. The French, with their backs to the nebulous light, loom out and show themselves to be already under arms ; LANNES holding the centre, NEY the right, SOULT the extreme right, and AUGEREAU the left. The Imperial Guard and MURAT'S cavalry are drawn up on the Landgrafenberg, behind the centre of the French position. In a valley stretching along to the rear of this height flows northward towards the Elbe the little river Saale, on which the town of Jena stands.

On the irregular plateaux in front of the French lines, and almost close to the latter, are the Prussians under TAUENZIEN ; and away on their right rear towards Weimar the bulk of the army under PRINCE HOHENLOHE. The DUKE OF BRUNSWICK (father of the Princess of Wales) is twelve miles off with his force at Auërstadt, in the valley of the Ilm.

Enter NAPOLÉON, and men bearing torches who escort him. He moves along the front of his troops, and is lost to view behind the mist and surrounding objects. But his voice is audible.

NAPOLÉON

Keep you good guard against their cavalry,
In past repute the formidablest known,
And such it may be now ; so asks our heed.
Receive it, then, in square, unflinchingly.—
Remember, men, last year you captured Ulm,
So make no doubt that you will vanquish these !

SOLDIERS

Long live the Emperor !   Advance, advance !

NAPOLÉON

Nay, caution, men !   'Tis mine to time your deeds
By light of long experience : yours to do them.

DUMB SHOW

Almost immediately glimpses reveal that LANNES' corps is moving forward, and amid an unbroken clatter of firelocks spreads out further and wider upon the stretch of country in front of the Landgrafenberg. The Prussians, surprised at discerning in the fog such masses of the enemy close at hand, recede towards the Ilm.

From PRINCE HOHENLOHE, who is with the body of the Prussians on the Weimar road to the south, comes perspiring the bulk of the infantry to rally the retreating regiments of TAUENZIEN, and he hastens up himself with the

cavalry and artillery.   The action is renewed between him and NEY as the
clocks of Jena strike ten.

But AUGEREAU is seen coming to NEY's assistance on one flank of the
Prussians, SOULT bearing down on the other, while NAPOLÉON on the Landgrafenberg orders the Imperial Guard to advance.   The doomed Prussians
are driven back, this time more decisively, falling in great numbers and losing
many as prisoners as they reel down the sloping land towards the banks of the
Ilm behind them.   GENERAL RUCHEL, in a last despairing effort to rally,
faces the French onset in person and alone.   He receives a bullet through the
chest and falls dead.

The crisis of the struggle is reached, though the battle is not over.
NAPOLÉON, discerning from the Landgrafenberg that the decisive moment
has come, directs MURAT to sweep forward with all his cavalry.   It engages
the shattered Prussians, surrounds them, and cuts them down by thousands.

From behind the horizon, a dozen miles off, between the din of guns in the
visible battle, there can be heard an ominous roar, as of a second invisible
battle in progress there.   Generals and other officers look at each other and
hazard conjectures between whiles, the French with exultation, the Prussians
gloomily.

HOHENLOHE

That means the Duke of Brunswick, I conceive,
Impacting on the enemy's further force
Led by, they say, Davout and Bernadotte. .
God grant his star less lurid rays than ours,
Or this too pregnant, hoarsely-groaning day
Shall, ere its loud delivery be done,
Have twinned disasters to the fatherland
That fifty years will fail to sepulchre !

Enter a straggler on horseback.

STRAGGLER

Prince, I have circuited by Auërstadt,
And bring ye dazzling tidings of the fight,
Which, if report by those who saw't be true,
Has raged thereat from clammy day-dawn on,
And left us victors !

HOHENLOHE

Thitherward go I,
And patch the mischief wrought upon us here !

Enter a second and then a third straggler.

Well, wet-faced men, whence come ye ?   What d'ye bring?

STRAGGLER II

Your Highness, I rode straight from Hassenhausen,
Across the stream of battle as it boiled
Betwixt that village and the banks of Saale,
And such the turmoil that no man could speak
On what the issue was!

HOHENLOHE (to Straggler III)
                      Can you add aught?

STRAGGLER III

Nothing that's clear, your Highness.

HOHENLOHE
                      Man, your mien
Is that of one who knows, but will not say.
Detain him here.

STRAGGLER III
                The blackness of my news,
Your Highness, darks my sense! . . . I saw this much:
The Duke of Brunswick, spurring on to head
His charging grenadiers, received in the face
A grape-shot stroke that gouged out half of it,
Proclaiming then and there his life fordone.

HOHENLOHE

Fallen? Brunswick! Reed in council, rock in fire . . .
Ah, this he looked for. Many a time of late
Has he, by some strange gift of foreknowing,
Declared his fate was hovering in such wise!

STRAGGLER III

His aged form being borne beyond the strife,
The gallant Moellendorf, in flushed despair,
Swore he would not survive; and, pressing on,
He, too, was slaughtered. Patriotic rage
Brimmed marshals' breasts and men's. The King himself
Fought like the commonest. But nothing served.
His horse is slain; his own doom yet unknown.
Prince William, too, is wounded. Brave Schmettau
Is broke; himself disabled. All give way,
And regiments crash like trees at felling-time!

HOHENLOHE

No more.   We match it here.   The yielding lines
Still sweep us backward.   Backward we must go !

[Exeunt HOHENLOHE, Staff, stragglers, etc.

The Prussian retreat from Jena quickens to a rout, many thousands being
taken prisoners by MURAT, who pursues them to Weimar, where the inhabitants
fly shrieking through the streets.

The October day closes in to evening.   By this time the troops retiring with
the King of Prussia from the second battlefield of Auërstadt have intersected
RUCHEL'S and HOHENLOHE'S flying battalions from Jena.   The crossing
streams of fugitives strike panic into each other, and the tumult increases with
the thickening darkness till night renders the scene invisible, and nothing
remains but a confused diminishing noise, and fitful lights here and there.

The fog of the morning returns, and curtains all.

SCENE V

BERLIN.   A ROOM OVERLOOKING A PUBLIC PLACE

A fluttering group of ladies is gathered at the window, gazing out and conversing anxiously.   The time draws towards noon, when the clatter of a
galloping horse's hoofs is heard echoing up the long Potsdamer-Strasse, and
presently turning into the Leipziger-Strasse reaches the open space commanded
by the ladies' outlook.   It ceases before a Government building opposite them,
and the rider disappears into the courtyard.

FIRST LADY

Yes : surely he is a courier from the field !

SECOND LADY

Shall we not hasten down, and take from him
The doom his tongue may deal us ?

THIRD LADY

                          We shall catch
As soon by watching here as hastening hence
The tenour of his news.   (They wait.)   Ah, yes : see—see
The bulletin is straightway to be nailed !
He was, then, from the field. . . .

They wait on while the bulletin is affixed.

SECOND LADY

I cannot scan the words the scroll proclaims ;
Peer as I will, these too quick-thronging dreads

Bring water to the eyes.   Grant us, good Heaven,
That victory be where she is needed most
To prove Thy goodness ! . . . What do you make of it ?

THIRD LADY (reading, through a glass)

" The battle strains us sorely ; but resolve
May save us even now.   Our last attack
Has failed, with fearful loss.   Once more we strive."

A long silence in the room.   Another rider is heard approaching, above the murmur of the gathering citizens.   The second lady looks out.

SECOND LADY

A straggler merely he. . . . But they decide,
At last, to post his news, wild-winged or no.

THIRD LADY (reading again through her glass)

" The Duke of Brunswick, leading on a charge,
Has met his death-doom.   Schmettau, too, is slain ;
Prince William wounded.   But we stand as yet,
Engaging with the last of our reserves."

The agitation in the street communicates itself to the room.   Some of the ladies weep silently as they wait, much longer this time.   Another horseman is at length heard clattering into the Platz, and they lean out again with painful eagerness.

SECOND LADY

An adjutant of Marshal Moellendorf's,
If I define him rightly.   Read—O read !—
Though reading draw them from their socket-holes
Use your eyes now !

THIRD LADY (glass up)
            As soon as 'tis affixed. . . .
Ah—this means much !   The people's air and gait
Too well betray disaster.   (Reading.)   " Berliners,
The King has lost the battle !   Bear it well.
The foremost duty of a citizen
Is to maintain a brave tranquillity.
This is what I, the Governor, demand
Of men and women now. . . . The King lives still."

They turn from the window and sit in a silence broken only by monosyllabic words, hearing abstractedly the dismay without that has followed the previous excitement and hope.

G

The stagnation is ended by a cheering outside, of subdued emotional quality, mixed with sounds of grief. They again look forth. QUEEN LOUISA is leaving the city with a very small escort, and the populace seem overcome. They strain their eyes after her as she disappears.

Enter fourth lady.

FIRST LADY

How does she bear it? Whither does she go?

FOURTH LADY

She goes to join the King at Custrin, there
To abide events—as we. Her heroism
So schools her sense of her calamities
As out of grief to carve new queenliness,
And turn a mobile mien to statuesque,
Save for a sliding tear.

The ladies leave the window severally.

SPIRIT IRONIC

So the Will plays at flux and reflux still.
This monarchy, one-half whose pedestal
Is built of Polish bones, has bones home-made!
Let the fair woman bear it. Poland did.

SPIRIT OF THE YEARS

Meanwhile the mighty Emperor nears apace,
And soon will glitter at the city gates
With palpitating drums, and breathing brass,
And rampant joyful-jingling retinue.

An evening mist cloaks the scene.

SCENE VI

THE SAME

It is a brilliant morning, with a fresh breeze, and not a cloud. The open Platz and the adjoining streets are filled with dense crowds of citizens, in whose upturned faces curiosity has mastered consternation and grief.

Martial music is heard, at first faint, then louder, followed by a trampling of innumerable horses and a clanking of arms and accoutrements. Through a street on the right hand of the view from the windows come troops of French dragoons heralding the arrival of BONAPARTE.

Re-enter the room hurriedly and cross to the windows several ladies as before, some in tears.

FIRST LADY

The kingdom late of Prussia, can it be
That thus it disappears ?—a patriot-cry,
A battle, bravery, ruin ; and no more ?

SECOND LADY

Thank God the Queen's gone !

THIRD LADY

           To what sanctuary ?
From earthquake shocks there is no sheltering cell !
—Is this what men call conquest ?   Must it close
As historied conquests do, or be annulled
By modern reason and the urbaner sense ?—
Such issue none would venture to predict,
Yet folly 'twere to nourish foreshaped fears
And suffer in conjecture and in deed.—
If verily our country be dislimbed,
Then at the mercy of his domination
The face of earth will lie, and vassal kings
Stand waiting on himself the Overking,
Who ruling them rules all ; till desperateness
Sting and excite a bonded last resistance,
And work its own release.

SECOND LADY

           He comes even now
From sacrilege.   I learn that, since the fight,
In marching here by Potsdam yesterday,
Sans-Souci Palace drew his curious feet,
Where even great Frederick's tomb was bared to him.

FOURTH LADY

All objects in the Palace—cared for, kept
Even as they were when our arch-monarch died—
The books, the chair, the inkhorn, and the pen
He quizzed with flippant curiosity ;
And entering where our hero's bones are urned
He seized the sword and standards treasured there,
And with a mixed effrontery and regard
Declared they should be all dispatched to Paris
As gifts to the Hôtel des Invalides.

Third Lady

Such rodomontade is cheap : what matters it !

A galaxy of marshals, forming Napoléon's staff, now enters the Platz immediately before the windows. In the midst rides the EMPEROR himself. The ladies are silent. The procession passes along the front until it reaches the entrance to the Royal Palace. At the door NAPOLÉON descends from his horse and goes into the building amid the resonant trumpetings of his soldiers and the silence of the crowd.

Second Lady (impressed)

O why does such a man debase himself
By countenancing loud scurrility
Against a queen who cannot make reprise !
A power so ponderous needs no littleness—
The last resort of feeble desperates !

Enter fifth lady.

Fifth Lady (breathlessly)

Humiliation grows acuter still.
He placards rhetoric to his soldiery
On their distress of us and our allies,
Declaring he'll not stack away his arms
Till he has choked the remaining foes of France
In their own gainful glut.—Whom means he, think you ?

First Lady

Us ?

Third Lady

Russia ? Austria ?

Fifth Lady

Neither : England.—Yea,
Her he still holds the master mischief-mind,
And marrer of the countries' quietude,
By exercising untold tyranny
Over all ports and seas.

Second Lady

Then England's doomed !
When he has overturned the Russian rule,
England comes next for wrack. They say that know ! . . .

Look—he has entered by the Royal doors
And makes the Palace his.—Now let us go !—
Our course, alas ! is—whither?

[*Exeunt ladies.*

The curtain drops temporarily.

SEMICHORUS I OF IRONIC SPIRITS (aerial music)

Deeming himself omnipotent
With the Kings of the Christian continent,
To warden the waves was his further bent.

SEMICHORUS II

But the weaving Will from eternity,
(Hemming them in by a circling sea)
Evolved the fleet of the Englishry.

SEMICHORUS I

The wane of his armaments ill-advised,
At Trafalgár, to a force despised,
Was a wound which never has cicatrized.

SEMICHORUS II

This, O this is the cramp that grips !
And freezes the Emperor's finger-tips
From signing a peace with the Land of Ships.

CHORUS

The Universal-empire plot
Demands the rule of that wave-walled spot ;
And peace with England cometh not !

THE SCENE REOPENS

A lurid gloom now envelops the Platz and city ; and Bonaparte is heard as from the Palace :

VOICE OF NAPOLÉON

These monstrous violations being in train
Of law and national integrities
By English arrogance in things marine,
(Which dares to capture simple merchant-craft,
In honest quest of harmless merchandize,
For crime of kinship to a hostile power)

Our vast, effectual, and majestic strokes
In this unmatched campaign, enable me
To bar from commerce with the Continent
All keels of English frame.   Hence I decree :—

SPIRIT OF RUMOUR

This outlines his renowned " Berlin Decree:"
Maybe he meditates its scheme in sleep,
Or hints it to his suite, or syllables it
While shaping, to his scribes.

VOICE OF NAPOLÉON (continuing)

All England's ports to suffer strict blockade ;
All traffic with that land to cease forthwith ;
All natives of her isles, wherever met,
To be detained as windfalls of the war.
All chattels of her make, material, mould,
To be good prize wherever pounced upon :
And never a bottom hailing from her shores
But shall be barred from every haven here.
This for her monstrous harms to human rights,
And shameless sauciness to neighbour powers !

SPIRIT SINISTER

I spell herein that our excellently high-coloured drama is not
played out yet !

SPIRIT OF THE YEARS

Nor will it be for many a month of moans,
And summer shocks, and winter-whitened bones.

The night gets darker, and the Palace outlines are lost.

SCENE VII

TILSIT AND THE RIVER NIEMEN

The scene is viewed from the windows of BONAPARTE'S temporary quarters.
Some sub-officers of his suite are looking out upon it.

It is the day after midsummer, about one o'clock.   A multitude of
soldiery and spectators lines each bank of the broad river which, stealing
slowly north-west, bears almost exactly in its midst a moored raft of bonded
timber.   On this as a floor stands a gorgeous pavilion of draped woodwork,
having at each side, facing the respective banks of the stream, a round-headed

doorway richly festooned. The cumbersome erection acquires from the current a rhythmical movement, as if it were breathing, and the breeze now and then produces a shiver on the face of the stream.

DUMB SHOW

On the south-west or Prussian side rides the EMPEROR NAPOLÉON in uniform, attended by the GRAND DUKE OF BERG, the PRINCE OF NEUFCHÂTEL, MARSHAL BESSIÈRES, DUROC Marshal of the Palace, and CAULAINCOURT Master of the Horse. The EMPEROR looks well, but is growing fat. They embark on an ornamental barge in front of them, which immediately puts off. It is now apparent to the watchers that a precisely similar enactment has simultaneously taken place on the opposite or Russian bank, the chief figure being the EMPEROR ALEXANDER—a graceful, flexible man of thirty, with a courteous manner and good-natured face. He has come out from an inn on that side, accompanied by the GRAND-DUKE CONSTANTINE, GENERAL BENNIGSEN, GENERAL OUWAROFF, PRINCE LABANOFF, and ADJUTANT-GENERAL COUNT LIEVEN.

The two barges draw towards the raft, reaching the opposite sides of it about the same time, amidst discharges of cannon. Each Emperor enters the door that faces him, and meeting in the centre of the pavilion they formally embrace each other. They retire together to the screened interior, the suite of each remaining in the outer half of the pavilion.

More than an hour passes while they are thus invisible. The French officers who have observed the scene from the lodging of NAPOLÉON walk about idly, and ever and anon go curiously to the windows, again to watch the raft.

CHORUS OF THE YEARS (aerial music)

The prelude to this smooth scene—mark well!—were the shocks
    whereof the times gave token
Vaguely to us ere last year's snows shut over Lithuanian pine
    and pool,
Which we told at the fall of the faded leaf, when the pride of
    Prussia was bruised and broken,
And the Man of Adventure sat in the seat of the Man of Method
    and rigid Rule.

SEMICHORUS I OF THE PITIES

Snows incarnadined were thine, O Eylau, field of the wide white
    spaces,
And frozen lakes, and frozen limbs, and blood iced hard as it left
    the veins :
Steel-cased squadrons swathed in cloud-drift, plunging to doom
    through pathless places,
And forty thousand dead and near dead, strewing the early-
    nighted plains.

Semichorus II

*Friedland to these adds its tale of victims, its midnight marches
    and hot collisions,*

*Its plunge, at his word, on the enemy hooped by the bended river
    and famed Mill stream,*

*As he shatters the moves of the loose-knit nations to curb his
    exploitful soul's ambitions,*

*And their great Confederacy dissolves like the diorama of a
    dream.*

DUMB SHOW (continues)

NAPOLÉON and ALEXANDER emerge from their seclusion, and each is
beheld talking to the suite of his companion apparently in flattering compli-
ment. An effusive parting, which signifies itself to be but temporary, is
followed by their return to the river shores amid the cheers of the spectators.

NAPOLÉON and his marshals arrive at the door of his quarters and enter,
and pass out of sight to other rooms than that of the foreground in which the
observers are loitering. Dumb show ends.

A murmured conversation grows audible, carried on by two persons in the
crowd beneath the open windows. Their dress being the native one, and
their tongue unfamiliar, they seem to the officers to be merely inhabitants
gossiping ; and their voices continue unheeded.

First English Spy [1] (below)

Did you get much for me to send on ?

Second English Spy [1]

I have got hold of the substance of their parley. Surely no
truce in European annals ever led to so odd an interview. They
were like a belle and her beau, by God ! But, queerly enough,
one of Alexander's staff said to him as he reached the raft :
"Sire, let me humbly ask you not to forget your father's fate !"
Grim—Eh ?

First Spy

Anything about the little island which shall be nameless ?

Second Spy

Much ; and startling, too. "Why are we at war ?" says
Napoléon when they met.—"Ah—why !" said t'other.—"Well,"
said Boney, "I am fighting you only as an ally of the English,
and you are simply serving them, and not yourself, in fighting
me."—"In that case," says Alexander, "we shall soon be friends,
for I owe her as great a grudge as you."

---

[1] It has been conjectured of late that these adventurous spirits were Sir Robert Wilson
and, possibly, Lord Hutchinson, present there at imminent risks of their lives.

FIRST SPY

Dammy, go that length, did they!

SECOND SPY

Then they plunged into the old story about English selfishness, and greed, and duplicity. But the climax related to Spain, and it amounted to this: they agreed that the Bourbons of the Spanish throne should be made to abdicate, and Bonaparte's relations set up as sovereigns instead of them.

FIRST SPY

Somebody must ride like hell to let our Cabinet know!

SECOND SPY

I have written it down in cipher, not to trust to memory, and to guard against accidents.—They also agreed that France should have the Pope's dominions, Malta, and Egypt; that Napoléon's brother Joseph should have Sicily as well as Naples, and that they would partition the Ottoman Empire between them.

FIRST SPY

Cutting up Europe like a plum-pudding. Par nobile fratrum!

SECOND SPY

Then the worthy pair came to poor Prussia, whom Alexander, they say, was anxious about, as he is under engagements to her. It seems that Napoléon agrees to restore to the King as many of his states as will cover Alexander's promise, so that the Tsar may feel free to strike out in this new line with his new friend.

FIRST SPY

Surely this is but surmise?

SECOND SPY

Not at all. One of the suite overheard, and I got round him. There was much more, which I did not learn. But they are going to soothe and flatter the unfortunate King and Queen by asking them to a banquet here.

FIRST SPY

Such a spirited woman will never come!

SECOND SPY

We shall see. Whom necessity compels needs must: and she has gone through an Iliad of woes!

FIRST SPY

It is this Spanish business that will stagger England, by God! And now to let her know it.

FRENCH SUBALTERN (looking out above)

What are those townspeople talking about so earnestly, I wonder? The lingo of this place has an accent akin to English.

SECOND SUBALTERN

No doubt because the races are both Teutonic.

The spies observe that they are noticed, and disappear in the crowd.

The curtain drops.

SCENE VIII

THE SAME

The midsummer sun is low, and a long table in the aforeshown apartment is laid out for a dinner, among the decorations being bunches of the season's roses.

At the vacant end of the room (divided from the dining end by folding-doors, now open) there are discovered the EMPEROR NAPOLÉON, the GRAND-DUKE CONSTANTINE, PRINCE HENRY OF PRUSSIA, the PRINCE ROYAL OF BAVARIA, the GRAND DUKE OF BERG, and attendant officers.

Enter the TSAR ALEXANDER. NAPOLÉON welcomes him, and the twain move apart from the rest, BONAPARTE placing a chair for his visitor and flinging himself down on another.

NAPOLÉON

The comforts I can offer are not great,
Nor is the accommodation more than scant
That falls to me for hospitality;
But, as it is, accept.

ALEXANDER

                          It serves me well.
And to unbrace the bandages of state
Is as clear air to incense-stifled souls.
What of the Queen?

NAPOLÉON

She's coming with the King.
We have some quarter-hour to spare or more
Before their Majesties are timed for us.

ALEXANDER

Good. I would speak of them. That she should show
    here
After the late events, betokens much!
Abasement in so proud a woman's heart

(His voice grows tremulous.)

Is not without a dash of painfulness.
And I beseech you, sire, that you hold out
Some soothing hope to her?

NAPOLÉON

I have, already!—
Now, sire, to those affairs we entered on:
Strong friendship, grown secure, bids me repeat
That you have been much duped by your allies.

ALEXANDER shows mortification.

Prussia's a shuffler, England a self-seeker,
Nobility has shone in you alone.
Your error grew of over-generous dreams,
And misbeliefs by dullard ministers.
By treating personally we speed affairs
More in an hour than they in blundering months.
Between us two, henceforth, must stand no third.
There's peril in it, while England's mean ambition
Still works to get us skewered by the ears;
And in this view your chiefs-of-staff concur.

ALEXANDER

The judgment of my officers I share.

NAPOLÉON

To recapitulate. Nothing can greaten you
Like this alliance. Providence has flung
My good friend Sultan Selim from his throne,
Leaving me free in dealings with the Porte;
And I discern the hour as one to end
A rule that Time no longer lets cohere,

If I abstain, its spoils will go to swell
The power of this same England, our annoy ;
That country which enchains the trade of towns
With such bold reach as to monopolize,
Among the rest, the whole of Petersburg's—
Ay !—through her purse, friend, as the lender there !—
Shutting that purse, she may incite to—what ?
Muscovy's fall, its ruler's murdering.
Her fleet at any minute can encoop
Yours in the Baltic ; in the Black Sea, too ;
And keep you snug as minnows in a glass !
   Hence we, fast-fellowed by our mutual foes,
Seaward the British, Germany by land,
And having compassed, for our common good,
The Turkish Empire's due partitioning,
As comrades can conjunctly rule the world
To its own gain and our eternal fame !

ALEXANDER (stirred and flushed)

I see vast prospects opened !—yet, in truth,
Ere you, sire, broached these themes, their outlines loomed
Not seldom in my own imaginings ;
But with less clear a vision than endows
So great a captain, statesman, philosoph,
As centre in yourself ; whom had I known
Sooner by some few years, months, even weeks,
I had been spared full many a fault of rule.
—Now as to Austria.   Should we call her in ?

NAPOLÉON

Two in a bed I have slept, but never three.

ALEXANDER

Ha-ha !   Delightful.   And, then nextly, Spain ?

NAPOLÉON

I lighted on some letters at Berlin,
Wherein King Carlos offered to attack me.
A Bourbon, minded thus, so near as Spain,
Is dangerous stuff.   He must be seen to soon ! . ,
A draft, then, of our treaty being penned,
We will peruse it later.   If King George

Will not, upon the terms there offered him,
Conclude a ready peace, he can be forced.
Trumpet yourself as France's firm ally,
And Austria will be fain to do the same :
England, left nude to such joint harassment,
Must shiver—fall.

     ALEXANDER (with naïve enthusiasm)
                 It is a great alliance !

        NAPOLÉON

Would it were one in blood as well as brain—
Of family hopes, and sweet domestic bliss !

        ALEXANDER

Ah—is it to my sister you refer ?

        NAPOLÉON

The launching of a lineal progeny
Has been much pressed upon me, much, of late,
For reasons which I will not dwell on now.
Staid counsellors, my brother Joseph, too,
Urge that I loose the Empress by divorce,
And re-wive promptly for the country's good.
Princesses even have been named for me !—
However this, to-day, is premature,
And 'twixt ourselves alone. . . .
    The Queen of Prussia must ere long be here :
Berthier escorts her.   And the King, too, comes.
She's one whom you admire ?

     ALEXANDER (reddening ingenuously)

            Yes. . . . Formerly
I had—did feel that some faint fascination
Vaguely adorned her form.   And, to be plain,
Certain reports have been calumnious,
And wronged an honest woman.

        NAPOLÉON

               As I knew !
But she is wearing thready : why, her years
Must be full one-and-thirty, if she's one.

ALEXANDER (quickly)

No, sire.   She's twenty-nine.   If traits teach more
It means that cruel memory gnaws at her
As fair inciter to that fatal war
Which broke her to the dust! . . . I do confess
(Since now we speak on't) that this sacrifice
Prussia is doomed to, still disquiets me.
Unhappy King!   When I recall the oaths
Sworn him upon great Frederick's sepulchre,
And—and my promises to his sad Queen,
It pricks me that his realm and revenues
Should be stript down to the mere half they were!

NAPOLÉON (coolly)

Believe me, 'tis but my regard for you
Which lets me leave him that!   Far easier 'twere
To leave him none at all.

> [He rises and goes to the window.
>   But here they are.

No; it's the Queen alone, with Berthier
As I directed.   Then the King will follow.

ALEXANDER

Let me, sire, urge your courtesy to bestow
Some gentle words on her?

NAPOLÉON

                Ay, ay; I will.

Enter QUEEN LOUISA OF PRUSSIA on the arm of BERTHIER.   She appears
in majestic garments and with a smile on her lips, so that her still great
beauty is impressive.   But her eyes bear traces of tears.   She accepts
NAPOLÉON'S attentions with the stormily sad air of a wounded beauty.
Whilst she is being received the KING arrives.   He is a plain, shy, honest-
faced, awkward man, with a wrecked and solitary look.   His manner to
NAPOLÉON is, nevertheless, dignified, and even stiff.

The company move into the inner half of the room, where the tables are,
and the folding-doors being shut, they seat themselves at dinner, the QUEEN
taking a place between NAPOLÉON and ALEXANDER.

NAPOLÉON

Madame, I love magnificent attire;
But in the present instance can but note
That each bright knot and jewel less adorns
The brighter wearer than the wearer it!

QUEEN (with a sigh)

You praise one, sire, whom now the wanton world
Has learnt to cease from praising ! But such words
From such a quarter are of worth no less.

NAPOLÉON

Of worth as candour, madame ; not as gauge.
Your reach in rarity outsoars my scope.
Yet, do you know, a troop of my hussars,
That last October day, nigh captured you ?

QUEEN

Nay ! Never a single Frenchman did I see.

NAPOLÉON

Not less it was that you exposed yourself,
And should have been protected. But at Weimar,
Had you but sought me, 'twould have bettered you.

QUEEN

I had no zeal to meet you, sire, alas !

NAPOLÉON (after a silence)

And how at Memel do you sport with time ?

QUEEN

Sport ? I !—I pore on musty chronicles,
And muse on usurpations long forgot,
And other historied dramas of high wrong !

NAPOLÉON

Why con not annals of your own rich age ?
They treasure acts well fit for pondering.

QUEEN

I am reminded too much of my age
By having had to live in it. May Heaven
Defend me now, and my wan ghost anon,
From conning it again !

NAPOLÉON

         Alas, alas!
Too grievous, this, for one who is yet a queen!

QUEEN

No; I have cause for vials more of grief.—
Prussia was blind in blazoning her power
Against the Mage of Earth! . . .
The embers of great Frederick's deeds inflamed her:
His glories swelled her to her ruining.
Too well has she been punished! (Emotion stops her.)

ALEXANDER (in a low voice, looking anxiously at her)

         Say not so.
You speak as all were lost. Things are not thus!
Such desperation has unreason in it,
And bleeds the hearts that crave to comfort you.

NAPOLÉON (to the King)

I trust the treaty, further pondered, sire,
Has consolations?

KING (curtly)

     I am a luckless man;
And muster strength to bear my lucklessness
Without vain hope of consolations now.
One thing, at least, I trust I have shown you, sire,
That *I* provoked not this calamity!
At Anspach first my feud with you began—
Anspach, my Eden, violated and shamed
By blushless tramplings of your legions there!

NAPOLÉON

It's rather late, methinks, to talk thus now.

KING (with more choler)

Never too late for truth and plainspeaking!

NAPOLÉON (blandly)

To your ally, the Tsar, I must refer you.
He was it, and not I, who tempted you

To push for war, when Eylau must have shown
Your every profit to have lain in peace.——
He can indemn ; yes, much or small ; and may.

KING (with a head-shake)

I would make up, would well make up, my mind
To half my kingdom's loss, could in such limb
But Magdeburg not lie.   Dear Magdeburg,
Place of my heart-hold ; *that* I would retain !

NAPOLÉON

Our words take not such pattern as is wont
To grace occasions of festivity.

[He turns brusquely from the King.

The banquet proceeds with a more general conversation.   When finished a
toast is proposed : '' The Freedom of the Seas,'' and drunk with enthusiasm.

SPIRIT SINISTER

Another hit at England and her tubs !
I hear harsh echoes from her chalky chines.

SPIRIT OF THE PITIES

O heed not England now !   Still read the Queen.
One grieves to see her spend her pretty spells
Upon the man who has so injured her.

They rise from table, and the folding-doors being opened they pass into
the adjoining part of the room.

Here are now assembled MURAT, TALLEYRAND, KOURAKIN, KALKREUTH,
BERTHIER, BESSIÈRES, CAULAINCOURT, LABANOFF, BENNIGSEN, and
others.   NAPOLÉON having spoken a few words here and there resumes his
conversation with QUEEN LOUISA, and parenthetically offers snuff to the
COUNTESS VOSS, her lady-in-waiting.   TALLEYRAND, who has observed
NAPOLÉON'S growing interest in the QUEEN, contrives to get near him.

TALLEYRAND (in a whisper)

Sire, is it possible that you can bend
To let one woman's fairness filch from you
All the resplendent fortune that attends
The grandest victory of your grand career ?

The QUEEN'S quick eye observes and flashes at the whisper, and she
obtains a word with the minister.

QUEEN (sarcastically)

I should infer, dear Monsieur Talleyrand,
Only two persons in the world regret
My having come to Tilsit.

TALLEYRAND

                                Madame, two?
Can any!—who may such sad rascals be?

QUEEN

You, and myself, Prince.   (Gravely.)   Yes! myself and you.

TALLEYRAND'S face becomes impassive, and he does not reply.

Soon the QUEEN prepares to leave, and NAPOLÉON rejoins her.

NAPOLÉON (taking a rose from a vase)

Dear Queen, do pray accept this little token
As souvenir of me before you go?

He offers her the rose, with his hand on his heart.   She hesitates, but
accepts it.

QUEEN (impulsively, with waiting tears)

Let Magdeburg come with it, sire!   O yes!

NAPOLÉON (with sudden frigidity)

It is for you to take what I can give.
And I give this—no more.[1]

She turns her head to hide her emotion, and withdraws.   NAPOLÉON
steps up to her, and offers his arm.   She takes it silently, and he perceives
the tears on her cheeks.   They cross towards the ante-room, away from the
other guests.

NAPOLÉON (softly)

Still weeping, dearest lady!   Why is this?

QUEEN (seizing his hand and pressing it)

Your speeches darn the tearings of your sword!—
Between us two, as man and woman now,
Is't even possible you question why!

---

[1] The traditional present of the rose was probably on this occasion, though it is not
quite matter of certainty.

O why did not the Greatest of the Age—
Of future ages—of the ages past,
This one time win a woman's worship—yea,
For all her little life!

NAPOLÉON (gravely)

      Know you, my Fair
That I—ay, I—in this deserve your pity.—
Some force within me, baffling mine intent,
Harries me onward, whether I will or no.
My star, my star is what's to blame—not I.
It is unswervable!

QUEEN

      Then now, alas!
My duty's done as mother, wife, and queen.—
I'll say no more—but that my heart is broken!

  [Exeunt NAPOLÉON, QUEEN, and LADY-IN-WAITING.

SPIRIT OF THE YEARS

He spoke thus at the Bridge of Lodi.   Strange,
He's of the few in Europe who discern
The working of the Will.

SPIRIT OF THE PITIES

     If that be so,
Better for Europe lacked he such discerning!

NAPOLÉON returns to the room and joins TALLEYRAND.

NAPOLÉON (aside to his minister)

 My God, it was touch-and-go that time, Talleyrand! She
was within an ace of getting over me. As she stepped into the
carriage she said in her pretty way, "O I have been cruelly
deceived by you!" And when she sank down inside, not
knowing I heard, she burst into sobs fit to move a statue. The
Devil take me if I hadn't a good mind to stop the horses, jump
in, give her a good kissing, and agree to all she wanted. Ha-ha,
well; a miss is as good as a mile. Had she come sooner with
those sweet, beseeching blue eyes of hers, who knows what
might not have happened! But she didn't come sooner, and I
have kept in my right mind.

The RUSSIAN EMPEROR, the KING OF PRUSSIA, and other guests advance to bid adieu. They depart severally. When they are gone NAPOLÉON turns to TALLEYRAND.

> Adhere, then, to the treaty as it stands :
> Change not therein a single article,
> But write it fair forthwith.

[Exeunt NAPOLÉON, TALLEYRAND, and other ministers and officers in waiting.

SHADE OF THE EARTH

Some surly voice afar I heard by now
Of an enisled Britannic quality ;
Wots any of the cause ?

SPIRIT IRONIC

> *Perchance I do !*
Britain is roused, in her slow, stolid style,
By Bonaparte's pronouncement at Berlin
Against her cargoes, commerce, life itself ;
And now from out her watery citadel
Blows counterblasting " Orders." Rumours tell.

RUMOUR I

" From havens of fierce France and her allies,
With poor or precious freight of merchandize
Whoso adventures, England pounds as prize ! "

RUMOUR II

Thereat Napoléon names her, furiously,
Curst Oligarch, Arch-pirate of the sea,
Who shall lack room to live while liveth he !

CHORUS OF THE PITIES (aerial music)

And peoples are enmeshed in new calamity !

Curtain of Evening Shades.

ACT SECOND

SCENE I

THE PYRENEES AND VALLEYS ADJOINING

The view is from upper air, immediately over the region that lies between Bayonne on the north, Pampeluna on the south, and San Sebastian on the west, including a portion of the Cantabrian mountains. The month is February, and snow covers not only the peaks but the lower slopes. The roads over the passes are well beaten.

DUMB SHOW

At various elevations multitudes of NAPOLÉON's soldiery, to the number of about thirty thousand, are discerned in a creeping progress across the frontier from the French to the Spanish side. The thin long columns serpentine along the roads, but are sometimes broken, while at others they disappear altogether behind vertical rocks and overhanging woods. The heavy guns and the whitey-brown tilts of the baggage-waggons seem the largest objects in the procession, which are dragged laboriously up the incline to the watershed, their lumbering being audible as high as the clouds.

Simultaneously the river Bidassoa, in a valley to the west, is being crossed by a train of artillery and another thirty thousand men, all forming part of the same systematic advance.

Along the great highway through Biscay the wondering native carters draw their sheep-skinned ox-teams aside, to let the regiments pass, and stray groups of peaceable field-workers in Navarre look inquiringly at the marching and prancing progress.

Time passes, and the various northern strongholds are approached by these legions. Their governors emerge at a summons, and when seeming explanations have been given the unwelcome comers are doubtfully admitted.

The chief places to which entrance is thus obtained are Pampeluna and San Sebastian at the front of the scene, and far away towards the shining horizon of the Mediterranean, Figueras and Barcelona.

Dumb Show concludes as the mountain mists close over.

SCENE II

ARANJUEZ, NEAR MADRID. A ROOM IN THE PALACE OF GODOY, THE "PRINCE OF PEACE"

A private chamber is disclosed, richly furnished with paintings, vases, mirrors, silk hangings, gilded lounges, and several lutes of rare workmanship. The hour is midnight, the room being lit by screened candelabra. In the centre at the back of the scene is a large window heavily curtained.

GODOY and the QUEEN MARÍA LUISA are dallying on a sofa. THE
PRINCE OF PEACE is a fine handsome man in middle life, with curled hair
and a mien of easy good-nature. The QUEEN is older, but looks younger in
the dim light, from the lavish use of beautifying arts. She has pronounced
features, dark eyes, low brows, black hair bound by a jewelled bandeau, and
brought forward in curls over her forehead and temples, long heavy ear-rings,
an open bodice, and sleeves puffed at the shoulders. A cloak and other
mufflers lie on a chair beside her.

GODOY (after a silence)

The life-guards still insist, Love, that the King
Shall not leave Aranjuez.

QUEEN

                        Let them insist.
Whether we stay, or whether we depart,
Napoléon soon draws hither with his host!

GODOY

He says he comes pacifically. . . . But no!

QUEEN

Dearest, we must away to Andalusia,
Thence to America when time shall serve.

GODOY

I hold seven thousand men to cover us,
And ships in Cadiz port. But then—the Prince
Flatly declines to go. He lauds the French
As true deliverers.

QUEEN

                Go Fernando *must*! . . .
O my sweet friend, that we—our sole two selves—
Could but escape and leave the rest to fate,
And in a western bower dream out our days!—
For the King's glass can run but briefly now,
Shattered and shaken as his vigour is.—
But ah—your love burns not in singleness!
Why, dear, caress Josefa Tudo still?
She does not solve her soul in yours as I.
And why those others even more than her? . . .
How little own I in thee!

GODOY

            Such must be.
I cannot quite forsake them.   Don't forget
The same scope has been yours in former years.

QUEEN

Yes, Love; I know.   I yield!   You cannot leave them;
But if you ever would bethink yourself
How long I have been yours, how truly all
Those other pleasures were my desperate shifts
To soften sorrow at your absences,
You would be faithful to me!

GODOY

           True, my dear.—
Yet I do passably keep troth with you,
And fond you with fair regularity;—
A week beside you, and a week away.
Such is not schemed without some risk and strain.—
And you agreed Josefa should be mine,
And, too, Thereza, without jealousy!

                  (A noise is heard without.)

Ah, what means that?

He jumps up from her side and crosses the room to a window, where he lifts the curtain cautiously. The Queen follows him with a scared look.

QUEEN

            A riot can it be?

GODOY

Let me put these out ere they notice them;
They think me at the Royal Palace yonder.

He hastily extinguishes the candles except one taper, which he places in a recess, so that the room is in shade. He then draws back the curtains, and she joins him at the window, where, enclosing her with his arm, he and she look out together.

In front of the house a guard of hussars is stationed, beyond them spreading the Pláza or Square. On the other side rises in the lamplight the white front of the Royal Palace. On the flank of the Palace is a wall enclosing gardens, bowered alleys, and orange groves, and in the wall a small door.

A mixed multitude of soldiery and populace fills the space in front of the King's Palace, and they shout and address each other vehemently. During a lull in their vociferations is heard the peaceful purl of the Tagus over a cascade in the Palace grounds.

QUEEN

Lingering, we've risked too long our chance of flight !
The Paris Terror will repeat it here.
Not for myself I fear.   No, no ; for thee !

(She clings to him.)

If they should hurt you, it would murder me
By heart-bleedings and stabs intolerable !

GODOY (kissing her)

The first thought now is how to get you back
Within the Palace walls.   Why would you risk
To come here on a night so critical ?

QUEEN (passionately)

I could not help it—nay, I *would* not help !
Rather than starve my soul I venture all.—
Our last love-night—last, maybe, of long years.
Why do you chide me now ?

GODOY

                    Dear Queen, I do not :
I shape these sharp regrets but for your sake.
Hence you must go, somehow, and quickly too.
They think not yet of you in threatening thus,
But of me solely. . . .   Where does your lady wait ?

QUEEN

Below.   One servant with her.   They are true,
And can be let know all.   But you—but you !

(Uproar continues.)

GODOY

I can escape.   Now call them.   All three cloak
And veil as when you came.

They retreat into the room.   QUEEN MARÍA LUISA's lady-in-waiting and
servant are summoned.   Enter both.   All three then muffle themselves up,
and GODOY prepares to conduct the QUEEN downstairs.

QUEEN

Nay, now !   I will not have it.   We are safe ;
Think of yourself.   Can you get out behind ?

GODOY

I judge so—when I have done what's needful here.—
The mob knows not the bye-door—slip across ;
Thence around sideways.—All's clear there as yet.

[The QUEEN, her lady-in-waiting, and the servant go out hurriedly.

GODOY looks again from the window. The mob is some way off, the immediate front being for the moment nearly free of loiterers ; and the three muffled figures are visible, crossing without hindrance towards the door in the wall of the Palace Gardens. The instant they reach it a sentinel springs up, challenging them.

GODOY

Ah—now they are doomed !   My God, why did she come !

A parley takes place. Something, apparently a bribe, is handed to the sentinel, and the three are allowed to slip in, the QUEEN having obviously been unrecognized. He breathes his relief.

Now for the others.   Then—ah, then Heaven knows !

He sounds a bell and a servant enters.

Where is the Countess of Castillofiel ?

SERVANT

She's looking for you, Prince.

GODOY

            Find her at once.
Ah—here she is —That's well.—Go watch the Pláza

                         (to servant).

GODOY's mistress, the DOÑA JOSEFA TUDO, enters. She is a young and beautiful woman, the vivacity of whose large dark eyes is now clouded. She is wrapped up for flight. The servant goes out.

JOSEFA (breathlessly)

I should have joined you sooner, but I knew
The Queen was fondling with you. She must needs
Come hampering you this night of all the rest,
As if not gorged with you at other times !

GODOY

Don't, pretty one ! needless it is in you,
Being so well aware who holds my love.—
I could not check her coming, since she would.
You well know how the old thing is, and how
I am compelled to let her have her mind !

He kisses her repeatedly.

JOSEFA

But look, the mob is swelling ! Pouring in
By thousands from Madrid—and all afoot.
Will they not come on hither from the King's?

GODOY

Not just yet, maybe. You should have sooner fled !
The coach is waiting and the baggage packed.

(He again peers out.)

Yes, there the coach is ; and the clamourers near,
Led by Montijo, if I see aright.
Yes, they cry " Uncle Peter ! "—that means him.
There will be time yet. Now I'll take you down
So far as I may venture.

[They leave the room.

In a few minutes GODOY, having taken her down, re-enters and again
looks out. JOSEFA'S coach is moving off with a small escort of GODOY'S
guards of honour. A sudden yelling begins, and the crowd rushes up and
stops the vehicle. An altercation ensues.

CROWD

Uncle Peter, it is the Favourite carrying off Prince Fernando.
Stop him !

JOSEFA (putting her head out of the coach)

Silence their uproar, please, Señor Count of Montijo ! It is
a lady only, the Countess of Castillofiel.

MONTIJO

Let her pass, let her pass, friends ! It is only that pretty
wench of his, Pepa Tudo, who calls herself a Countess. Our
titles are put to comical uses in these days. We shall catch the
cock-bird presently !

CROWD (to each other)

The King and Queen and Fernando are at their own Palace—
not here !

The DOÑA JOSEFA'S carriage is allowed to pass on, as a shout from some
who have remained before the Royal Palace attracts the attention of the
multitude, which surges back thither.

CROWD (nearing the Palace)

Call out the King and the Prince. Long live the King! He shall not go. Hola! He is gone! Let us see him! He shall abandon Godoy!

The clamour before the Royal Palace still increasing, a figure emerges upon a balcony, whom GODOY recognizes by the lamplight to be FERNANDO, Prince of Asturias. He can be seen waving his hand. The mob grows suddenly silent.

FERNANDO (in a shaken voice)

Citizens! the King my father is in the palace with the Queen. He has been much tried to-day.

CROWD

Promise, Prince, that he shall not leave us. Promise!

FERNANDO

I do. I promise in his name. He has mistaken you, thinking you wanted his head. He knows better now.

CROWD

The villain Godoy misrepresented us to him! Throw out the Prince of Peace!

FERNANDO

He is not here, my friends.

CROWD

Then the King shall announce to us that he has dismissed him! Let us see him. The King; the King!

FERNANDO goes in. KING CARLOS comes out reluctantly, and bows to their cheering. He produces a paper with a trembling hand.

KING (reading)

" As it is the wish of the people——"

CROWD

Speak up, your Majesty!

KING (more loudly)

"As it is the wish of the people, I release Don Manuel Godoy, Prince of Peace, from the posts of Generalissimo of the Army and Grand Admiral of the Fleet, and give him leave to withdraw whither he pleases."

CROWD

Huzza !

KING

Citizens, to-morrow the decree is to be posted in Madrid.

CROWD

Huzza !   Long life to the King, and death to Godoy !

KING CARLOS disappears from the balcony, and the populace, still increasing in numbers, look towards GODOY's mansion, as if deliberating how
to attack it.   GODOY retreats from the window into the room, and gazing
round him starts.   A pale, worn, but placid lady, in a sombre though elegant
robe, stands here in the gloom.   She is THEREZA OF BOURBON, the Princess
of Peace.

PRINCESS

It is only your unhappy wife, Manuel.   She will not hurt you !

GODOY (shrugging his shoulders)

Nor will *they* hurt *you* !   Why did you not stay in the Royal
Palace ?   You would have been more comfortable there.

PRINCESS

I don't recognize why you should specially value my comfort.
You have saved your real wives.   How can it matter what
happens to your titular one ?

GODOY

Much, dear.   I always play fair.   But it being your blest
privilege not to need my saving I was left free to practise it on
those who did.   (Mob heard approaching.)   Would that I were in
no more danger than you !

PRINCESS

Puf !

He again peers out.   His guard of hussars stands firmly in front of the
mansion ; but the life-guards from the adjoining barracks, who have joined
the people, endeavour to break the hussars of GODOY.   A shot is fired,
GODOY's guard yields, and the gate and door are battered in.

CROWD (without)

Murder him ! murder him !   Death to Manuel Godoy !

They are heard rushing into the court and house.

PRINCESS

Go, I beseech you! You can do nothing for me, and I pray
you to save yourself! The heap of mats in the lumber-room will
hide you!

GODOY hastes to a jib-door concealed by sham book-shelves, presses the
spring of it, returns, kisses her, and then slips out.

His wife sits down with her back against the jib-door, and fans herself.
She hears the crowd trampling up the stairs, but she does not move, and in
a moment people burst in. The leaders are armed with stakes, daggers,
and various improvised weapons, and some guards in undress appear with
halberds.

FIRST CITIZEN (peering into the dim light)

Where is he? Murder him! (Noticing the Princess.) Come,
where is he?

PRINCESS

The Prince of Peace is gone. I know not whither.

SECOND CITIZEN

Who is this lady?

LIFE-GUARDSMAN

Manuel Godoy's Princess.

CITIZENS (uncovering)

Princess, a thousand pardons grant us!—you
An injured wife—an injured people we!
Common misfortune makes us more than kin.
No single hair of yours shall suffer harm.

The PRINCESS bows.

FIRST CITIZEN

But this, Señora, is no place for you,
For we mean mischief here! Yet first will grant
Safe conduct for you to the Palace gates,
Or elsewhere, as you wish.

PRINCESS

My wish is nought.
Do what you will with me. But he's not here.

Several of them form an escort, and accompany her from the room and
out of the house. Those remaining, now a great throng, begin searching the
room, and in bands invade other parts of the mansion.

SOME CITIZENS (returning)

It is no use searching.   She said he was not here, and she's a woman of honour.

FIRST CITIZEN (drily)

She's his wife.

They leave the room for another search, but return still baffled.

SEVERAL CITIZENS

He must have slipped out somehow!   Smash his nicknacks, since we can't smash him.

They begin knocking the furniture to pieces, tearing down the hangings, trampling on the musical instruments, and kicking holes through the paintings they have unhung from the walls. These, with clocks, vases, carvings, and other movables, they throw out of the window, till the chamber is a scene of utter wreck and desolation. In the rout a musical box is swept off a table, and starts playing a serenade as it falls on the floor.

Enter the COUNT OF MONTIJO.

MONTIJO

Stop, friends ; stop this !   There is no sense in it—
It shows but useless spite !   I have much to say :
The French Ambassador, de Beauharnais,
Has come, and sought the King.   And next Murat,
With thirty thousand men, half cavalry,
Is closing in upon our doomed Madrid !
I know not what he means, this Bonaparte ;
He makes pretence to gain us Portugal,
But what want we with her ?   'Tis like as not
His aim's to noose us vassals all to him !
The King will abdicate, and shortly too,
As those will live to see who live not long.—
We have saved our nation from the Favourite,
But who is going to save us from our Friend ?

The mob desists dubiously and goes out ; the musical box upon the floor plays on, the taper burns to its socket, and the room becomes wrapt in the shades of night.

SCENE III

LONDON : THE MARCHIONESS OF SALISBURY'S

A large reception-room is disclosed, arranged for a conversazione. It is an evening in the summer following, and at present the chamber is empty and in gloom. At one end is an elaborate device, representing Britannia offering her assistance to Spain, and at the other a figure of Time crowning the Spanish Patriots' flag with laurel.

SPIRIT OF THE YEARS

> *O clarionists of human welterings,*
> *Relate how Europe's madding movement brings*
> *This easeful haunt into the path of palpitating things!*

RUMOURS (chanting)

I

> *The Spanish King has bowed unto the Fate*
> *Which bade him abdicate:*
> *The sensual Queen, whose passionate caprice*
> *Has held her chambering with " the Prince of Peace,"*
> *And wrought the Bourbons' fall,*
> *Holds to her Love in all;*
> *And Bonaparte has ruled that his and he*
> *Henceforth displace the Bourbon dynasty.*

II

> *The Spanish people, handled in such sort,*
> *As chattels of a Court,*
> *Dream dreams of England. Messengers are sent*
> *In secret to the assembled Parliament,*
> *In faith that England's hand*
> *Will stouten them to stand,*
> *And crown a cause which, hold they, bond and free*
> *Must advocate enthusiastically.*

SPIRIT OF THE YEARS

> *So the Will heaves through Space, and moulds the times,*
> *With mortals for Its fingers! We shall see*
> *Again men's passions, virtues, visions, crimes,*
> *Obey resistlessly*
> *The purposive, unmotived, dominant Thing*
> *Which sways in brooding dark their wayfaring!*

The reception-room is lighted up, and the hostess comes in. There arrive Ambassadors and their wives, the Dukes and Duchesses of RUTLAND and SOMERSET, the Marquis and Marchioness of STAFFORD, the Earls of STAIR, WESTMORELAND, GOWER, ESSEX, Viscounts and Viscountesses CRANLEY and MORPETH, Viscount MELBOURNE, Lord and Lady KINNAIRD, Baron de ROLLE, Lady CHARLES GREVILLE, the Ladies CAVENDISH, Mr. and Mrs.

THOMAS HOPE, Mr. GUNNING, Mrs. FITZHERBERT, and many other notable personages. Lastly, she goes to the door to welcome severally the PRINCE OF WALES, the PRINCES OF FRANCE, and the PRINCESS CASTELCICALA.

LADY SALISBURY (to the Prince of Wales)

I am sorry to say, sir, that the Spanish Patriots are not yet arrived. I doubt not but that they have been delayed by their ignorance of the town, and will soon be here.

PRINCE OF WALES

No hurry whatever, my dear hostess. Gad, we've enough to talk about! I understand that the arrangement between our ministers and these noblemen will include the liberation of Spanish prisoners in this country, and the providing 'em with arms, to go back and fight for their independence.

LADY SALISBURY

It will be a blessed event if they do check the career of this infamous Corsican. I have just heard that that poor foreigner Guillet de la Gevrillière, who proposed to Mr. Fox to assassinate him, died a miserable death a few days ago in the Bicêtre— probably by torture, though nobody knows. Really one almost wishes Mr. Fox had——. O here they are!

Enter the Spanish Viscount de MATEROSA and DON DIEGO de la VEGA. They are introduced by CAPTAIN HILL and Mr. BAGOT, who escort them. LADY SALISBURY presents them to the PRINCE and others.

PRINCE OF WALES

By Gad, Viscount, we were just talking of 'ee. You have had some adventures in getting to this country?

MATEROSA (assisted by Bagot as interpreter)

Sir, it has indeed been a trying experience for us. But here we are, impressed by a deep sense of gratitude for the signal marks of attachment your country shows us.

PRINCE OF WALES

You represent, practically, the Spanish people?

MATEROSA

We are immediately deputed, sir,
By the Assembly of Asturias,
More sailing soon from other provinces.

We bring official writings, charging us
To clinch and solder Treaties with this realm
That may promote our cause against the foe.
Nextly a letter to your gracious King ;
Also a Proclamation, soon to sound
And swell the pulse of the Peninsula,
Declaring that the act by which King Carlos
And his son Prince Fernando cede the throne
To whomsoever Napoléon may appoint,
Being an act of cheatery, not of choice,
Unfetters us from our allegiant oath.

Mrs. Fitzherbert

The usurpation began, I suppose, with the divisions in the Royal Family ?

Materosa

Yes, madam, and the protection they foolishly requested from the Emperor ; and their timid intent of flying secretly helped it on. It was an opportunity he had been awaiting for years.

Mrs. Fitzherbert

All brought about by this man Godoy, Prince of Peace !

Prince of Wales

Dash my wig, mighty much you know about it, Maria ! Why, sure, Boney thought to himself, " This Spain is a pretty place ; 'twill just suit me as an extra acre or two ; so here goes."

Don Diego (aside to Bagot)

This lady is the Princess of Wales ?

Bagot

Hsh ! no, Señor. The Princess lives at large at Kensington and other places, and has parties of her own, and doesn't keep house with her husband. This lady is—well, really his wife, you know, in the opinion of many ; but——

Don Diego

Ah ! Ladies a little mixed, as they were at our Court ! She's the Pepa Tudo to *this* Prince of Peace ?

H

BAGOT

O no——not exactly that, Señor.

DON DIEGO

Ya, ya. Good. I'll be careful, my friend. You are not saints in England more than we are in Spain!

BAGOT

We are not. Only you sin with naked faces, and we with masks on.

DON DIEGO

Virtuous country!

DUCHESS OF RUTLAND

It was understood that Ferdinand, Prince of Asturias, was to marry a French princess, and so unite the countries peacefully?

MATEROSA

It was. And our credulous prince was tempted to meet Napoléon at Bayonne. Also the poor simple King, and the infatuated Queen, and Manuel Godoy.

DUCHESS OF RUTLAND

Then Godoy escaped from Aranjuez?

MATEROSA

Yes, by hiding in the garret. Then they all threw themselves upon Napoléon's protection. In his presence the Queen swore that the King was not Fernando's father! Altogether they form a queer little menagerie. What will happen to them nobody knows.

PRINCE OF WALES

And do you wish us to send an army at once?

MATEROSA

What we most want, sir, are arms and ammunition. But we leave the English Ministry to co-operate in its own wise way, anyhow, so as to sustain us in resenting these insults from the Tyrant of the Earth.

DUCHESS OF RUTLAND (to the Prince of Wales)

What sort of aid shall we send, sir?

PRINCE OF WALES

We are going to vote fifty millions, I hear. We'll whack him, and preserve your noble country for 'ee, Señor Viscount. The debate thereon is to come off to-morrow. It will be the finest thing the Commons have had since Pitt's time. Sheridan, who is to open it, says he and Canning are to be absolutely unanimous; and, by God, like the parties in his "Critic," when Government and Opposition do agree, their unanimity is wonderful! Viscount Materosa, you and your friends must be in the Gallery. O dammy, you must!

MATEROSA

Sir, we are already pledged to be there.

PRINCE OF WALES

And hark ye, Señor Viscount. You will then learn what a mighty fine thing a debate in the English Parliament is! No Continental humbug there. Not but that the Court has a trouble to keep 'em in their places sometimes; and I would it had been one in the Lords instead. However, Sheridan says he has been learning his speech these two days, and has hunted his father's dictionary through for some stunning long words.—Now, Maria (to Mrs. Fitzherbert), I am going home.

LADY SALISBURY

At last, then, England will take her place in the forefront of this mortal struggle, and in pure disinterestedness fight with all her strength for the European deliverance. God defend the right!

The Prince of Wales leaves, and the other guests begin to depart.

SEMICHORUS I OF THE YEARS (aerial music)

Leave this glib throng to its conjecturing,
And let four burdened weeks uncover what they bring!

SEMICHORUS II

The said Debate, to wit; its close in deeds;
Till England stands enlisted for the Patriots' needs.

SEMICHORUS I

And transports in the docks gulp down their freight
Of buckled fighting-flesh, and, gale-bound, watch and wait.

SEMICHORUS II

Till gracious zephyrs shoulder on their sails
To where the brine of Biscay moans its tragic tales.

CHORUS

Bear we, too, south, as we were swallow-vanned,
And mark the game now played there by the Master-hand!

The reception-chamber is shut over by the night without, and the point of view rapidly recedes south, London and its streets and lights diminishing till they are lost in the distance, and its noises being succeeded by the babble of the Channel and Biscay waves.

SCENE IV

MADRID AND ITS ENVIRONS

The view is from the housetops of the city on a dusty evening in this July, following a day of suffocating heat. The sunburnt roofs, warm ochreous walls, and blue shadows of the capital, wear their usual aspect except for a few feeble attempts at decoration.

DUMB SHOW

Gazers gather in the central streets, and particularly in the Puerta del Sol. They show curiosity, but no enthusiasm. Patrols of French soldiery move up and down in front of the people, and seem to awe them into quietude.

There is a discharge of artillery in the outskirts, and the church bells begin ringing ; but the peals dwindle away to a melancholy jangle, and then to silence. Simultaneously, on the northern horizon of the arid, unenclosed, and treeless plain swept by the eye around the city, a cloud of dust arises, and a Royal procession is seen nearing. It means the new king, JOSEPH BONAPARTE.

He comes on, escorted by a clanking guard of four thousand Italian troops, and the brilliant royal carriage is followed by a hundred coaches bearing his suite. As the procession enters the city many houses reveal themselves to be closed, many citizens leave the route and walk elsewhere, while many of those who remain turn their backs upon the spectacle.

KING JOSEPH proceeds thus through the Pláza Oriente to the granite-walled Royal Palace, where he alights and is received by some of the nobility, the French generals who are in occupation there, and some clergy. Heralds emerge from the Palace, and hasten to divers points in the city, where trumpets are blown and the Proclamation of JOSEPH as KING OF SPAIN is read in a loud voice. It is received in silence.

The sun sets, and the curtain falls.

SCENE V

THE OPEN SEA BETWEEN THE ENGLISH COASTS
AND THE SPANISH PENINSULA

From high aloft, in the same July weather, and facing east, the vision swoops over the ocean and its coast-lines, from Cork Harbour on the extreme left, to Mondego Bay, Portugal, on the extreme right. Land's End and the Scilly Isles, Ushant and Cape Finisterre, are projecting features along the middle distance of the picture, and the English Channel recedes endwise as a tapering avenue near the centre.

DUMB SHOW

Four groups of moth-like transport ships are discovered silently skimming this wide liquid plain. The first group, to the right, is just vanishing behind Cape Mondego to enter Mondego Bay; the second, in the midst, has come out from Plymouth Sound, and is preparing to stand down Channel; the third is clearing St. Helen's point for the same course; and the fourth, much further up Channel, is obviously to follow on considerably in the rear of the two preceding. A south-east wind is blowing strong, and, according to the part of their course reached, they either sail direct with the wind on their larboard quarter, or labour forward by tacking in zigzags.

SPIRIT OF THE PITIES

What are these fleets that cross the sea
*   From British ports and bays*
To coasts that glister southwardly
*   Behind the dog-day haze?*

RUMOURS (chanting)

SEMICHORUS I

They are the shipped battalions sent
To bar the bold Belligerent
*   Who stalks the Dancers' Land.*
Within these hulls, like sheep a-pen,
Are packed in thousands fighting-men
*   And colonels in command.*

SEMICHORUS II

The fleet that leans each aëry fin
Far south, where Mondego mouths in,
Bears Wellesley and his aides therein,
*   And Hill, and Crauford too;*

With Torrens, Ferguson, and Fane,
And majors, captains, clerks, in train,
And those grim needs that appertain—
    The surgeons—not a few!
To them add near twelve thousand souls
In linesmen that the list enrolls,
Borne onward by those sheeted poles
    As war's red retinue!

Semichorus I

The fleet that clears St. Helen's shore
Holds Burrard, Hope, ill-omened Moore,
    Clinton and Paget; while
The transports that pertain to those
Count six-score sail, whose planks enclose
    Ten thousand rank and file.

Semichorus II

The third-sent ships, from Plymouth Sound,
With Acland, Anstruther, impound
    Souls to six thousand strong.
While those, the fourth fleet, that we see
Far back, are lined with cavalry,
And guns of girth, wheeled heavily
    To roll the routes along.

Spirit of the Years

Enough, and more, of inventories and names!
Many will fail; many earn doubtful fames.
Await the fruitage of their acts and aims.

DUMB SHOW (continuing)

In the spacious scene visible the far-separated groups of transports, convoyed by battleships, float on before the wind almost imperceptibly, like preened duck-feathers across a pond. The southernmost expedition, under Sir Arthur Wellesley, soon comes to anchor within the Bay of Mondego aforesaid, and the soldiery are indefinitely discernible landing upon the beach from boats. Simultaneously the division commanded by Moore, as yet in the Chops of the Channel, is seen to be beaten back by contrary winds. It gallantly puts to sea again, and being joined by the division under Anstruther that has set out from Plymouth, labours round Ushant, and stands to the south in the track of WELLESLEY. The rearward transports do the same.

A moving stratum of summer cloud beneath the point of view covers up the spectacle like an awning.

SCENE VI

ST. CLOUD. THE BOUDOIR OF JOSÉPHINE

It is the dusk of an evening in the latter summer of this year, and from the windows at the back of the stage, which are still uncurtained, can be seen the EMPRESS with NAPOLÉON and some ladies and officers of the Court playing Catch-me-if-you-can by torchlight on the lawn. The moving torches throw bizarre lights and shadows into the apartment, where only a remote candle or two are burning.

Enter JOSÉPHINE and NAPOLÉON together, somewhat out of breath. With careless suppleness she slides down on a couch and fans herself. Now that the candle-rays reach her they show her mellow complexion, her velvety eyes with long lashes, mouth with pointed corners and excessive mobility beneath its *duvet*, and curls of dark hair pressed down upon the temples by a gold band.

The EMPEROR drops into a seat near her, and they remain in silence till he jumps up, knocks over some nicknacks with his elbow, and begins walking about the boudoir.

NAPOLÉON (with sudden gloom)

These mindless games are very well, my friend ;
But ours to-night marks, not improbably,
The last we play together.

JOSÉPHINE (starting)

Can you say it !
Why raise that ghastly nightmare on me now,
When, for a moment, my poor brain had dreams
Denied it all the earlier anxious day ?

NAPOLÉON

Things that verge nigh, my simple Joséphine,
Are not shoved off by wilful winking at.
Better quiz evils with too strained an eye
Than have them leap from disregarded lairs.

JOSÉPHINE

Maybe 'tis true, and you shall have it so !—
Yet there's no joy save sorrow waived awhile.

NAPOLÉON

Ha, ha !   That's like you.   Well, each day by day
I get sour news.   Each hour since we returned
From this queer Spanish business at Bayonne,
I have had nothing else ; and hence my brooding.

JOSÉPHINE

But all went well throughout our touring-time ?

NAPOLÉON

Not so—behind the scenes.   Our arms at Baylen
Have been smirched badly.   Twenty thousand shamed
All through Dupont's ill-luck !   The selfsame day
My brother Joseph's progress to Madrid
Was glorious as a sodden rocket's fizz !
Since when his letters creak with querulousness.
" Napoléon el chico " 'tis they call him—
" Napoléon the Little," so he says.
Then notice Austria.   Much looks louring there,
And her sly new regard for England grows.
The English, next, have shipped an army down
To Mondego, under one Wellesley,
A man from India, and his march is south
To Lisbon, by Vimiero.   On he'll go
And do the devil's mischief ere he is met
By unaware Junot, and chevyed back
To English fogs and fumes !

JOSÉPHINE

                              My dearest one,
You have mused on worse reports with better grace
Full many and many a time.   Ah—there is more ! . . ,
I know ; I know !   •

NAPOLÉON (kicking away a stool)

                    There is, of course ; that worm
Time ever keeps in hand for gnawing me !—
The question of my dynasty—which bites
Closer and closer as the years wheel on.

JOSÉPHINE

Of course it's that!   For nothing else could hang
My lord on tenterhooks through nights and days ;—
Or rather, not the question, but the tongues
That keep the question stirring.   Nought recked you
Of throne-succession or dynastic lines
When gloriously engaged in Italy !
I was your fairy then : they labelled me
Your Lady of Victories ; and much I joyed,
Till dangerous ones drew near and daily sowed
These choking tares within your fecund brain,—
Making me tremble if a panel crack,
Or mouse but cheep, or silent leaf sail down,
And murdering my melodious hours with dreads
That my late happiness, and my late hope,
Will oversoon be knelled !

NAPOLÉON (genially nearing her)

But years have passed since first we talked of it;
And now, with loss of dear Hortense's son
Who won me as my own, it looms forth more.
And selfish 'tis in my good Joséphine
To blind her vision to the weal of France,
And this great Empire's solidarity.
The grandeur of your sacrifice would gild
Your life's whole shape.

JOSÉPHINE

          Were I as coarse a wife
As I am limned in English caricature—
(Those cruel effigies they draw of me !)—
You could not speak more aridly.

NAPOLÉON

              Nay, nay !
You know, my comrade, how I love you still
Were there a long-notorious dislike
Betwixt us, reason might be in your dreads.
But all earth knows our conjugality.
There's not a bourgeois couple in the land
Who, should dire duty rule their severance,
Could part with scanter scandal than could we.

JOSÉPHINE (pouting)

Nevertheless there's one.

NAPOLÉON

    A scandal ? What ?

JOSÉPHINE

Madame Walewska ! How could you pretend
When, after Jena, I'd have come to you,
" The weather was so wild, the roads so rough,
That no one of my sex and delicate nerve
Could hope to face the dangers and fatigues."
Yes—so you wrote me, dear. They hurt not her !

NAPOLÉON (blandly)

She was a week's adventure—not worth words !
I say 'tis France.—I have held out for years
Against the constant pressure brought on me
To null this sterile marriage.

JOSÉPHINE (bursting into sobs)

    Me you blame !
But how know you that you are not the culprit ?

NAPOLÉON

I have reason so to know—if I must say.
The Polish lady you have chosen to name
Has proved the fault not mine.

      (JOSÉPHINE sobs more violently.)
    Don't cry, my cherished ;
It is not really amiable of you,
Or prudent, my good little Joséphine,
With so much in the balance.

JOSÉPHINE

    How—know you—
What may not happen ! Wait a—little longer !

NAPOLÉON (playfully pinching her arm)

O come, now, my adored ! Haven't I already !
Nature's a dial whose shade no hand puts back,

Trick as we may!   My friend, you are forty-three
This very year in the world—

> (JOSÉPHINE breaks out sobbing again.)

                              And vain it is
To think of waiting longer; pitiful
To dream of coaxing shy fecundity
To an unlikely freak by physicking
With superstitious drugs and quackeries
That work you harm, not good.   The fact being so,
I have looked it squarely down—against my heart!
Solicitations voiced repeatedly
At length have shown the soundness of their shape,
And left me no denial.   You, at times,
My dear one, have been used to handle it.
My brother Joseph, years back, frankly gave
His honest view that something should be done;
And he, you well may know, shows no ill tinct
In his regard of you.

JOSÉPHINE

                    And what princess?

NAPOLÉON

For wiving with?   No thought was given to that,
She shapes as vaguely as the Veiled—

JOSÉPHINE

                              No, no;
It's Alexander's sister, I'm full sure!—
But why this craze for home-made manikins
And lineage mere of flesh?   You have said yourself
It mattered not.   Great Caesar, you declared,
Sank sonless to his rest; was greater deemed
Even for the isolation.   Frederick
Saw, too, no heir.   It is the fate of such,
Often, to be denied the common hope
As fine for fulness in the rarer gifts
That Nature yields them.   O my husband long,
Will you not purge your soul to value best
That high heredity from brain to brain
Which supersedes mere sequences of blood,

That often vary more from sire to son
Than between furthest strangers ! . . .
Napoléon's offspring in his like must lie ;
The second of his line be he who shows
Napoléon's soul in later bodiment,
The household father happening as he may !

NAPOLÉON (smilingly wiping her eyes)

Little guessed I my dear would prove her rammed
With such a charge of apt philosophy
When tutoring me gay arts in earlier times !
She who at home coquetted through the years
In which I vainly penned her wishful words
To come and comfort me in Italy,
Might, faith, have urged it then effectually !
But never would you stir from Paris joys,
                              (With some bitterness).
And so, when arguments like this could move me,
I heard them not ; and get them only now
When their weight dully falls.   But I have said
'Tis not for me, but France—Good-bye an hour.
                              (Kissing her.)
I must dictate some letters.   This new move
Of England on Madrid may mean some trouble.
Come, dwell not gloomily on this cold need
Of waiving private joy for policy.
We are but thistle-globes on Heaven's high gales,
And whither blown, or when, or how, or why,
Can choose us not at all ! . . .
I'll come to you anon, dear : staunch Roustan
Will light me in.

                              [Exit NAPOLÉON.

          The scene shuts in shadow.

SCENE VII

VIMIERO

A village among the hills of Portugal, about fifty miles north of Lisbon.
Around it are disclosed, as ten on Sunday morning strikes, a blue army of
fourteen thousand men in isolated columns, and a red army of eighteen
thousand in line formation, drawn up in order of battle.   The blue army is
a French one under JUNOT ; the other an English one under SIR ARTHUR
WELLESLEY—portion of that recently landed.

The August sun glares on the shaven faces, white gaiters, and white cross-belts of the English, who are to fight for their lives while sweating under a quarter-hundredweight in knapsack and pouches, and with firelocks heavy as putlogs. They occupy a group of heights, but their position is one of great danger, the land abruptly terminating two miles behind their backs in lofty cliffs overhanging the Atlantic. The French occupy the valleys in the English front, and this distinction between the two forces strikes the eye—the red army is accompanied by scarce any cavalry, while the blue is strong in that arm.

DUMB SHOW

The battle is begun with alternate moves that match each other like those of a chess opening. JUNOT makes an oblique attack by moving a division to his right ; WELLESLEY moves several brigades to his left to balance it.

A column of six thousand French then climbs the hill against the English centre, and drives in those who are planted there. The English artillery checks its adversaries, and the infantry recover and charge the baffled French down the slopes. Meanwhile the latter's cavalry and artillery are attacking the village itself, and, rushing on a few squadrons of English dragoons stationed there, cut them to pieces. A dust is raised by this ado, and moans of men and shrieks of horses are heard. Close by the carnage the little Maceira stream continues to trickle unconcernedly to the sea.

On the English left five thousand French infantry, having ascended to the ridge and maintained a stinging musket-fire as sharply returned, are driven down by the bayonets of six English regiments. Thereafter a brigade of the French, the northernmost, finding that the others have pursued to the bottom and are resting after the effort, surprise them and bayonet them back to their original summit. The see-saw is continued by the recovery of the English, who again drive their assailants down.

The French army pauses stultified, till, the columns uniting, they fall back towards the opposite hills. The English, seeing that their chance has come, are about to pursue and settle the fortunes of the day. But a messenger dispatched from a distant group is marked riding up to the large-nosed man with a telescope and an Indian sword who, his staff around him, has been directing the English movements. He seems astonished at the message, appears to resent it, and pauses with a gloomy look. But he sends countermands to his generals, and the pursuit ends abortively.

The French retreat without further molestation by a circuitous march into the great road to Torrès Védras by which they came, leaving nearly two thousand dead and wounded on the slopes they have quitted.

Dumb Show ends and the curtain draws

ACT THIRD

SCENE I

SPAIN.   A ROAD NEAR ASTORGA

The eye of the spectator rakes the road from the interior of a cellar which opens upon it, and forms the basement of a deserted house, the roof, doors, and shutters of which have been pulled down and burnt for bivouac fires. The season is the beginning of January, and the country is covered with a sticky snow.   The road itself is intermittently encumbered with heavy traffic, the surface being churned to a yellow mud that lies half knee-deep, and at the numerous holes in the track forming still deeper quagmires.

In the gloom of the cellar are heaps of damp straw, in which ragged figures are lying half-buried, many of the men in the uniform of English line-regiments, and the women and children in clouts of all descriptions, some being nearly naked.   At the back of the cellar is revealed, through a burst door, an inner vault, where are discernible some wooden-hooped wine-casks ; in one sticks a gimlet, and the broaching-cork of another has been driven in. The wine runs into pitchers, washing-basins, shards, chamber-vessels, and other extemporized receptacles.   Most of the inmates are drunk ; some to insensibility.

So far as the characters are doing anything they are contemplating the almost incessant traffic outside, passing in one direction.   It includes a medley of stragglers from the Marquis of ROMANA's Spanish forces and the retreating English army under SIR JOHN MOORE—to which the concealed deserters belong.

FIRST DESERTER

Now he's one of the Eighty-first, and I'd gladly let that poor blade know that we've all that man can wish for here—good wine and buxom women.   But if I do, we shan't have room for ourselves—hey ?

He signifies a man limping past with neither fire-lock nor knapsack. Where the discarded knapsack has rubbed for weeks against his shoulder-blades the jacket and shirt are fretted away, leaving his skin exposed.

SECOND DESERTER (drowsily)

He may be the Eighty-firsht, or th' Eighty-second ; but what I say is, without fear of contradiction, I wish to the Lord I was back in old Bristol again.   I'd sooner have a nipperkin of our own real " Bristol milk " than a mash-tub full of this barbarian wine !

THIRD DESERTER

'Tis like thee to be ungrateful, after putting away such a skinful on't. I am as much Bristol as thee, but would as soon be here as there. There ain't near such willing women, that are strict respectable too, there as hereabout, and no open cellars.— As there's many a slip in this country I'll have the rest of my allowance now.

He crawls on his elbows to one of the barrels, and turning on his back lets the wine run down his throat.

FOURTH DESERTER (to a fifth, who is snoring)

Don't treat us to such a snoaching there, mate. Here's some more coming, and they'll sight us if we don't mind!

Enter without a straggling flock of military objects, some with fragments of shoes on, others bare-footed, many of the latter's feet bleeding. The arms and waists of some are clutched by women as tattered and bare-footed as themselves. They pass on.

The Retreat continues. More of ROMANA's Spanish limp along in disorder; then enters a miscellaneous group of English cavalry soldiers, some on foot, some mounted, the rearmost of the latter bestriding a shoeless foundered creature whose neck is vertebræ and mane only. While passing it falls from exhaustion; the trooper extricates himself and pistols the animal through the head. He and the rest pass on.

FIRST DESERTER (a new plashing of feet being heard)

Here's something more in order, or I am much mistaken. (*He cranes out.*) Yes, a sergeant of the Forty-third, and what's left of their second battalion. And, by God, not far behind I see shining helmets. 'Tis a whole squadron of French dragoons!

Enter the sergeant. He has a racking cough, but endeavours, by stiffening himself up, to hide how it is wasting away his life. He halts, and looks back, till the remains of the Forty-third are abreast, to the number of some three hundred, about half of whom are crippled invalids, the other half being presentable and armed soldiery.

SERGEANT

Now show yer nerve, and be men. If you die to-day you won't have to die to-morrow. Fall in! (*The miscellany falls in.*) All invalids and men without arms march ahead as well as they can. Quick—maw-w-w-ch! (*Exeunt invalids, etc.*) Now! Tention! Shoulder-r-r-r—fawlocks! (*Order obeyed.*)

The sergeant hastily forms these into platoons, who prime and load, and seem preternaturally changed from what they were into alert soldiers.

Enter French dragoons at the left-back of the scene. The rear platoon of

the Forty-third turns, fires, and proceeds. The next platoon covering them
does the same. This is repeated several times, staggering the pursuers.
Exeunt French dragoons, giving up the pursuit. The coughing sergeant and
the remnant of the Forty-third march on.

FOURTH DESERTER (to a woman lying beside him)

What d'ye think o' that, my honey? It fairly makes me a
man again. Come, wake up! We must be getting along
somehow. (He regards the woman more closely.) Why—my little
chick? Look here, friends. (They look, and the woman is found to
be dead.) If I didn't think that her poor knees felt cold! . . .
And only an hour ago I swore I'd marry her!

They remain silent. The Retreat continues in the snow without, now in
the form of a file of ox-carts, followed by a mixed rabble of English and
Spanish, and mules and muleteers hired by English officers to carry their
baggage. The muleteers, looking about and seeing that the French dragoons
have been there, cut the bands which hold on the heavy packs, and scamper
off with their mules.

A VOICE (behind)

The Commander-in-Chief is determined to maintain discipline,
and they must suffer. No more pillaging here. It is the worst
case of brutality and plunder that we have had in this wretched
time!

Enter an English captain of hussars, a lieutenant, a guard of about a
dozen, and three men as prisoners.

CAPTAIN

If they choose to draw lots, only one need be made an example
of. But they must be quick about it. The advance-guard of the
enemy is not far behind.

The three prisoners appear to draw lots, and the one on whom the lot
falls is blindfolded. Exeunt the hussars behind a wall, with carbines. A
volley is heard and something falls. The wretches in the cellar shudder.

FOURTH DESERTER

'Tis the same for us but for this heap of straw. Ah—my
doxy is the only one of us who is safe and sound!

(He kisses the dead woman.)

Retreat continues. A train of six-horse baggage-waggons lumbers past, a
mounted sergeant alongside. Among the baggage lie wounded soldiers and
sick women.

SERGEANT OF THE WAGGON-TRAIN

If so be they are dead, ye may as well drop 'em over the tail-board. 'Tis no use straining the horses unnecessary.

Waggons halt. Two of the wounded who have just died are taken out, laid down by the roadside, and some muddy snow scraped over them. Exeunt waggons and sergeant.

An interval. More English troops pass on horses, mostly shoeless and foundered.

Enter SIR JOHN MOORE *and officers.* MOORE *appears in the pale evening light as a handsome man, far on in the forties, the orbits of his dark eyes showing marks of deep anxiety. He is talking to some of his staff with vehement emphasis and gesture. They cross the scene and go on out of sight, and the squashing of their horses' hoofs in the snowy mud dies away.*

FIFTH DESERTER (incoherently in his sleep)

Poise fawlocks—open pans—right hands to pouch—handle ca'tridge—bring it—quick motion—bite top well off—prime—shut pans—cast about—load——

FIRST DESERTER (throwing a shoe at the sleeper)

Shut up that! D'ye think you are a 'cruity in the awkward squad still?

SECOND DESERTER

I don't know what he thinks, but I know what I feel! Would that I were at home in England again, where there's old-fashioned tipple, and a proper God A'mighty instead of this eternal 'Ooman and baby;—ay, at home a-leaning against old Bristol Bridge, and no questions asked, and the winter sun slanting friendly over Baldwin Street as 'a used to do! 'Tis my very belief, though I have lost all sure reckoning, that if I wer there, and in good health, 'twould be New Year's day about now. What it is over here I don't know. Ay, to-night we should be a-setting in the tap of the "Adam and Eve"—lifting up the tune of "The Light o' the Moon." 'Twer a romantical thing enough. 'A used to go som'at like this (*he sings in a nasal tone*):—

> "O I thought it had been day,
> And I stole from her away;
> But it proved to be the light o' the moon!"

Retreat continues, with infantry in good order. Hearing the singing, one of the officers looks around, and detaching a patrol enters the ruined house with the file of men, the body of soldiers marching on. The inmates of the cellar bury themselves in the straw. The officer peers about, and seeing no one prods the straw with his sword.

VOICES (under the straw)

Oh! Hell! Stop it! We'll come out! Mercy! Quarter!

[The lurkers are uncovered.

OFFICER

If you are well enough to sing bawdy songs, you are well enough to march. So out of it—or you'll be shot, here and now!

SEVERAL

You may shoot us, captain, or the French may shoot us, or the devil may take us; we don't care which! Only we can't stir. Pity the women, captain, but do what you will with us!

The searchers pass over the wounded, and stir out those capable of marching, both men and women, so far as they discover them. They are pricked on by the patrol. Exeunt patrol and deserters in its charge.

Those who remain look stolidly at the highway. The English Rear-guard of cavalry crosses the scene and passes out. An interval. It grows dusk.

SPIRIT IRONIC

Quaint poesy, and real romance of war!

SPIRIT OF THE PITIES

Mock on, Shade, if thou wilt! But others find
Poesy ever lurk where pit-pats poor mankind!

The scene is cloaked in darkness.

SCENE II

THE SAME

It is nearly midnight. The fugitives who remain in the cellar having slept off the effects of the wine, are awakened by a new tramping of cavalry, which becomes more and more persistent. It is the French, who now fill the road. The advance-guard having passed by, DELABORDE's division, LORGE's division, MERLE's division, and others, successively cross the gloom.

Presently come the outlines of the Imperial Guard, and then, with a start, those in hiding realize their situation, and are wide awake. NAPOLÉON enters with his staff. He has just been overtaken by a courier, and orders those round him to halt.

NAPOLÉON

Let there a fire be lit: ay, here and now.
The lines within these letters brook no pause
In mastering their purport.

Some of the French approach the ruined house and, appropriating what wood is still left there, heap it by the roadside and set it alight. A mixed rain and snow falls, and the sputtering flames throw a glare all round.

SECOND DESERTER (under his voice)

We be shot corpses! Ay, faith, we be! Why didn't I stick
to England, and true doxology, and leave foreign doxies and
their wine alone! . . . Mate, can ye squeeze another shardful
from the cask there, for I feel my time is come! . . . O that I
had but the barrel of that firelock I throwed away, and that
wasted powder to prime and load! This bullet I chaw to
squench my hunger would do the rest! . . . Yes, I could pick
him off now!

FIRST DESERTER

You lie low with your picking off, or he may pick off you!
Thank God the babies are gone. Maybe we shan't be noticed,
if we've but the courage to do nothing, and keep hid.

NAPOLÉON dismounts, approaches the fire, and looks around.

NAPOLÉON

Another of their dead horses here, I see.

OFFICER

Yes, sire. We have counted eighteen hundred odd
From Benavente hither, pistoled thus.
Some we'd to finish for them : headlong haste
Spared them no time for mercy to their brutes.
One-half their cavalry now tramps afoot.

NAPOLÉON

And what's the tale of waggons we've picked up?

OFFICER

Spanish and all abandoned, some four hundred ;
Of magazines and firelocks, full ten load ;
And stragglers and their girls a numerous crew.

NAPOLÉON

Ay, devil—plenty those! Licentious ones
These English, as all canting peoples are.—
And prisoners?

OFFICER

            Seven hundred English, sire ;
Spaniards five thousand more.

NAPOLÉON

                        'Tis not amiss.
To keep the new year up they run away !

(He soliloquizes as he begins tearing open the dispatches)

Nor Pitt nor Fox displayed such blundering
As glares in this campaign !   It is, indeed,
Enlarging Folly to Foolhardiness
To combat France by land !   But how expect
Aught that can claim the name of government
From Canning, Castlereagh, and Perceval,
Caballers all—poor sorry politicians—
To whom has fallen the luck of reaping in
The harvestings of Pitt's bold husbandry.

He unfolds a dispatch, and looks for something to sit on.   A cloak is thrown over a log, and he settles to reading by the firelight.   The others stand round.   The light, crossed by the snow-flakes, flickers on his unhealthy face and stoutening figure.   He sinks into the rigidity of profound thought, till his features lour.

So this is their reply !   They have done with me !
Britain declines negotiating further—
Flouts France and Russia indiscriminately.
"Since one dethrones and keeps as prisoners
The most legitimate kings"—that means myself—
"The other suffers their unworthy treatment
For sordid interests"—that's for Alexander ! . . .
And what is Georgy made to say besides ?—
"Pacific overtures to us are wiles
Woven to unnerve the generous nations round
Lately escaped the galling yoke of France,
Or waiting so to do.   Such, then, being seen,
These tentatives must be regarded now
As finally forgone ; and crimson war
Be faced to its fell worst, unflinchingly."
—The devil take their lecture !   What am I,
That England should return such insolence ?

He jumps up, furious, and walks to and fro beside the fire.   By and by cooling he sits down again.

Now as to hostile signs in Austria. . . .

(He breaks another seal and reads)

Ah,—swords to cross with her some day in spring !
Thinking me cornered over here in Spain

She speaks without disguise, the covert pact
'Twixt her and England owning now quite frankly,
Careless how works its knowledge upon me.
She, England, Germany : well—I can front them !
That there is no sufficient force of French
Between the Elbe and Rhine to prostrate her,
Let new and terrible experience
Soon disillude her of !   Yea ; she may arm :
The opportunity she late let slip
Will not subserve her now !

SPIRIT OF THE PITIES

Has he no heart-hints that this Austrian court,
Whereon his mood takes mould so masterful,
Is rearing naïvely in its nursery-room
A future wife for him ?

SPIRIT OF THE YEARS

Thou dost but guess it,
And how should his heart know ?

NAPOLÉON (opening and reading another dispatch)

Now eastward.   Ohè !—
The Orient likewise looms full sombrely. . . .
The Turk declines pacifically to yield
What I have promised Alexander.   Ah ! . . .
As for Constantinople being his prize
I'll see him frozen first.   His flight's too high !
And showing that I think so makes him cool.   (Rises.)
Is Soult the Duke Dalmatia yet at hand ?

OFFICER

He has arrived along the Leon road
Just now, your Majesty ; and only waits
The close of your perusals.

Enter SOULT, who is greeted by NAPOLÉON.

FIRST DESERTER

Good Lord deliver us from all great men, and take me back
again to humble life !   That's Marshal Soult the Duke of
Dalmatia !

SECOND DESERTER

The Duke of Damnation for our poor rear, by the look on't!

FIRST DESERTER

Yes—he'll make 'em rub their poor rears before he has done
with 'em! But we must overtake 'em to-morrow by a cross-cut,
please God!

NAPOLÉON (pointing to the dispatches)

Here's matter enough for me, Duke, and to spare.
The ominous contents are like the threats
The ancient prophets dealt rebellious Judah!
Austria we soon shall have upon our hands,
And England still is fierce for fighting on,—
Strange humour in a concord-loving land!
So now I must to Paris straight away—
At least, to Valladolid ; so as to stand
More apt for couriers than I do out here
In this far western corner, and to mark
The veerings of these new developments,
And blow a counter-breeze. . . .
    Then, too, there's Lannes, still sweating at the siege
Of sullen Zaragoza as 'twere hell.
Him I must further counsel how to close
His twice too tedious battery.—You, then, Soult—
Ney is not yet, I gather, quite come up?

SOULT

He's near, sire, on the Benavente road ;
But some hours to the rear I reckon, still.

NAPOLÉON

Him I'll direct to come to your support
In this pursuit and harassment of Moore
Wherein you take my place. You'll follow up
And chase the flying English to the sea.
Bear hard on them, the bayonet at their loins.
With Merle's and Mermet's corps just gone ahead,
And Delaborde's, and Heudelet's here at hand.
While Lorge's and Lahoussaye's picked dragoons
Will follow, and Franceschi's cavalry.
To Ney I am writing that, in case of need,
He will support, with Marchand and Mathieu.—

Your total thus of seventy thousand odd,
Ten thousand horse, and cannon to five score,
Should near annihilate this British force,
And carve a triumph large in history.

(He bends over the fire and makes some notes rapidly.)

I move into Astorga ; then turn back,
(Though only in my person do I turn)
And leave to you the destinies of Spain.

SPIRIT OF THE YEARS

More turning may be here than he designs.
In this small, sudden, swift turn backward, he
Suggests one turning from his apogee !

The characters disperse, the fire sinks, and snowflakes and darkness blot
out all.

SCENE III

BEFORE CORUÑA

The town, harbour, and hills at the back are viewed from an aerial point
to the north, over the lighthouse known as the Tower of Hercules, rising at
the extremity of the tongue of land on which La Coruña stands, the open
ocean being in the spectator's rear.

In the foreground the most prominent feature is the walled old town, with
its white towers and houses, shaping itself aloft over the harbour.   The new
town, and its painted fronts, show bright below, even on this cloudy winter
afternoon.   Further off, behind the harbour—now crowded with British
transports of all sizes—is a series of low broken hills, intersected by hedges
and stone walls.

A mile behind these low inner hills is beheld a rocky chain of outer and
loftier heights that completely command the former.   Nothing behind them is
seen but grey sky.

DUMB SHOW

On the inner hills aforesaid the little English army—a pathetic fourteen
thousand of foot only—is just deploying into line : HOPE'S division on the left,
BAIRD'S to the right.   PAGET with the reserve is in the hollow to the left
behind them ; and FRASER'S division still further back shapes out on a slight
rise to the right.

This harassed force now appears as if composed of quite other than the
men observed in the Retreat insubordinately straggling along like vagabonds.
Yet they are the same men, suddenly stiffened and grown amenable to
discipline by the satisfaction of standing to the enemy at last.   They resemble
a double palisade of red stakes, the only gaps being those that the melancholy
necessity of scant numbers entails here and there.

Over the heads of these red men is beheld on the outer hills the twenty thousand French that have been pushed along the road at the heels of the English by SOULT. They have an ominous superiority, both in position and in their abundance of cavalry and artillery, over the slender lines of English foot. The left of this background, facing HOPE, is made up of DELABORDE'S and MERLE'S divisions, while in a deadly arc round BAIRD, from whom they are divided only by the village of Elvina, are placed MERMET'S division, LAHOUSSAYE'S and LORGE'S dragoons, FRANCESCHI'S cavalry, and, highest up of all, a formidable battery of eleven great guns that rake the whole British line.

It is now getting on for two o'clock, and a stir of activity has lately been noticed along the French front. Three columns are discerned descending from their position, the first towards the division of SIR DAVID BAIRD, the weakest point in the English line, the next towards the centre, the third towards the left. A heavy cannonade from the battery supports this advance.

The clash ensues, the English being swept down in swathes by the enemy's artillery. The opponents meet face to face at the village in the valley between them, and the fight there grows furious.

SIR JOHN MOORE is seen galloping to the front under the gloomy sky.

SPIRIT OF THE PITIES

I seem to vision in San Carlos' garden,
That rises salient in the upper town,
His name, and date, and doing, set within
A filmy outline like a monument,
Which yet is but the insubstantial air.

SPIRIT OF THE YEARS

Read visions as conjectures; not as more.

When MOORE arrives at the front, FRASER and PAGET move to the right, where the English are most sorely pressed. A grape-shot strikes off BAIRD'S arm. There is a little confusion, and he is borne to the rear; while MAJOR NAPIER disappears, a prisoner.

Intelligence of these misfortunes is brought to SIR JOHN MOORE. He goes further forward, and precedes in person the Forty-second regiment and a battalion of the Guards who, with fixed bayonets, bear the enemy back, MOORE'S gestures in cheering them being notably energetic. Pursuers, pursued, and SIR JOHN himself pass out of sight behind the hill. Dumb Show ends.

The point of vision descends to the immediate rear of the English position. The early January evening has begun to spread its shades, and shouts of dismay are heard from behind the hill over which MOORE and the advancing lines have vanished.

Straggling soldiers cross in the gloom.

FIRST STRAGGLER

He's struck by a cannon-ball, that I know; but he's not killed, that I pray God A'mighty.

SECOND STRAGGLER

Better he were. His shoulder is knocked to a bag of splinters. As Sir David was wownded, Sir John was anxious that the right should not give way, and went forward to keep it firm.

FIRST STRAGGLER

He didn't keep *you* firm, howsomever.

SECOND STRAGGLER

Nor you, for that matter.

FIRST STRAGGLER

Well, 'twas a serious place for a man with no priming-horn, and a character to lose, so I judged it best to fall to the rear by lying down. A man can't fight by the regulations without his priming-horn, and I am none of your slovenly anyhow fighters.

SECOND STRAGGLER

'Nation, having dropped my flint-pouch, I was the same. If you'd had your priming-horn, and I my flints, mind ye, we should have been there now? Then, forty-whory, that we are not is the fault o' Government for not supplying new ones from the reserve!

FIRST STRAGGLER

What did he say as he led us on?

SECOND STRAGGLER

" Forty-second, remember Egypt!" I heard it with my own ears. Yes, that was his strict testament.

FIRST STRAGGLER

" Remember Egypt." Ay, and I do, for I was there! . . . Upon my salvation, here's for back again, whether or no!

SECOND STRAGGLER

But here. " Forty-second, remember Egypt," he said in the very eye of that French battery playing through us. And the next omen was that he was struck off his horse, and fell on his back to the ground. I remembered Egypt, and what had just happened too, so thorough well that I remembered the way over

this wall !—Captain Hardinge, who was close to him, jumped off
his horse, and he and one in the ranks lifted him, and are now
bringing him along.

FIRST STRAGGLER

Nevertheless, here's for back again, come what will. Remember
Egypt ! Hurrah !

[Exit First straggler.

Second straggler ponders, then suddenly follows First. Enter COLONEL
ANDERSON and others hastily.

AN OFFICER

Now fetch a blanket. He must be carried in.

[Shouts heard.

COLONEL ANDERSON

That means we are gaining ground ! Had fate but left
This last blow undecreed, the hour had shone
A star amid these girdling days of gloom !

[Exit.

Enter in the obscurity six soldiers of the Forty-second bearing SIR JOHN
MOORE on their joined hands. CAPTAIN HARDINGE walks beside and
steadies him. He is temporarily laid down in the shelter of a wall, his left
shoulder being pounded away, the arm dangling by a shred of flesh.

Enter COLONEL GRAHAM and CAPTAIN WOODFORD.

GRAHAM

The wound is more than serious, Woodford, far.
Ride for a surgeon—one of those, perhaps,
Who tend Sir David Baird ? (Exit Captain Woodford.)
His blood throbs forth so fast, that I have dark fears
He'll drain to death ere anything can be done !

HARDINGE

I'll try to staunch it—since no skill's in call.

(He takes off his sash and endeavours to bind the wound with it. MOORE
smiles and shakes his head.)

There's not much checking it ! The rent's too gross.
A dozen lives could pass that thoroughfare !

Enter a soldier with a blanket. They lift MOORE into it. During the
operation the pommel of his sword, which he still wears, is accidentally thrust
into the wound.

I'll loose the sword—it bruises you, Sir John.

[He begins to unbuckle it.

MOORE

No.   Let it be !   One hurt more matters not.
I wish it to go off the field with me.

HARDINGE

I like the sound of that.   It augurs well
For your much-hoped recovery.

MOORE (looking sadly at his wound)

                              Hardinge, no :
Nature is nonplussed there !   My shoulder's gone,
And this left side laid open to my lungs.
There's but a brief breath now for me, at most. . . .
Could you—move me along—that I may glimpse
Still how the battle's going ?

HARDINGE

                              Ay, Sir John—
A few yards higher up, where·we can see.

He is borne in the blanket a little way onward, and lifted so that he can
view the valley and the action.

MOORE (brightly)

They seem to be advancing.   Yes, it is so !

Enter SIR JOHN HOPE.

Ah, Hope !—I am doing badly here enough ;
But they are doing rarely well out there.

                              (Presses Hope's hand.)

Don't leave ! my speech may flag with this fierce pain,
But you can talk to me.—Are the French checked ?

HOPE

My dear friend, they are borne back steadily.

MOORE (his voice weakening)

I hope that England—will be satisfied—
I hope my native land—will do me justice ! . . .
I shall be blamed for sending Craufurd off
Along the Orense road.   But had I not,
Bonaparte would have headed us that way. . . .

HOPE

O would that Soult had but accepted battle
By Lugo town! We should have crushed him there.

MOORE

Yes . . . yes.—But it has never been my lot
To owe much to good luck ; nor was it then.
Good fortune has been mine, but, (bitterly) mostly so
By the exhaustion of all shapes of bad ! . . .
Well, this does not become a dying man ;
And others have been chastened more than I
By Him who holds us in His hollowed hand ! . . .
    I grieve for Zaragoza if, as said,
The siege goes sorely with her, which it must.
I heard when at Dahagun that late day
That she was holding out heroically.
But I must leave such now.—You'll see my friends
As early as you can ? Tell them the whole ;
Say to my mother. . . . (His voice fails.)
Hope, Hope, I have so much to charge you with,
But weakness clams my tongue ! . . . If I must die
Without a word with Stanhope, ask him, Hope,
To—name me to his sister. You may know
Of what there was between us ? . . .
Is Colonel Graham well, and all my aides ?
My will I have made—it is in Colborne's charge
With other papers.

HOPE

He's now coming up.

Enter MAJOR COLBORNE, principal aide-de-camp.

MOORE

Are the French beaten, Colborne, or repulsed ?
Alas ! you see what they have done to me !

COLBORNE

I do, Sir John : I am more than sad thereat !
In brief time now the surgeon will be here.
The French retreat—pushed from Elvina far.

MOORE

That's good ! Is Paget anywhere about ?

COLBORNE

He's at the front, Sir John.

MOORE

                    Remembrance to him !

Enter two surgeons.

Ah, doctors,—you can scarcely mend up me.—
And yet I feel so tough—I have feverish fears
My dying will waste a long and tedious while ;
But not too long, I hope !

SURGEONS (*after a hasty examination*)

                    You must be borne
In to your lodgings instantly, Sir John.
Please strive to stand the motion—if you can ;
They will keep step, and bear you steadily.

MOORE

Anything. . . . Surely fainter ebbs that fire ?

COLBORNE

Yes : we must be advancing everywhere :
Colbert their General, too, they have lost, I learn.

*They lift him by stretching their sashes under the blanket, and begin
moving off.   A light waggon enters.*

MOORE

Who's in that waggon ?

HARDINGE

                    Colonel Wynch, Sir John.
He's wounded, but he urges you to take it.

MOORE

No.   I will not.   This suits. . . . Don't come with me ;
There's more for you to do out here as yet.

                              (*Cheerful shouts.*)

A-ha !   'Tis *this* way I have wished to die !

Exeunt slowly in the twilight MOORE, *bearers, surgeons, etc., towards*
Coruña.

The scene darkens.

SCENE IV

CORUÑA.   NEAR THE RAMPARTS

It is just before dawn on the following morning, objects being still indistinct. The features of the elevated enclosure of San Carlos can be recognized in dim outline, and also those of the Old Town of Coruña around, though scarcely a lamp is shining. The numerous transports in the harbour beneath have still their riding-lights burning.

In a nook of the town walls a lantern glimmers. Some English soldiers of the Ninth regiment are hastily digging a grave there with extemporized tools.

A VOICE (from the gloom some distance off)

"I am the resurrection and the life, saith the Lord : he that believeth in me, though he were dead, yet shall he live."

The soldiers look up, and see entering at the further end of the patch of ground a slow procession. It advances by the light of lanterns in the hands of some members of it. At moments the fitful rays fall upon bearers carrying a coffinless body rolled in a blanket, with a military cloak roughly thrown over by way of pall. It is brought towards the incomplete grave, and followed by HOPE, GRAHAM, ANDERSON, COLBORNE, HARDINGE, and several aides-de-camp, a chaplain preceding.

FIRST SOLDIER

They are here, almost as quickly as ourselves.
There is no time to dig much deeper now :
Level a bottom just as far's we've got.
He'll couch as calmly in this scrabbled hole
As in a royal vault !

SECOND SOLDIER

Would it had been a foot deeper, here among foreigners, with strange manures manufactured out of no one knows what ! Surely we can give him another six inches ?

FIRST SOLDIER

There is no time.   Just make the bottom true.

The meagre procession approaches the spot, and waits while the half-dug grave is roughly finished by the men of the Ninth. They step out of it, and another of them holds a lantern to the chaplain's book. The winter day slowly dawns.

CHAPLAIN

" Man that is born of a woman hath but a short time to live,
and is full of misery.   He cometh up, and is cut down, like a
flower ; he fleeth as it were a shadow, and never continueth in
one stay."

A gun is fired from the French battery not far off ; then another.   The
ships in the harbour take in their riding-lights.

COLBORNE (in a low voice)

I knew that dawn would see them open fire.

HOPE

We must perforce make swift use of our time.
Would we had closed our too sad office sooner !

As the body is lowered another discharge echoes.   They glance gloomily
at the heights where the French are ranged, and then into the grave.

CHAPLAIN

" We therefore commit his body to the ground.   Earth to
earth, ashes to ashes, dust to dust."   (Another gun.)

A spent ball falls not far off.   They put out their lanterns.   Continued
firing, some shot splashing into the harbour below them.

HOPE

In mercy to the living, who are thrust
Upon our care for their deliverance,
And run much hazard till they are embarked,
We must abridge these duties to the dead,
Who will not mind be they abridged or no.

HARDINGE

And could he mind, would be the man to bid it. . . .

HOPE

We shall do well, then, curtly to conclude
These mutilated prayers—our hurried best !—
And what's left unsaid, feel.

CHAPLAIN (his words broken by the cannonade)

" . . . . We give Thee hearty thanks for that it hath pleased
Thee to deliver this our brother out of the miseries of this sinful
world. . . . Who also hath taught us not to be sorry, as men

without hope, for them that sleep in Him. . . . Grant this,
through Jesus Christ our Mediator and Redeemer."

OFFICERS AND SOLDIERS

Amen !

*The diggers of the Ninth hastily fill in the grave, and the scene shuts as
the mournful figures retire.*

SCENE V

VIENNA.   A CAFÉ IN THE STEPHANS-PLATZ

*An evening between light and dark is disclosed, some lamps being lit.
The huge body and tower of St. Stephen's rise into the sky some way off, the
western gleam still touching the upper stonework. Groups of people are
seated at the tables, drinking and reading the newspapers.   One very
animated group, which includes an Englishman, is talking loudly.   A citizen
near looks up from his newspaper.*

CITIZEN (to the Englishman)

I read, sir, here, the troubles you discuss
Of your so gallant army under Moore.
His was a spirit baffled but not quelled,
And in his death there shone a stoicism
That lent retreat the rays of victory.

ENGLISHMAN

It was so.   While men chide they will admire him,
And frowning, praise.   I could nigh prophesy
That the unwonted crosses he has borne
In his career of sharp vicissitude
Will tinct his story with a tender charm,
And grant the memory of his strenuous feats
As long a lease within the minds of men
As conquerors hold there.—Does the sheet give news
Of how the troops reached home ?

CITIZEN (looking again at the paper)

Yes ; from your press
It quotes that they arrived at Plymouth Sound
Mid dreadful weather and much suffering.
It states they looked the very ghosts of men,
So heavily had hunger told on them,
And the fatigues and toils of the retreat.

Several were landed dead, and many died
As they were borne along.   At Portsmouth, too,
Sir David Baird, still helpless from his wound,
Was carried in a cot, sheet-pale and thin,
And Sir John Hope, lank as a skeleton.—
Thereto is added, with authority,
That a new expedition soon will fit,
And start again for Spain.

ENGLISHMAN

                I have heard as much.

CITIZEN

You'll do it next time, sir.   And so shall we !

SECOND CITIZEN (regarding the church tower opposite)
You witnessed the High Service over there
They held this morning ?   (To the Englishman.)

ENGLISHMAN

            Ay ; I did get in ;
Though not without hard striving, such the throng ;
But travellers roam to waste who shyly roam
And I pushed like the rest.

SECOND CITIZEN

            Our young Archduchess
Maria Louisa was, they tell me, present ?

ENGLISHMAN

O yes : the whole Imperial family,
And when the Bishop called all blessings down
Upon the Landwehr colours there displayed,
Enthusiasm touched the sky—she sharing it.

SECOND CITIZEN

Commendable in her, and spirited,
After the graceless insults to the Court
The Paris journals flaunt—not voluntarily,
But by his ordering.   Magician-like
He holds them in his fist, and at his squeeze
They bubble what he wills ! . . . Yes, she's a girl
Of patriotic build, and hates the French.

I

Quite lately she was overheard to say
She had met with most convincing auguries
That this year Bonaparte was starred to die.

ENGLISHMAN

Your arms must render its fulfilment sure.

SECOND CITIZEN

Right !   And we have the opportunity,
By upping to the war in suddenness,
And catching him unaware.   The pink and flower
Of all his veteran troops are now in Spain
Fully engaged with yours ; while those he holds
In Germany are scattered far and wide.

FIRST CITIZEN (looking up again from his newspaper)

I see here that he vows and guarantees
Inviolate bounds to all our territories
If we but pledge to carry out forthwith
A prompt disarmament.   Since that's his price
Hell burn his guarantees !   Too long he has fooled us.
(To the Englishman) I drink, sir, to your land's consistency.
While we and all the kindred Europe States
Alternately have wooed and warred with him,
You have not bent to blowing hot and cold,
But held you sturdily inimical !

ENGLISHMAN (laughing)

Less Christian-like forgiveness mellows us
Than Continental souls !   (They drink.)

A band is heard in a distant street, with shouting.   Enter third and fourth
citizens, followed by others.

FIRST CITIZEN
                    More news afloat ?

THIRD AND FOURTH CITIZENS

Yea ; an announcement that the Archduke Charles
Is given the chief command.

FIRST, SECOND, ETC., CITIZENS
                    Huzza !   Right so !

A clinking of glasses, rising from seats, and general enthusiasm.

SECOND CITIZEN

If war had not so patly been declared,
Our howitzers and firelocks of themselves
Would have gone off to shame us !   This forenoon
Some of the Landwehr met me ; they are hot
For setting out, though but few months enrolled.

ENGLISHMAN

That moves reflection somewhat.   They are young
For measuring with the veteran files of France !

FIRST CITIZEN

Napoléon's army swarms with tender youth,
His last conscription besomed into it
Thousands of merest boys.   But he contrives
To mix them in the field with seasoned frames.

SECOND CITIZEN

The sadly-seen mistake this country made
Was that of grounding hostile arms at all.
We should have fought irreconcilably—
Have been consistent as the English are.
The French are our hereditary foes,
And this adventurer of the saucy sword,
This sacrilegious slighter of our shrines,
Stands author of all our ills . . .
Our harvest fields and fruits he tramples on,
Accumulating ruin in our land.
Think of what mournings in the last sad war
'Twas his to instigate and answer for !
Time never can efface the glint of tears
In palaces, in shops, in fields, in cots,
From women widowed, sonless, fatherless,
That then oppressed our eyes.   There is no salve
For such deep harrowings but to fight again ;
The enfranchisement of Europe hangs thereon,
And long she has lingered for the sign to crush him :
That signal we have given ; the time is come !

                                    (Thumping on the tables.)

FIFTH CITIZEN (at another table, looking up from his paper
                        and speaking across)

I see that Russia has declined to aid us,
And says she knows that Prussia likewise must ;
So that the mission of Prince Schwarzenberg
To Alexander's Court has closed in failure.

THIRD CITIZEN

Ay—through his being honest—fatal sin !—
Probing too plainly for the Emperor's ears
His ominous friendship with Napoléon.

ENGLISHMAN

Some say he was more than honest with the Tsar
Hinting that his becoming an ally
Makes him accomplice of the Corsican
In the unprincipled dark overthrow
Of his poor trusting childish Spanish friends—
Which gave the Tsar offence.

THIRD CITIZEN

                        And our best bid—
The last, most delicate dish—a tastelessness.

FIRST CITIZEN

What was Prince Schwarzenberg's best bid, I pray ?

THIRD CITIZEN

The offer of the heir of Austria's hand
For Alexander's sister the Grand-Duchess.

ENGLISHMAN

He could not have accepted, if or no :
She is inscribed as wife for Bonaparte.

FIRST CITIZEN

I doubt that text !

ENGLISHMAN

                Time's context soon will show.

SECOND CITIZEN

The Russian Cabinet can not for long
Resist the ardour of the Russian ranks
To march with us the moment we achieve
Our first loud victory!

A band is heard playing afar, and shouting. People are seen hurrying past in the direction of the sounds. Enter sixth citizen.

SIXTH CITIZEN

                The Archduke Charles
Is passing the Ringstrasse just by now,
His regiment at his heels!

The younger sitters jump up with animation, and go out, the elder mostly remaining.

SECOND CITIZEN

                    Realm never faced
The grin of a more fierce necessity
For horrid war, than ours at this tense time!

The sounds of band-playing and huzzaing wane away. Citizens return.

FIRST CITIZEN

More news, my friends, of swiftly swelling zeal?

RE-ENTERED CITIZENS

Ere passing down the Ring, the Archduke paused
And gave the soldiers speech, enkindling them
As sunrise a confronting throng of panes
That glaze a many-windowed east façade:
Hot volunteers vamp in from vill and plain—
More than we need in furthest sacrifice!

FIRST, SECOND, ETC., CITIZENS

Huzza! Right so! Good! Forwards! God be praised!

They stand up, and a clinking of glasses follows, till they subside to quietude and a reperusal of newspapers. Nightfall succeeds. Dancing-rooms are lit up in an opposite street, and dancing begins. The figures are seen gracefully moving round to the throbbing strains of a string-band, which plays a new waltzing movement with a warlike name, soon to spread over Europe. The dancers sing patriotic words as they whirl.

The night closes over.

ACT FOURTH

SCENE I

A ROAD OUT OF VIENNA

It is a morning in early May. Rain descends in torrents, accompanied by peals of thunder. The tepid downpour has caused the trees to assume as by magic a clothing of limp green leafage, and has turned the ruts of the uneven highway into little canals.

A drenched travelling-chariot is passing, with a meagre escort. In the interior are seated four women : the ARCHDUCHESS MARIA LOUISA, in age about eighteen ; her stepmother the EMPRESS OF AUSTRIA, third wife of FRANCIS, only four years older than the ARCHDUCHESS ; and two ladies of the Austrian Court. Behind come attendant carriages bearing servants and luggage.

The inmates remain for the most part silent, and appear to be in a gloomy frame of mind. From time to time they glance at the moist spring scenes which pass without in a perspective distorted by the rain-drops that slide down the panes, and by the blurring effect of the travellers' breathings. Of the four the one who keeps in the best spirits is the ARCHDUCHESS, a fair, blue-eyed, full-figured, round-lipped maiden.

MARIA LOUISA

Whether the rain comes in or not I must open the window. Please allow me.   (She straightway opens it.)

EMPRESS (groaning)

Yes——open or shut it—I don't care.   I am too ill to care for anything !   (The carriage jolts into a hole.)   O woe !   To think that I am driven away from my husband's home in such a miserable conveyance, along such a road, and in such weather as this. (Peal of thunder.)   There are his guns !

MARIA LOUISA

No, my dear one.   It cannot be his guns.   They told us when we started that he was only half-way from Ratisbon hither, so that he must be nearly a hundred miles off as yet ; and a large army cannot move fast.

EMPRESS

He should never have been let come nearer than Ratisbon ! The victory at Echmühl was fatal for us.   O Echmühl, Echmühl ! I believe he will overtake us before we get to Buda.

FIRST LADY-IN-WAITING

If so, your Majesty, shall we be claimed as prisoners and marched to Paris?

EMPRESS

Undoubtedly.   But I shouldn't much care.   It would not be worse than this. . . . I feel sodden all through me, and frowzy, and broken!   (She closes her eyes as if to doze.)

MARIA LOUISA

It is dreadful to see her suffer so!   (Shutting the window.)   If the roads were not so bad I should not mind.   I almost wish we had stayed; though when he arrives the cannonade will be terrible.

FIRST LADY-IN-WAITING

I wonder if he will get into Vienna.   Will his men knock down all the houses, madam?

MARIA LOUISA

If he do get in, I am sure his triumph will not be for long. My uncle the Archduke Charles is at his heels!   I have been told many important prophecies about Bonaparte's end, which is fast nearing, it is asserted.   It is he, they say, who is referred to in the Apocalypse.   He is doomed to die this year at Cologne, in an inn called "The Red Crab."   I don't attach too much importance to all these predictions, but O, how glad I should be to see them come true!

SECOND LADY-IN-WAITING

So should we all, madam.   What would become of his divorce-scheme then?

MARIA LOUISA

Perhaps there is nothing in that report.   One can hardly believe such gossip.

SECOND LADY-IN-WAITING

But they say, your Imperial Highness, that he certainly has decided to sacrifice the Empress Joséphine, and that at the meeting last October with the Emperor Alexander at Erfurt, it was even settled that he should marry as his second wife the Grand-Duchess Anne.

MARIA LOUISA

I am sure that the Empress her mother will never allow one of the house of Romanoff to marry with a bourgeois Corsican. I wouldn't if I were she!

FIRST LADY-IN-WAITING

Perhaps, your Highness, they are not so particular in Russia, where they are rather new themselves, as we in Austria, with your ancient dynasty, are in such matters.

MARIA LOUISA

Perhaps not. Though the Empress-mother is a pompous old thing, as I have been told by Prince Schwarzenberg, who was negotiating there last winter. My father says it would be a dreadful misfortune for our country if they were to marry. Though if we are to be exiled I don't see how anything of that sort can matter much. . . . I hope my father is safe!

An officer of the escort rides up to the carriage window, which is opened.

EMPRESS (unclosing her eyes)

Any more misfortunes?

OFFICER

A rumour is a-wind, your Majesty,
That the French host, the Emperor in its midst,
Lannes, Masséna, and Bessières in its van,
Advancing hither along the Ratisbon road,
Has seized the castle and town of Ebersberg,
And burnt all down, with frightful massacre,
Vast heaps of dead and wounded being consumed,
So that the streets stink strong with frizzled flesh.—
The enemy, ere this, has crossed the Traun,
Hurling brave Hiller's army back on us,
And marches on Amstetten—thirty miles
Less distant from Vienna than before!

EMPRESS

The Lord show mercy to us! But O why
Did not the Archdukes intercept the foe?

OFFICER

His Highness Archduke Charles, your Majesty,
After his sore repulse Bohemia-wards,
Could not proceed with strength and speed enough
To close in junction with the Archduke John
And Archduke Louis, as was their intent.
So Marshall Lannes swings swiftly on Vienna,
With Oudinot's and Demont's might of foot ;
Then Masséna and all his mounted men,
And then Napoléon, Guards, Cuirassiers,
And the main body of the Imperial force.

EMPRESS

Alas for poor Vienna !

OFFICER

Even so !
Your Majesty has fled it none too soon.

The window is shut, and the procession disappears behind the sheets of rain.

SCENE II

THE ISLAND OF LOBAU, WITH WAGRAM BEYOND

The north horizon at the back of the bird's-eye prospect is the high ground stretching from the Bisamberg on the left to the plateau of Wagram on the right. In front of these elevations spreads the wide plain of the Marchfeld, open, treeless, and with scarcely a house upon it.[1]

In the foreground the Danube crosses the scene with a graceful slowness, looping itself round the numerous wooded islands therein. The largest of these, immediately under the eye, is the Lobau, which stands like a knot in the gnarled grain represented by the running river.

On this island can be discerned, closely packed, an enormous dark multitude of foot, horse, and artillery in French uniforms, the numbers reaching to a hundred and seventy thousand.

Lifting our eyes to discover what may be opposed to them we perceive on the Wagram plateau aforesaid, and right and left in front of it, extended lines of Austrians, whitish and glittering, to the number of a hundred and forty thousand.

The July afternoon turns to evening, the evening to twilight. A species of simmer which pervades the living spectacle raises expectation till the very air itself seems strained with suspense. A huge event of some kind is awaiting birth.

---

[1] At this date.

DUMB SHOW

The first change under the cloak of night is that the tightly packed regiments on the island are got under arms. The soldiery are like a thicket of reeds in which every reed should be a man.

A large bridge connects the island with the further shore, as well as some smaller bridges. Opposite are high redoubts and ravelins that the Austrians have constructed for opposing the passage across, which the French ostentatiously set themselves to attempt by the large bridge, amid heavy cannonading.

But the movement is a feint, though this is not perceived by the Austrians as yet. The real movement is on the right hand of the foreground, behind a spur of the isle, and out of sight of the enemy ; where several large rafts and flat boats, each capable of carrying three hundred men, are floated out from a screened creek.

Chosen battalions enter upon these, which immediately begin to cross with their burden. Simultaneously from other screened nooks secretly prepared floating bridges, in sections, are moved forth, joined together, and defended by those who crossed on the rafts.

At two o'clock in the morning the thousands of cooped soldiers begin to cross the bridges, producing a scene which, on such a scale, was never before witnessed in the history of war. A great discharge from the batteries accompanies this manœuvre, arousing the Austrians to a like cannonade.

The night has been obscure for summer-time, and there is no moon. The storm now breaks in a tempestuous downpour, with lightning and thunder. The tumult of nature mingles so fantastically with the tumult of projectiles that flaming bombs and forked flashes cut the air in company, and the noise from the mortars alternates with the noise from the clouds.

From bridge to bridge and back again a gloomy-eyed figure stalks, as it has stalked the whole night long, with the restlessness of a wild animal. Plastered with mud, and dribbling with rain-water, it bears no resemblance to anything dignified or official. The figure is that of NAPOLÉON, urging his multitudes over.

By daylight the great mass of the men is across the water. At six the rain ceases, the mist uncovers the face of the sun, which bristles on the helmets and bayonets of the French. A hum of amazement rises from the Austrian hosts, who turn staring faces southward and perceive what has happened, and the columns of their enemies standing to arms on the same side of the stream with themselves, and preparing to turn their left wing.

NAPOLÉON rides along the front of his forces, which now spread out upon the plain, and are ranged in order of battle.

Dumb Show ends, and the point of view changes.

SCENE III

THE FIELD OF WAGRAM

The battlefield is now viewed reversely, from the windows of a mansion at Wolkersdorf, to the rear of the Austrian position. The aspect of the windows is nearly south, and the prospect includes the plain of the Marchfeld, with the isled Danube and Lobau in the extreme distance. Ten miles to the south-west, rightwards, the faint summit of the tower of St. Stephen's, Vienna, appears. On the middle-left stands the compact plateau of Wagram, so regularly shaped as to seem as if constructed by art. On the extreme left the July sun has lately risen.

Inside the room are discovered the EMPEROR FRANCIS and some household officers in attendance; with the War-Minister and Secretaries at a table at the back. Through open doors can be seen in an outer apartment adjutants, equerries, aides, and other military men. An officer in waiting enters.

OFFICER

During the night the French have shifted, sire,
And much revised their stations of the eve
By thwart and wheeling moves upon our left,
And on our centre—projects unforeseen
Till near accomplished.

FRANCIS

But I am advised
By oral message that the Archduke Charles,
Since the sharp strife last night, has mended, too,
His earlier dispositions, and has sped
Strong orders to the Archduke John, to bring
In swiftest marches all the force he holds,
And fall with heavy impact on the French
From nigh their rear?

OFFICER

'Tis good, sire; such a swoop
Will raise an obstacle to their retreat
And refuge in the fastness of the isle;
And show this victory-gorged adventurer
That striking with a river in his rear
·Is not the safest tactic to be played
Against an Austrian front equipt like ours!

The EMPEROR FRANCIS and others scrutinize through their glasses the positions and movements of the Austrian divisions, which appear on the plain as pale masses, emitting flashes from arms and helmets under the July rays, and reaching from the Tower of Neusiedel on the left, past Wagram, into the village of Stammersdorf on the right. Beyond their lines are spread out the darker-hued French, almost parallel to the Austrians.

FRANCIS

Those moving masses toward the right I deem
The forces of Klenau and Kollowrath,

Sent to support Prince John of Lichtenstein
In his attack that way?

An interval.

Now that they've gained
The right there, why is not the attack begun?

OFFICER

They are beginning on the left wing, sire.

The EMPEROR *resumes his glass and beholds bodies of men descending from the hills by Neusiedel, and crossing the Russbach river towards the French—a movement which has been going on for some time.*

Meanwhile the French stride stoutly on our midst!

FRANCIS (turning thither)

Where we are weakest! It surpasses me
To understand why was our centre thinned
To pillar up our right already strong,
Where nought is doing, while our left assault
Stands ill-supported?

Time passes in silence.

Yes; it is so. See,
The enemy strikes Rossenberg in flank,
Compelling him to fall behind the Russbach!

The EMPEROR *gets excited, and his face perspires. At length he cannot watch through his glass, and walks up and down.*

Penned useless here my nerves annoy my sight!
Inform me what you note.—I should opine
The Wagram height behind impregnable?

Another silence, broken by the distant roar of the guns.

OFFICER (at his glass)

Klenau and Kollowrath are pounding on!
To turn the enemy's left with our strong right
Is, after all, a plan that works out well.
Hiller and Lichtenstein conjoin therein.

FRANCIS

I hear from thence appalling cannonades.

OFFICER

'Tis theirs, your Majesty. Now we shall see
If the French read that there the danger lies.

FRANCIS

I only pray that Bonaparte refrain
From spying danger there till all too late !

OFFICER (involuntarily, after a pause)

Ah, Heaven !

FRANCIS (turning sharply)

Well, well ?   What changes figure now ?

OFFICER

They pierce our centre, sire !   We are, despite,
Not centrally so weak as I supposed.
Well done, Bellegarde !

FRANCIS (glancing to the centre)

And what has he well done ?

OFFICER

The French in fierce fume broke through Aderklaa ;
But Bellegarde, pricking along the plain behind,
Has charged and driven them back disorderedly.
The Archduke Charles bounds thither, as I shape,
In person to support him !

The EMPEROR returns to his spyglass ; and they and others watch in
silence, sometimes the right of their front, sometimes the centre.

FRANCIS

It is so !
That right attack of ours spells victory,
And Austria's grand salvation ! . . . (Time passes.)   Turn
        your glass,
And closely scan Napoléon and his aides
Hand-galloping towards his centre-left
To strengthen it against the brave Bellegarde.
Does your eye reach him ?—That white horse, alone
In front of those that move so rapidly.

OFFICER

It does, sire ; though my glass can conjure not
So cunningly as yours. . . . That horse must be

The famed Euphrates—him the Persian king
Sent Bonaparte as gift.

A silence. NAPOLÉON *reaches a carriage that is moving across.   It bears*
MASSÉNA, *who, having received a recent wound, is unable to ride.*

FRANCIS

See, the white horse and horseman pause beside
A coach for some strange reason rolling there. . . .
That white-horsed rider—yes !—is Bonaparte,
By the aides hovering round. . . .
New war-wiles have been worded ; we shall spell
Their purport soon enough !   (*An interval.*)
                       The French take heart
To stand to our battalions steadfastly,
And hold their ground, having the Emperor near !

Time passes.   An aide-de-camp enters.

AIDE

The Archduke Charles is pierced in the shoulder, sire ;
He strove too far in beating back the French
At Aderklaa, and was nearly ta'en.
The wound's not serious.—On our right we win,
And deem the battle ours.

Enter another aide-de-camp.

SECOND AIDE

                  Your Majesty,
We have borne them back through Aspern village-street
And Essling is recovered.   What counts more,
Their bridges to the rear we have nearly grasped,
And panic-struck they crowd the few left free,
Choking the track, with cries of " All is lost ! "

FRANCIS

Then is the land delivered.   God be praised !

                          [*Exeunt aides.*

An interval, during which the EMPEROR *and his companions again*
remain anxiously at their glasses.

There is a curious feature I discern
To have come upon the battle.   On our right
We gain ground rapidly ; towards the left

We lose it ; and the unjudged consequence
Is that the armies' whole commingling mass
Moves like a monstrous wheel.   I like it not !

Enter another aide-de-camp.

THIRD AIDE

Our left wing, sire, recedes before Davout,
Whom nothing can withstand !   Two corps he threw
Across the Russbach up to Neusiedel,
While he himself assailed the place in front.
Of the divisions one pressed on and on,
Till lodged atop.   They would have been hurled back——

FRANCIS

But how goes it with us in sum ? pray say !

THIRD AIDE

We have been battered off the eastern side
Of Wagram plateau.

FRANCIS

                Where's the Archduke John ?
Why comes he not ?   One man of his here now
Were worth a host anon.   And yet he tarries !

[*Exit third aide.*

Time passes, while they reconnoitre the field with strained eyes.

Our centre-right, it seems, round Neusiedel,
Is being repulsed !   May the kind Heaven forbid
That Hesse Homberg should be yielding there !

The Minister in attendance comes forward, and the EMPEROR *consults him ; then walking up and down in silence.   Another aide-de-camp enters.*

FOURTH AIDE

Sire, Neusiedel has just been wrenched from us,
And the French right is on the Wagram crest ;
Nordmann has fallen, and Veczay : Hesse Homberg,
Warteachben, Muger—almost all our best—
Bleed more or less profusely !

A gloomy silence.   Exit fourth aide.   Ten minutes pass.   Enter an officer in waiting.

FRANCIS

What guns are those that groan from Wagram height?

OFFICER

Alas, Davout's!   I have climbed the roof-top, sire,
And there discerned the truth.

Cannonade continues. A long interval of suspense. The EMPEROR
returns to his glass.

FRANCIS

                A part of it!
There seems to be a grim, concerted lunge
By the whole strength of France upon our right,
Centre, and left wing simultaneously!

OFFICER

Most viciously upon the centre, sire,
If I mistook not, hard by Sussenbrunn;
The assault is led by Bonaparte in person,
Who shows himself with marvellous recklessness,
Yet like a phantom-fiend receives no hurt.

FRANCIS (still gazing)

Ha! Now the Archduke Charles has seen the intent,
And taken steps against it.   Sussenbrunn
Must be the threatened thing. (Silence.) What an
    advance!—
Straight hitherward.   Our centre girdles them.—
Surely they'll not persist?   Who heads that charge?

OFFICER

They say Macdonald, sire.

FRANCIS

              Meagrest remains
Will there be soon of those in that advance!
We are burning them to bones by our hot fire.
They are almost circumscribed: if fully so
The battle's ours!   What's that behind them, eh?

OFFICER

Their last reserves, that they may feed the front,
And sterilize our hope!

FRANCIS

                    Yes, their reserve—
Dragoons and cuirassiers—charge in support.
You see their metal gleaming as they come.
Well, it is neck or nothing for them now!

OFFICER

It's nothing, sire.   Their charge of cavalry
Has desperately failed.

FRANCIS

                    Their foot press on,
However, with a battery in front
Which deals the foulest damage done us yet.
                    (Time passes.)
They *are* effecting lodgment, after all.
Who would have reckoned on't—our men so firm!
                    Re-enter first aide-de-camp.

FIRST AIDE

The Archduke Charles retreats, your Majesty;
And the issue wears a dirty look just now.

FRANCIS (gloomily)

Yes: I have seen the signs for some good while.
But he retreats with blows, and orderly.

Time passes, till the sun has rounded far towards the west.   The features
of the battle now materially change.   The French have regained Aspern and
Essling; the Austrian army is doubled back from the Danube and from the
heights of Wagram, which, as viewed from Wolkersdorf, face the afternoon
shine, the French established thereon glittering in the rays.

FRANCIS (choking a sigh)

The turn has passed. We are worsted, but not whelmed! . . .
The French advance is laboured, and but slow.
—This might have been another-coloured day
If but the Archduke John had joined up promptly;
Yet still he lags!

ANOTHER OFFICER (lately entered)

                    He's just now coming, sire.
His columns glimmer in the Frenchmen's rear,
Past Siebenbrunn's and Loebensdorf's smoked hills.

FRANCIS (impatiently)

Ay—coming *now*!   Why could he not be *come*!

(They watch intently.)

We can see nothing of that side from here.

Enter a general officer, who speaks to the Minister at the back of the room.

MINISTER (coming forward)

Your Majesty, I now have to suggest,
Pursuant to conclusions reached this morn,
That since the front and flower of all our force
Is seen receding to the Bisamberg,
These walls no longer yield safe shade for you,
Or facile outlook.   Scouts returning say
Either Davout, or Bonaparte himself,
With the mid-columns of his forward corps,
Will bear up hitherward in fierce pursuit,
And may intrude beneath this very roof.
Not yet, I think; it may not be to-night;
But we should stand prepared.

FRANCIS

                              If we must go
We'll go with a good grace, unfeignedly!
Who knows to-morrow may not see regained
What we have lost to-day?

Re-enter fourth aide-de-camp.

FOURTH AIDE (breathlessly)

                         The Archduke John,
Discerning our main musters in retreat,
Abandons an advance that throws on him
The enemy's whole brunt if he bear on.

FRANCIS

Alas for his devotion!   Let us go.
Such weight of sadness as we shoulder now
Will wring us down to sleep in stall or stye,
If even that be found! . . . . Think! Bonaparte,
By reckless riskings of his life and limb,
Has turned the steelyard of our strength to-day,

Whilst I have idled here! . . . May brighter times
Attend the cause of Europe far in Spain,
And British blood flow not, as ours, in vain!

[Exeunt the EMPEROR FRANCIS, ministers, officers, and attendants.

The night comes, and the scene is obscured.

SCENE IV

THE FIELD OF TALAVERA

It is the same month and weather as in the preceding scene.

Talavera town, on the river Tagus, is at the extreme right of the fore-ground; a mountain range on the extreme left.

The allied army under SIR ARTHUR WELLESLEY stretches between—the English on the left, the Spanish on the right—part holding a hill to the left-centre of the scene, divided from the mountains by a valley, and part holding a redoubt to the right-centre. This army of more than fifty thousand all told, of which twenty-two thousand only are English, has its back to the spectator.

Beyond, in a wood of olive, oak, and cork, are the fifty to sixty thousand French, facing the spectator and the allies. Their right includes a strong battery upon a hill which fronts the one on the English left.

Behind all, the heights of Salinas close the prospect, the small river Alberche flowing at their foot from left to right into the Tagus, which advances in foreshortened perspective to the town at the right front corner of the scene as aforesaid.

DUMB SHOW

The hot and dusty July afternoon having turned to twilight, shady masses of men start into motion from the French position, come towards the fore-ground, silently ascend the hill on the left of the English, and assail the latter in a violent outburst of fire and lead. They nearly gain possession of the hill ascended.

CHORUS OF RUMOURS (aerial music)

Talavera tongues it as ten o' the night-time:
Now come Ruffin's slaughterers surging upward,
Backed by bold Vilatte's! From the vale Lapisse, too,
Darkly outswells there!—

Down the vague veiled incline the English fling them,
Bended bayonets prodding opponents backward:
So the first fierce charge of the ardent Frenchmen
England repels there!

Having fallen back into the darkness the French presently reascend in yet larger masses. The high square knapsack which every English foot-soldier carries, and his shako, and its tuft, outline themselves against the dim light as the ranks stand awaiting the shock.

Chorus of Rumours

Pushing spread they !—shout as they reach the summit !—
Strength and stir new-primed in their plump battalions :
Puffs of barbed flame blown on the lines opposing
*   Higher and higher.*

There those hold them mute, though at speaking distance—
Mute, while clicking flints, and the crash of volleys
Whelm the weighted gloom with immense distraction
*   Pending their fire.*

Fronting heads, helms, brows can each ranksman read there,
Epaulettes, hot cheeks, and the shining eyeball,
(Called a trice from gloom by the fleeting pan-flash)
*   Pressing them nigher !*

The French again fall back in disorder into the hollow, and LAPISSE draws off on the right. As the sinking sound of the muskets tells what has happened the English raise a shout.

Chorus of Pities

Thus the dim nocturnal embroil of conflict
Closes with the roar of receding gun-fire.
Harness loosened then, and their day-long strenuous
*   Temper unbending,*

Worn-out lines lie down where they late stood staunchly—
Cloaks around them rolled—by the bivouac embers :
There at dawn to stake in the dynasts' death-game
*   All, till the ending !*

SCENE V

THE SAME

DUMB SHOW (continued)

The morning breaks. There is another murderous attempt to dislodge the English from the hill, the assault being pressed with a determination that excites the admiration of the English themselves.

The French are seen descending into the valley, crossing it, and climbing it on the English side under the fire of HILL'S whole division, all to no purpose. In their retreat they leave behind them on the slopes nearly two thousand lying.

The day advances to noon, and the air trembles in the intense heat. The combat flags, and is suspended.

Spirit of the Pities

What do I see but thirsty, throbbing bands
From these inimic hosts defiling down
In homely need towards the little stream
That parts their enmities, and drinking there!
They get to grasping hands across the rill,
Sealing their sameness as earth's sojourners.—
What more could plead the wryness of the times
Than such unstudied piteous pantomines!

Spirit Ironic

It is only that Life's queer mechanics chance to work out in
this grotesque shape just now. The groping tentativeness of an
Immanent Will (as grey old Years describes it) cannot be asked to
learn logic at this time of day! The spectacle of Its instruments,
set to riddle one another through, and then to drink together in peace
and concord, is where the humour comes in, and makes the play
worth seeing!

Spirit Sinister

Come, Sprite, don't carry your ironies too far, or you may
wake up the Unconscious Itself, and tempt It to let all the gory
clock-work of the show run down to spite me!

The drums roll, and the men of the two nations part from their comradeship at the Alberche brook, the dark masses of the French army assembling anew. Sir Arthur Wellesley has seated himself on a mound that commands a full view of the contested hill, and remains there motionless a long time. When the French form for battle he is seen to have come to a conclusion. He mounts, gives his orders, and the aides ride off.

The French advance steadily through the sultry atmosphere, the skirmishers in front, and the columns after, moving, yet seemingly motionless. Their eighty cannon peal out and their shots mow every space in the line of them. Up the great valley and the terraces of the hill whose fame is at that moment being woven, comes Vilatte, boring his way with foot and horse, and Ruffin's men following behind.

According to the order given, the Twenty-third Light Dragoons and the German Hussars advance at a chosen moment against the head of these columns. On the way they disappear.

Spirit of the Pities

Why this bedevilment? What can have chanced?

Spirit of Rumour

It so befalls that as their chargers near
The inimical wall of flesh with its iron frise,

A treacherous chasm uptrips them : zealous men
And docile horses roll to dismal death
And horrid mutilation.

SPIRIT OF THE PITIES

                              Those who live
Even now advance !   I'll see no more.   Relate.

SPIRIT OF RUMOUR

Yes, those pant on.   Then further Frenchmen cross,
And Polish Lancers, and Westphalian Horse,
Who ring around these luckless Islanders,
And sweep them down like reeds by the river-brink
In scouring floods ; till scarce a man remains.

Meanwhile on the British right SEBASTIANI'S corps has precipitated
itself in column against GENERAL CAMPBELL'S division, the division of LAPISSE
against the centre, and at the same time the hill on the English left is again
assaulted.   The English and their allies are pressed sorely here, the bellow-
ing battery tearing lanes through their masses.

SPIRIT OF RUMOUR (continuing)

The French reserves of foot and horse now on,
Smiting the Islanders in breast and brain
Till their mid-lines are shattered. . . . Now there ticks
The moment of the crisis; now the next,
Which brings the turning stroke.

SIR ARTHUR WELLESLEY sends down the Forty-eighth regiment under
COLONEL DONELLAN to support the wasting troops.   It advances amid
those retreating, opening to let them pass.

SPIRIT OF RUMOUR (continuing)

                              Then pales, enerved,
The hitherto unflinching enemy !
Lapisse is pierced to death ; the flagging French
Decline into the hollows whence they came.
The too exhausted English and reduced
Lack strength to follow.— Now the western sun,
Conning with unmoved visage quick and dead,
Gilds horsemen slackening, and footmen stilled,
Till all around breathes drowsed hostility.
    Last, the swealed herbage lifts a leering light,
And flames traverse the field ; and hurt and slain
Opposed, opposers, in a common plight
Are scorched together on the dusk champaign.

The fire dies down, and darkness enwraps the scene.

SCENE VI

BRIGHTON. THE ROYAL PAVILION

It is the birthday dinner-party of the PRINCE OF WALES. In the floridly decorated banqueting-room stretch tables spread with gold and silver plate, and having artificial fountains in their midst.

Seated at the tables are the PRINCE himself as host—rosy, well curled, and affable—the DUKES OF YORK, CLARENCE, KENT, SUSSEX, CUMBERLAND, and CAMBRIDGE, with many noblemen, including LORDS HEADFORT, BERKELEY, EGREMONT, CHICHESTER, DUDLEY, SAY AND SELE, SOUTH-AMPTON, HEATHFIELD, ERSKINE, KEITH, C. SOMERSET, G. CAVENDISH, R. SEYMOUR, and others; SIR C. POLE, SIR E. G. DE CRESPIGNY, MR. SHERIDAN; Generals, Colonels, and Admirals, and the REV. MR. SCOTT.

The PRINCE'S band plays in the adjoining room. The banquet is drawing to its close, and a boisterous conversation is in progress.

Enter COLONEL BLOOMFIELD with a dispatch for the PRINCE, who looks it over amid great excitement in the company. In a few moments silence is called.

PRINCE OF WALES

I have the joy, my lords and gentlemen,
To rouse you with the just imported tidings
From General Wellesley through Lord Castlereagh
Of a vast victory (noisy cheers) over the French in Spain.
The place—called Talavera de la Reyna
(If I pronounce it rightly)—long unknown,
Wears now the crest and blazonry of fame!   (Cheers.)
The heads and chief contents of the dispatch
I read you as succinctly as I can.   (Cheers.)

SHERIDAN (singing sotto voce)

" Now foreign foemen die and fly,
Dammy, we'll drink little England dry ! "

The PRINCE reads the parts of the dispatch that describe the battle, amid intermittent cheers.

PRINCE OF WALES (continuing)

Such is the substance of the news received,
Which, after Wagram, strikes us genially
As sudden sunrise through befogged night shades !

SHERIDAN (privately)

By God, that's good, sir ! You are a poet born, while the rest of us are but made, and bad at that.

The health of the army in Spain is drunk with acclamations.

Prince of Wales (continuing)

In this achievement we, alas ! have lost
Too many !   Yet such blanks must ever be.——
Mackenzie, Langworth, Beckett of the Guards,
Have fallen of ours ; while of the enemy
Generals Lapisse and Morlot are laid low.——
Drink to their memories !

They drink in silence.

                Other news, my friends,
Received to-day is of like hopeful kind.
The Great War-Expedition to the Scheldt (cheers)
Which lately sailed, has found a favouring wind,
And by this hour has touched its destined shores.
The enterprise will soon be hot aglow,
The invaders making first the Cadsand coast,
And then descending on Walcheren Isle.
But items of the next step are withheld
Till later days, from obvious policy.   (Cheers.)

Faint throbbing sounds, like the notes of violoncellos and contrabassos reach the ear from some building without as the speaker pauses.

In worthy emulation of us here
The county holds to-night a birthday ball,
Which flames with all the fashion of the town.
I have been asked to patronize their revel,
And sup with them, and likewise you, my guests.
We have good reason, with such news to bear !
Thither we haste and join our loyal friends,
And stir them with this live intelligence
Of our staunch regiments on the Spanish plains.

                              (Applause.)

With them we'll now knit hands and beat the ground,
And bring in dawn as we whirl round and round !
There are some fair ones in their set to-night,
And such we need here in our bachelor-plight.   (Applause.)

The Prince, his brothers, and a large proportion of the other Pavilion guests, swagger out in the direction of the Castle assembly-rooms adjoining, and the deserted banqueting-hall grows dark.   In a few moments the back of the scene opens, revealing the assembly-rooms behind.

SCENE VII

THE SAME.   THE ASSEMBLY ROOMS

The rooms are lighted with candles in brass chandeliers, and a dance is in full movement to the strains of a string-band. A signal is given, shortly after the clock has struck eleven, by MR. FORTH, Master of Ceremonies.

FORTH

His Royal Highness comes, though somewhat late,
But never too late for welcome! (Applause.)   Dancers, stand,
That we may do fit homage to the Prince
Who soon may shine our country's gracious king.

After a brief stillness a commotion is heard at the door, the band strikes up the National air, and the PRINCE enters, accompanied by the rest of the visitors from the Pavilion. The guests who have been temporarily absent now crowd in, till there is hardly space to stand.

PRINCE OF WALES (wiping his face and whispering to Sheridan)

What shall I say to fit their feelings here?
Damn me, that other speech has stumped me quite!

SHERIDAN (whispering)

If heat be evidence of loy——

PRINCE OF WALES

If what?

SHERIDAN

If heat be evidence of loyalty,
Et cætera—something quaint like that might please 'em.

PRINCE OF WALES (to the company)

If heat be evidence of loyalty,
This room affords it truly without question;
If heat be not, then its accompaniment
Most surely 'tis to-night.   The news I bring,
Good ladies, friends, and gentlemen, perchance
You have divined already?   That our arms——
Engaged to thwart Napoléon's tyranny
Over the jaunty, jocund land of Spain
Even to the highest apex of our strength——
Are rayed with victory!   (Cheers.)   Lengthy was the strife.

And fierce, and hot ; and sore the suffering ;
But proudly we endured it ; and shall hear,
No doubt, of its far consequence
Ere many days.   I'll read the details sent.   (Cheers.)

He reads again from the dispatch amid more cheering, the ball-room guests crowding round. When he has done he answers questions ; then continuing :

Meanwhile our interest is, if possible,
As keenly waked elsewhere.   Into the Scheldt
Some forty thousand bayonets and swords,
And twoscore ships o' the line, with frigates, sloops,
And gunboats sixty more, make headway now,
Bleaching the waters with their bellying sails ;
Or maybe they already anchor there,
And that the level ooze of Walcheren shore
Ring with the voices of that landing host
In every twang of British dialect,
Clamorous to loosen fettered Europe's chain !   (Cheers.)

A Noble Lord (aside to Sheridan)

Prinny's outpouring tastes suspiciously like your brew, Sheridan.
I'll be damned if it is his own concoction.   How d'ye sell it a gallon ?

Sheridan

I don't deal that way nowadays.   I give the recipe, and charge a duty on the gauging.   It is more artistic, and saves trouble.

The company proceed to the supper-rooms, and the ball-room sinks into solitude.

Spirit of the Pities

So they pass on.   Let be !—But what is this—
A moan ?—all frailly floating from the east
To usward, even from the forenamed isle ? . . .
Would I had not broke nescience, to inspect
A world so ill-contrived !

Spirit of the Years

                    But since thou hast
We'll hasten to the isle ; and thou'lt behold—
Such as it is—the scene its coasts enfold.

SCENE VIII

WALCHEREN

A marshy island at the mouth of the Scheldt, lit by the low sunshine of an evening in late summer. The horizontal rays from the west lie in yellow sheaves across the vapours that the day's heat has drawn from the sweating soil. Sour grasses grow in places, and strange fishy smells, now warm, now cold, pass along. Brass-hued and opalescent bubbles, compounded of many gases, rise where passing feet have trodden the damper spots. At night the place is the haunt of the Jack-lantern.

DUMB SHOW

A vast army is encamped here, and in the open spaces are infantry on parade—skeletoned men, some flushed, some shivering, who are kept moving because it is dangerous to stay still. Every now and then one falls down, and is carried away to a hospital with no roof, where he is laid, bedless, on the ground.

In the distance soldiers are digging graves for the funerals which are to take place after dark, delayed till then that the sight of so many may not drive the living melancholy-mad. Faint noises are heard in the air.

SHADE OF THE EARTH

What storm is this of souls dissolved in sighs,
And what the dingy doom it signifies?

SPIRIT OF THE PITIES

We catch a lamentation shaped thuswise:

CHORUS OF PITIES (aerial music)

" *We who withstood the blasting blaze of war*
When marshalled by the gallant Moore awhile,
Beheld the grazing death-bolt with a smile,
Closed combat edge to edge and bore to bore,
        Now rot upon this Isle!

" *The ever wan morass, the dune, the blear*
Sandweed, and tepid pool, and putrid smell,
Emaciate purpose to a fractious fear,
Beckon the body to its last low cell—
        A chink no chart will tell.

" *O ancient Delta, where the fen-lights flit!*
Ignoble sediment of loftier lands,

Thy humour clings about our hearts and hands
And solves us to its softness, till we sit
    As we were part of it.

" *Such force as fever leaves is maddened now,*
With tidings trickling in from day to day
Of others' differing fortunes, wording how
They yield their lives to baulk a tyrant's sway—
    Yield them not vainly, they !

" *In champaigns green and purple, far and near,*
In town and thorpe where quiet spire-cocks turn,
Through vales, by rocks, beside the brooding burn
Echoes the aggressor's arrogant career;
    And we pent pithless here !

" *Here, where each creeping day the creeping file*
Draws past with shouldered comrades score on score,
Bearing them to their lightless last asile,
Where weary wave-wails from the clammy shore
    Will reach their ears no more.

" *We might have fought, and had we died, died well,*
Even if in dynasts' discords not our own;
Our death-spot some sad haunter might have shown,
Some tongue have asked our sires or sons to tell
    The tale of how we fell;

" *But such bechanced not.   Like the mist we fade,*
No lustrous lines engrave in story we,
Our country's chiefs, for their own fames afraid,
Will leave our names and fates by this pale sea
    To perish silently ! "

SPIRIT OF THE YEARS

Why must ye echo as mechanic mimes
These mortal minions' bootless cadences,
Played on the stops of their anatomy
As is the mewling music on the strings
Of yonder ship-masts by the unweeting wind,
Or the frail tune upon this withering sedge
That holds its papery blades against the gale ?

—Men pass to dark corruption, at the best,
Ere I can count five score : these why not now ?—
The Immanent Shaper builds Its beings so
Whether ye sigh their sighs with them or no !

The night fog enwraps the isle and the dying English army.

ACT FIFTH

SCENE I

PARIS.   A BALLROOM IN THE HOUSE OF CAMBACÉRÈS

The many-candled saloon at the ARCH-CHANCELLOR'S is visible through a draped opening, and a crowd of masked dancers in fantastic costumes revolve, sway, and intermingle to the music that proceeds from an alcove at the further end of the same apartment.   The front of the scene is a withdrawing-room of smaller size, now vacant, save for the presence of one sombre figure, that of NAPOLÉON, seated, and apparently watching the moving masquerade.

SPIRIT OF THE PITIES

Napoléon even now unbraces not
From stress of state affairs, which hold him grave
Through revels that might win the King of Spleen
To toe a measure !   I would speak with him.

SPIRIT OF THE YEARS

Speak if thou wilt whose speech nor mars nor mends !

SPIRIT OF THE PITIES (into Napoléon's ear)

Why thus and thus Napoléon ?   Can it be
That Wagram with its glories, shocks, and shames,
Still leaves athirst the palate of thy pride ?

NAPOLÉON (answering as in soliloquy)

The trustless, timorous lease of human life
Warns me to hedge in my diplomacy.
The sooner, then, the safer !   Ay, this eve,
This very night, will I take steps to rid
My morrows of the weird contingencies
That vision round and make one hollow-eyed. . . .
The unexpected, lurid death of Lannes—

Rigid as iron, reaped down like a straw—
Tiptoed Assassination haunting round
In unthought thoroughfares, the near success
Of Staps the madman, argue to forbid
The riskful blood of my previsioned line
And potence for dynastic empery
To linger vialled in my veins alone.
Perhaps within this very house and hour,
Under an innocent mask of Love or Hope,
Some enemy queues my ways to coffin me. . . .
When at the first clash of the late campaign,
A bold belief in Austria's star prevailed,
There pulsed quick pants of expectation round
Among the cowering kings, that too well told
What would have fared had I been overthrown !
So ; I must send down shoots to future time
Who'll plant my standard and my story there ;
And a way opens.—Better I had not
Bespoke a wife from Alexander's house.
Not there now lies my look.   But done is done !

The dance ends and masks enter, BERTHIER among them.   NAPOLÉON
beckons to him, and he comes forward.

God send you find amid this motley crew
Frivolities enough, friend Berthier—eh ?
My thoughts have worn oppressive shades despite such !
What scandals of me do they bandy here ?
These close disguises render women bold—
Their shames being of the light, not of the thing—
And your sagacity has garnered much,
I make no doubt, of ill and good report,
That marked our absence from the capital ?

BERTHIER

Methinks, your Majesty, the enormous tale
Of your campaign, like Aaron's serpent-rod,
Has swallowed up the smaller of its kind.
Some speak, 'tis true, in counterpoise thereto,
Of English deeds by Talavera town,
Though blurred by their exploit at Walcheren,
And all its crazy, crass futilities.

NAPOLÉON

Yet was the exploit well featured in design,
Large in idea, and imaginative ;
I had not deemed the blinkered English folk
So capable of view.   Their fate contrived
To place an idiot at the helm of it,
Who marred its working, else it had been hard
If things had not gone seriously for us.
—But see, a lady saunters hitherward
Whose gait proclaims her Madame Metternich,
One that I fain would speak with.

NAPOLÉON rises and crosses the room towards a lady-masker who has
just appeared in the opening.   BERTHIER draws off, and the EMPEROR,
unceremoniously taking the lady's arm, brings her forward to a chair, and
sits down beside her as dancing is resumed.

MADAME METTERNICH

                                In a flash
I recognized you, sire ; as who would not
The bearer of such deep-delved charactery ?

NAPOLÉON

The devil, madame, take your piercing eyes !
It's hard I cannot prosper in a game
That every coxcomb plays successfully.
—So here you are still, though your loving lord
Disports him at Vienna ?

MADAME METTERNICH

                                Paris, true,
Still holds me ; though in quiet, save to-night,
When I have been expressly prayed come hither,
Or I had not left home.

NAPOLÉON

                                I sped that prayer !—
I have a wish to put a case to you,
Wherein a woman's judgment, such as yours,
May be of signal service.   (He lapses into reverie.)

MADAME METTERNICH

                                Well ?   The case—

NAPOLÉON

Is marriage—mine.

MADAME METTERNICH

It is beyond me, sire!

NAPOLÉON

You glean that I have decided to dissolve
(Pursuant to monitions murmured long)
My union with the present Empress—formed
Without the Church's due authority?

MADAME METTERNICH

Vaguely.   And that light tentatives have winged
Betwixt your Majesty and Russia's court,
To moot that one of their Grand-Duchesses
Should be your Empress-wife.   Nought else I know.

NAPOLÉON

There have been such approachings ; more, worse luck.
Last week Champagny wrote to Alexander
Asking him for his sister—yes or no.

MADAME METTERNICH

What "worse luck" lies in that, your Majesty,
If severance from the Empress Joséphine
Be fixed unalterably?

NAPOLÉON

This worse luck lies there :
If your Archduchess, Marie Louise the fair,
Would straight accept my hand, I'd offer it,
And throw the other over.   Faith, the Tsar
Has shown such backwardness in answering me,
Time meanwhile trotting, that I have ample ground
For such withdrawal.—Madame, now, again,
Will your Archduchess marry me or no ?
That is, will her good sire assent thereto ?

MADAME METTERNICH

Your sudden questions quite confound my sense!
It is impossible to answer them.

NAPOLÉON

Well, madame, now I'll put it to you thus :
Were you in the Archduchess Marie's place
Would you accept my hand—and heart therewith ?

MADAME METTERNICH

I should refuse you—most assuredly ! [1]

NAPOLÉON (laughing roughly)

Ha-ha !   That's frank,   And devilish cruel too !
—Well, write to your husband.   Ask him what he thinks,
And let me know.

MADAME METTERNICH

                    Indeed, sire, why should I ?
There goes the Ambassador, Prince Schwarzenberg,
Successor to my spouse.   He's now the groove
And proper conduit of diplomacy
Through whom to broach this matter to his Court.

NAPOLÉON

Do you, then, broach it through him, madame, pray ;
Now, here, to-night.

MADAME METTERNICH

                    I will, informally,
To humour you, on this recognizance,
That you leave not the business in my hands,
But clothe your project in official guise
Through him to-morrow ; so safeguarding me
From foolish seeming, as the babbler forth
Of a fantastic and unheard of dream.

NAPOLÉON

I'll send Eugène to him, as you suggest.
Meanwhile prepare him.   Make your stand-point this :
Children are needful to my dynasty,
And if one woman cannot mould them for me,
Why, then, another must.

                              [Exit NAPOLÉON abruptly.
    Dancing continues.   Madame METTERNICH sits on, musing.   Enter
SCHWARZENBERG.

_____

[1] So Madame Metternich to her husband in reporting this interview.   But who
shall say !

                                                                    K

MADAME METTERNICH

The Emperor has just left me.   We have tapped
This theme and that ; his Empress and—his next.
Ay, so !   Now, guess you anything ?

SCHWARZENBERG

                                        Of her ?

No more than that the stock of Romanoff
Will not supply the spruce commodity.

MADAME METTERNICH

And that the would-be customer turns toe
To our shop in Vienna.

SCHWARZENBERG

                                        Marvellous ;

And comprehensible but as the dream
Of Delaborde, of which I have lately heard.
It will not work !—What think you, madame, on't ?

MADAME METTERNICH

That it will work, and is as good as wrought !—
I break it to you thus, at his request.
In brief time Prince Eugène will wait on you,
And make the formal offer in his name.

SCHWARZENBERG

Which I can but receive *ad referendum*,
And shall initially make clear as much,
Disclosing not a glimpse of my own mind !
Meanwhile you make good Metternich aware ?

MADAME METTERNICH

I write this midnight, that amaze may pitch
To coolness ere your messenger arrives.

SCHWARZENBERG

This radiant revelation flicks a gleam
On many circling things !—the courtesies
Which graced his bearing towards our officers
Amid the tumults of the late campaign,

His wish for peace with England, his affront
At Alexander's tedious-timed reply . . .
Well, it will thrust a thorn in Russia's side,
If I err not, whatever else betide !   [Exeunt.

The maskers surge into the foreground of the scene, and their motions
become more and more fantastic. A strange gloom begins and intensifies,
until only the high lights of their grinning figures are visible. These also,
with the whole ball-room, gradually darken, and the music softens to silence.

SCENE II

PARIS.   THE TUILERIES

The evening of the next day. A saloon of the Palace, with folding-doors
communicating with a dining-room. The doors are flung open, revealing on
the dining-table an untouched dinner, NAPOLÉON and JOSÉPHINE rising
from it, and DE BAUSSET, chamberlain-in-waiting, pacing up and down.
The EMPEROR and EMPRESS come forward into the saloon, the latter pale
and distressed, and patting her eyes with her handkerchief.

The doors are closed behind them ; a page brings in coffee ; NAPOLÉON
signals to him to leave. JOSÉPHINE goes to pour out the coffee, but
NAPOLÉON pushes her aside and pours it out himself, looking at her in a
way which causes her to sink cowering into a chair like a frightened animal.

JOSÉPHINE

I see my doom, my friend, upon your face !

NAPOLÉON

You see me bored by Cambacérès' ball.

JOSÉPHINE

It means divorce !—a thing more terrible
Than carrying elsewhere the dalliances
That formerly were mine.   I kicked at that ;
But now agree, as I for long have done,
To any infidelities of act
May I be yours in name !

NAPOLÉON

               My mind must bend
To other things than our domestic pettings :
The Empire orbs above our happiness,
And 'tis the Empire dictates this divorce.

I reckon on your courage and calm sense
To breast with me the law's formalities,
And get it through before the year has flown.

JOSÉPHINE

But are you *really* going to part from me?
O no, no, my dear husband; no, in truth,
It cannot be my Love will serve me so!

NAPOLÉON

I mean but mere divorcement, as I said,
On simple grounds of sapient sovereignty.

JOSÉPHINE

But nothing have I done save good to you:—
Since the fond day we wedded into one
I never even have *thought* you jot of harm!
Many the happy junctures when you have said
I stood as guardian-angel over you,
As your Dame Fortune, too, and endless things
Of such-like pretty tenour—yes, you have!
Then how can you so gird against me now?
You had not pricked upon it much of late,
And so I hoped and hoped the ugly spectre
Had been laid dead and still.

NAPOLÉON (impatiently)

                                        I tell you, dear,
The thing's decreed, and even the princess chosen.

JOSÉPHINE

Ah—so—the princess chosen! . . . I surmise
It is none else than the Grand-Duchess Anne:
Gossip was right—though I would not believe.
She's young; but no great beauty!—Yes, I see
Her silly, soulless eyes and horrid hair;
In which new gauderies you'll forget sad me!

NAPOLÉON

Upon my soul you are childish, Joséphine:
A woman of your years to pout it so!—
I say it's not the Tsar's Grand-Duchess Anne.

JOSÉPHINE

Some other Fair, then.   You whose name can nod
The flower of all the world's virginity
Into your bed, will well take care of that!
(Spitefully.)   She may not have a child, friend, after all.

NAPOLÉON (drily)

You hope she won't, I know!—But don't forget
Madame Walewska did, and had she shown
Such cleverness as yours, poor little fool,
Her withered husband might have been displaced,
And her boy made my heir.—Well, let that be.
The severing parchments will be signed by us
Upon the fifteenth, prompt.

JOSÉPHINE

                 What—I have to sign
My putting away upon the fifteenth next?

NAPOLÉON

Ay—both of us.

JOSÉPHINE (falling on her knees)
             So far advanced—so far!
Fixed?—for the fifteenth?   O I do implore you,
My very dear one, by our old, old love,
By my devotion, don't, don't cast me off
Now, after these long years!

NAPOLÉON
            Heavens, how you jade me!
Must I repeat that I don't cast you off;
We merely formally arrange divorce—
We live and love, but call ourselves divided.

A silence.

JOSÉPHINE (with sudden calm)

Very well.   Let it be.   I must submit!   (Rises.)

NAPOLÉON

And this much likewise you must promise me,
To act in the formalities thereof
As if you shaped them of your own free will.

JOSÉPHINE

How can I—when no freewill's left in me?

NAPOLÉON

You are a willing party—do you hear?

JOSÉPHINE (quivering)

I hardly—can—bear this!—It is—too much
For a poor weak and broken woman's strength!
But—but I yield!—I am so helpless now:
I give up all—ay, kill me if you will,
I won't cry out!

NAPOLÉON

And one thing further still,
You'll help me in my marriage overtures
To win the Duchess—Austrian Marie she,—
Concentring all your force to forward them.

JOSÉPHINE

It is the—last humiliating blow!—
I cannot—O, I will not!

NAPOLÉON (fiercely)

But you *shall*!
And from your past experience you may know
That what I say I mean!

JOSÉPHINE (breaking into sobs)

O my dear husband—do not make me—don't!
If you but cared for me—the hundredth part
Of how—I care for you, you could not be
So cruel as to lay this torture on me.
It hurts me so!—it cuts me like a sword.
Don't make me, dear! Don't, will you! O, O, O!

(She sinks down in a hysterical fit.)

NAPOLÉON (calling)

Bausset!

Enter DE BAUSSET, Chamberlain-in-waiting.

Bausset, come in and shut the door.
Assist me here. The Empress has fallen ill.

Don't call for help.   We two can carry her
By the small private staircase to her rooms.
Here—I will take her feet.

They lift JOSÉPHINE *between them and carry her out.   Her moans die
away as they recede towards the stairs.*

Enter two servants, who remove coffee-service, readjust chairs, etc.

FIRST SERVANT

So, poor old girl, she's wailed her *Miserere Mei*, as Mother
Church says.   I knew she was to get the sack ever since he
came back.

SECOND SERVANT

Well, there will be a little civil huzzaing, a little crowing and
cackling among the Bonapartes at the downfall of the Beauharnais
family at last, mark me there will!   They've had their little
hour, as the poets say, and now 'twill be somebody else's turn.
O it is droll!   Well, Father Time is a great philosopher, if you
take him right.   Who is to be the new woman?

FIRST SERVANT

She that contains in her own corporation the necessary
particulars.

SECOND SERVANT

And what may they be?

FIRST SERVANT

She must be young.

SECOND SERVANT

Good.   She must.   The country must see to that.

FIRST SERVANT

And she must be strong.

SECOND SERVANT

Good again.   She must be strong.   The doctors will see to
that.

FIRST SERVANT

And she must be fruitful as the vine.

SECOND SERVANT

Ay, by God.   She must be fruitful as the vine.   That, Heaven
help him, he must see to himself, like the meanest multiplying
man in Paris.

[*Exeunt servants.*

Re-enter NAPOLÉON *with his stepdaughter,* QUEEN HORTENSE.

NAPOLÉON

Your mother is too rash and reasonless—
Wailing and fainting over statesmanship
Which is no personal caprice of mine,
But policy most painful—forced on me
By the necessities of this country's charge.
Go to her ; see if she be saner now ;
Explain it to her once and once again,
And bring me word what impress you may make.

HORTENSE *goes out.*   CHAMPAGNY *is shown in.*

Champagny, I have something clear to say
Now, on our process after the divorce.
The question of the Russian Duchess Anne
Was quite inept for further toying with.
The years rush on, and I grow nothing younger.
So I have made up my mind—committed me
To Austria and the Hapsburgs—good or ill !
It was the best, most practicable plunge,
And I have plunged it.

CHAMPAGNY

　　　　　　Austria, say you, sire ?
I reckoned that but as a scurrying dream !

NAPOLÉON

Well, so it was.   But such a pretty dream
That its own charm transfixed it to a notion,
That showed itself in time a sanity,
Which hardened in its turn to a resolve
As firm as any built by mortal mind.—
The Emperor's consent must needs be won ;
But I foresee no difficulty there.
The young Archduchess is a bright blond thing

By general story ; and considering, too,
That her good mother childed seventeen times,
It will be hard if she can not produce
The modest one or two that I require.

Enter DE BAUSSET with dispatches.

DE BAUSSET

The courier, sire, from Petersburg is here,
And brings these letters for your Majesty.

[Exit DE BAUSSET.

NAPOLÉON (after silently reading)

Ha-ha !   It never rains unless it pours :
Now I can have the other readily.
The proverb hits me aptly : " Well they do
Who doff the old love ere they don the new ! "

(He glances again over the letter.)

Yes, Caulaincourt now writes he has every hope
Of quick success in settling the alliance !
The Tsar is willing—even is anxious for it,
His sister's youth the single obstacle.
The Empress-mother, hitherto against me,
Ambition-fired, verges on suave consent,
Likewise the whole Imperial family.
What irony is all this to me now !
Time lately was when I had leapt thereat.

CHAMPAGNY

You might, of course, sire, give th' Archduchess up,
Seeing she looms uncertainly as yet,
While this does so no longer.

NAPOLÉON

No—not I.

My sense of my own dignity forbids
My watching the slow clocks of Muscovy !
Why have they dallied with my tentatives
In pompous silence since the Erfurt day ?
—And Austria, too, affords a safer hope.
The young Archduchess is much less a child
Than is the other, who, Caulaincourt says,
Will be incapable of motherhood
For six months yet or more—a grave delay

K 2

CHAMPAGNY

Your Majesty appears to have trimmed your sail
For Austria ; and no more is to be said !

NAPOLÉON

Except that there's the house of Saxony
If Austria fail.—Then, very well, Champagny,
Write you to Caulaincourt accordingly.

CHAMPAGNY

I will, your Majesty.

[Exit CHAMPAGNY.

Re-enter QUEEN HORTENSE.

NAPOLÉON

        Ah, dear Hortense,
How is your mother now ?

HORTENSE

        Calm ; quite calm, sire.
I pledge me you need have no further fret
From her entreating tears.   She bids me say
That now, as always, she submits herself
With chastened dignity to circumstance,
And will descend, at notice, from your throne—
As in days earlier she ascended it—
In questionless obedience to your will.
It was your hand that crowned her ; let it be
Likewise your hand that takes her crown away
As for her children, we shall be but glad
To follow and withdraw ourselves with her,
The tenderest mother children ever knew,
From grandeurs that have brought no happiness !

NAPOLÉON (taking her hand)

But, Hortense, dear, it is not to be so !
You must stay with me, as I said before.
Your mother, too, must keep her royal state,
Since no repudiation stains this need.
Equal magnificence will orb her round
In aftertime as now.   A palace here,
A palace in the country, wealth to match,

A rank in order next my future wife's,
And conference with me as my truest friend.
Now we will seek her—Eugène, you, and I—
And make the project clear.

                           [Exeunt NAPOLÉON and HORTENSE.

          The scene darkens and shuts.

SCENE III

VIENNA.   A PRIVATE APARTMENT IN THE IMPERIAL PALACE

   The EMPEROR FRANCIS discovered, paler than usual, and somewhat flurried.

   Enter METTERNICH the Prime Minister—a thin-lipped, long-nosed man with inquisitive eyes.

FRANCIS

I have been expecting you some minutes here,
The thing that fronts us brooking brief delay.—
Well, what say you by now on this strange offer?

METTERNICH

My views remain the same, your Majesty:
The policy of peace that I have upheld,
Both while in Paris and of late time here,
Points to this step as heralding sweet balm
And bandaged veins for our late crimsoned realm.

FRANCIS

Agreed.   As monarch I perceive therein
A happy doorway for my purposings.
It seems to guarantee the Hapsburg crown
A quittance of distractions such as those
That leave their shade on many a backward year!—
There is, forsooth, a suddenness about it,
And it would aid us had we clearly keyed
The cryptologues of which the world has heard
Between Napoléon and the Russian Court—
Begun there with the selfsame motiving.

METTERNICH

I would not, sire, one second ponder it
It was an obvious first crude cast-about
In the important reckoning of means
For his great end, a strong monarchic line.
The more advanced the more it profits us ;
For sharper, then, the quashing of such views,
And wreck of that conjunction in the aims
Of France and Russia, marked so much of late
As jeopardizing quiet neighbours' thrones.

FRANCIS

If that be so, on the domestic side
There seems no bar.   Speaking as father solely,
I see secured to her the proudest fate
That woman can daydream.   And I could hope
That private bliss would not be wanting her !

METTERNICH

A hope well seated, sire.   The Emperor,
Imperious and determined in his rule,
Is easy-natured in domestic life,
As my long time in Paris amply proved.
Moreover, the accessories of his glory
Have been, and will be, admirably designed
To fire the fancy of a young princess.

FRANCIS

Thus far you satisfy me. . . . So, to close,
Or not to close with him, is now the thing.

METTERNICH

Your Majesty commands the issue quite :
The Father of his people can alone
In such a case give answer—yes or no.
Vagueness and doubt have ruined Russia's chance ;
Let not, then, such be ours.

FRANCIS

                         You mean, if I,
You'd answer straight.   What would that answer be ?

METTERNICH

In state affairs, sire, as in private life,
Times will arise when even the faithfullest squire
Finds him unfit to jog his chieftain's choice,
On whom responsibility must lastly rest.
And such times are pre-eminently, sire,
Those wherein thought alone is not enough
To serve the head as guide.   As Emperor,
As father, both, to you, to you in sole
Must appertain the privilege to pronounce
Which track stern duty bids you tread herein.

FRANCIS

Affection is my duty, heart my guide.—
Without constraint or prompting I shall leave
The big decision in my daughter's hands.
Before my obligations to my people
Must stand her wish.   Go, find her, Metternich,
Take her the tidings.   She is free with you,
And will speak out.

> (Looking forth upon the terrace.)

                              She's here at hand, I see :
I'll call her in.   Then tell me what's her mind.

He beckons from the window, and goes out in another direction.

METTERNICH

So much for form's sake !   Can the river-flower
The current drags, direct its face up-stream ?
What she must do she will ; nought else at all.

Enter through one of the windows MARIA LOUISA *in garden-costume,
fresh-coloured, girlish, and smiling.*   METTERNICH *bends.*

MARIA LOUISA

O how, dear Chancellor, you startled me !
Please pardon my so brusquely bursting in.
I saw you not.—Those five poor little birds
That haunt out there beneath the pediment,
Snugly defended from the north-east wind,
Have lately disappeared.   I sought a trace
Of scattered feathers, which I dread to find !

METTERNICH

They are gone, I ween, the way of tender flesh
At the assaults of winter, want, and foes.

MARIA LOUISA

It is too melancholy thinking, that!
Don't say it.—But I saw the Emperor here?
Surely he beckoned to me?

METTERNICH

             Sure, he did,
Your gracious Highness; and he has left me here
To break vast news that will make good his call.

MARIA LOUISA

Then do. I'll listen. News from near or far?

                    [She seats herself.

METTERNICH

From far—though of such distance-dwarfing might
That far may read as near eventually.
But, dear Archduchess, with your kindly leave
I'll speak straight out. The Emperor of the French
Has sent to-day to make, through Schwarzenberg,
A formal offer of his heart and hand,
His honours, dignities, imperial throne,
To you, whom he admires above all those
The world can show elsewhere.

MARIA LOUISA (frightened)

            My husband—he?
What, an old man like him!

METTERNICH (cautiously)

            He's scarcely old,
Dear lady. True, deeds densely crowd in him;
Turn months to years in calendaring his span;
Yet by Time's common clockwork he's but young.

MARIA LOUISA

So wicked, too!

METTERNICH (nettled)

        Well—that's a point of view.

MARIA LOUISA

But, Chancellor, think what things I have said of him!
Can women marry where they have taunted so?

METTERNICH

Things?   Nothing inexpungeable, I deem,
By time and true good humour.

MARIA LOUISA

                              O I have!
Horrible things.   Why—ay, a hundred times—
I have said I wished him dead!   At that strained hour
When the first voicings of the late war came,
Thrilling out how the French were smitten sore
And Bonaparte retreating, I clapped hands
And answered that I hoped he'd lose his head
As well as lose the battle!

METTERNICH

                    Words.   But words!
Born like the bubbles of a spring that come
Of zest for springing—aimless in their shape.

MARIA LOUISA

It seems indecent, mean, to wed a man
Whom one has held such fierce opinions of!

METTERNICH

My much beloved Archduchess, and revered,
Such things have been!   In Spain and Portugal
Like enmities have led to intermarriage.
In England, after warring thirty years
The Red and White Rose wedded.

MARIA LOUISA (after a silence)

                              Tell me, now,
What does my father wish?

METTERNICH

                              His wish is yours.
Whatever your Imperial Highness feels
On this grave verdict of your destiny,

Home, title, future sphere, he bids you think
Not of himself, but of your own desire.

MARIA LOUISA (reflecting)

My wish is what my duty bids me wish.
Where a wide Empire's welfare is in poise,
That welfare must be pondered, not my will.
I ask of you, then, Chancellor Metternich,
Straightway to beg the Emperor my father
That he fulfil his duty to the realm,
And quite subordinate thereto all thought
Of how it personally impinge on me.

A slight noise as of something falling is heard in the room. They glance momentarily, and see that a small enamel portrait of MARIE ANTOINETTE, which was standing on a console-table, has slipped down on its face.

SPIRIT OF THE YEARS

What mischief's this? The Will must have its way.

SPIRIT SINISTER

Perhaps Earth shivered at the lady's say?

SHADE OF THE EARTH

*I own thereto. When France and Austria wed
My echoes are men's groans, my dews are red;
So I have reason for a passing dread!*

METTERNICH

Right nobly phrased, Archduchess; wisely too.
I will acquaint your sire the Emperor
With these your views. He waits them anxiously.

(Going.)

MARIA LOUISA

Let me go first. It much confuses me
To think—But I would fain let thinking be!

[She goes out trembling.

Enter FRANCIS by another door.

METTERNICH

I was about to seek your Majesty.
The good Archduchess luminously holds
That in this weighty question you regard
The Empire. Best for it is best for her.

FRANCIS (moved)

My daughter's views thereon do not surprise me.
She is too staunch to pit a private whim
Against the fortunes of a commonwealth.
During your speech with her I have taken thought
To shape decision sagely.   An assent
Would yield the Empire many years of peace,
And leave me scope to heal those still green sores
Which linger from our late unhappy moils.
Therefore, my daughter not being disinclined,
I know no basis for a negative.
Send, then, a courier prompt to Paris : say
The offer made for the Archduchess' hand
I do accept—with this defined reserve,
That no condition, treaty, bond, attach
To such alliance save the tie itself.
There are some sacrifices whose grave rites
No bargain must contaminate.   This is one—
This personal gift of a beloved child !

METTERNICH (leaving)

I'll see to it this hour, your Majesty,
And cast the words in keeping with your wish.
 (To himself as he goes)
Decently done ! . . . He slipped out " sacrifice,"
And scarce could hide his heartache for his girl.
Well ached it !—But when these things have to be
It is as well to breast them stoically.
                                    [Exit METTERNICH.
          The clouds draw over.

SCENE IV

LONDON.   A CLUB IN ST. JAMES'S STREET

A winter midnight.   Two members are conversing by the fire, and others
are seen lolling in the background, some of them snoring.

FIRST MEMBER

I learn from a private letter that it was carried out in the
Emperor's Cabinet at the Tuileries—just off the throne-room,
where they all assembled in the evening,—Boney and the wife

of his bosom (in pure white muslin from head to foot, they say),
the Kings and Queens of Holland, Westphalia, and Naples, the
Princess Pauline, and one or two more ; the officials present
being Cambacérès the Chancellor, and Count Regnaud.   Quite a
small party.   It was over in a few minutes—short and sweet,
like a donkey's gallop.

SECOND MEMBER

Anything but sweet for her.   How did she stand it ?

FIRST MEMBER

Serenely, I believe, while the Emperor was making his speech
renouncing her ; but when it came to her turn to say she
renounced him she began sobbing mightily, and was so completely choked up that she couldn't get out a word.

SECOND MEMBER

Poor old dame !   I pity her, by God ; though she had a
rattling good spell while it lasted.

FIRST MEMBER

They say he was a bit upset, too, at sight of her tears.   But I
dare vow that was put on.   Fancy Boney caring a curse what a
woman feels.   She had learnt her speech by heart, but that did
not help her : Regnaud had to finish it for her, the ditch that
overturned her being where she was made to say that she no
longer preserved any hope of having children, and that she was
pleased to show her attachment by enabling him to obtain them
by another woman.   She was led off fainting.   A turning of the
tables, considering how madly jealous she used to make him by
her flirtations !

Enter a third member.

SECOND MEMBER

How is the debate going ?   Still braying the Government in
a mortar ?

THIRD MEMBER

They are.   Though one thing everybody admits : young Peel
has made a wonderful first speech in seconding the address.
There has been nothing like it since Pitt.   He spoke rousingly
of Austria's misfortunes—went on about Spain, of course, showing
that we must still go on supporting her, winding up with a

brilliant peroration about—what were the words—"the fiery glance of freedom which flashed incessantly from the indignant eyes of the British soldier!"—Oh, well: it was all learnt beforehand, of course.

SECOND MEMBER

I wish I had gone down. But the wind soon blew the other way.

THIRD MEMBER

Then Gower rapped out his amendment. That was good, too, by God.

SECOND MEMBER

Well, the war must go on. And that being the general conviction this censure and that censure are only so many blank cartridges.

THIRD MEMBER

Blank? Damn me, were they! Gower's was a palpable hit when he said that Parliament had placed unheard-of resources in the hands of Ministers last year, to make this year's results to the country worse than if they had been afforded no resources at all. Every single enterprise of theirs had been a beggarly failure.

SECOND MEMBER

Anybody could have said it, come to that.

THIRD MEMBER

Yes, because it is so true. However, when he began to lay on with such rhetoric as "the treasures of the nation lavished in wasteful thoughtlessness,"—"thousands of our troops sacrificed wantonly in the pestilential swamps of Walcheren," and gave the details we know so well, Ministers wriggled a good one, though 'twas no news to 'em. Castlereagh kept on starting forward as if he were going to jump up and interrupt, taking the strictures entirely as a personal affront.

Enter a fourth member.

SEVERAL MEMBERS

Who's speaking now?

FOURTH MEMBER

I don't know. I have heard of nobody later than Ward.

SECOND MEMBER

The fact is that, as Whitbread said to me to-day, the materials for condemnation are so prodigious that we can scarce marshal them into argument. We are just able to pour 'em out one upon t'other.

THIRD MEMBER

Ward said, with the blandest air in the world: "Censure? Do his Majesty's Ministers expect censure? Not a bit. They are going about asking in tremulous tones if anybody has heard when their impeachment is going to begin."

SEVERAL MEMBERS

Haw-haw-haw!

THIRD MEMBER

Then he made another point. After enumerating our frightful failures — Spain, Walcheren, and the rest — he said: "But Ministers have not failed in everything. No; in one thing they have been strikingly successful. They have been successful in their attack upon Copenhagen—because it was directed against an ally!" Mighty fine, wasn't it?

SECOND MEMBER

How did Castlereagh stomach that?

THIRD MEMBER

He replied then. Donning his air of injured innocence he proved the honesty of his intentions—no doubt truly enough. But when he came to Walcheren nothing could be done. The case was hopeless, and he knew it, and foundered. However, at the division, when he saw what a majority was going out on his side he was as frisky as a child. Canning's speech was grave, with bits of shiny ornament stuck on—like the brass nails on a coffin, Sheridan says.

Fifth and sixth members stagger in, arm-and-arm.

FIFTH MEMBER

The 'vision is——'jority of ninety-six againsht—Gov'ment—I mean—againsht us. Which is it—hey?   (*To his companion.*)

SIXTH MEMBER

Damn majority of—damn ninety-six—against damn amendment!

        (*They sink down on a sofa.*)

SECOND MEMBER

Gad, I didn't expect the figure would have been quite so high!

THIRD MEMBER

The one conviction is that the war in the Peninsula is to go on, and as we are all agreed upon that, what the hell does it matter what their majority is?

Enter SHERIDAN. *They all turn inquiringly.*

SHERIDAN

Have ye heard the latest?

SECOND MEMBER

Ninety-six against us.

SHERIDAN

O no—that's ancient history. I'd forgot it.

THIRD MEMBER

A revolution, because Ministers are not impeached and hanged?

SHERIDAN

That's in contemplation, when we've got their confessions. But what I meant was from over the water—it is a deuced sight more serious to us than a debate and division that are only like the Liturgy on a Sunday—known beforehand to all the congregation. Why, Bonaparte is going to marry Austria forthwith—the Emperor's daughter Maria Louisa.

THIRD MEMBER

The Lord look down! Our late respected crony Austria! Why, in this very night's debate they have been talking about the laudable principles we have been acting upon in affording assistance to the Emperor Francis in his struggle against the violence and ambition of France!

SECOND MEMBER

Boney safe on that side, what may not befall!

THIRD MEMBER

We had better make it up with him, and shake hands all round.

SECOND MEMBER

Shake heads seems most natural in the case.   O House of
Hapsburg, how hast thou fallen !

Enter WHITBREAD, LORD HUTCHINSON, LORD GEORGE CAVENDISH,
GEORGE PONSONBY, WINDHAM, LORD GREY, BARING, ELLIOT, *and other
members, some drunk. The conversation becomes animated and noisy ;
several move off to the card-room, and the scene closes.*

SCENE V

THE OLD WEST HIGHWAY OUT OF VIENNA

The spot is where the road passes under the slopes of the *Wiener Wald,*
with its beautiful forest scenery.

DUMB SHOW

A procession of enormous length, composed of eighty carriages—many of
them drawn by six horses and one by eight—and escorted by detachments of
cuirassiers, yeomanry, and other cavalry, is quickening its speed along the
highway from the city.

The six-horse carriages contain a multitude of Court officials, ladies of the
Court, and other Austrian nobility.   The eight-horse coach contains a rosy,
blue-eyed girl of eighteen, with full red lips, round figure, and pale auburn
hair.   She is MARIA LOUISA, and her eyes are red from recent weeping.
The COUNTESS DE LAZANSKY, Grand Mistress of the Household, in the
carriage with her, and the other ladies of the Palace behind, have a pale,
proud, yet resigned look, as if conscious that upon their sex had been laid
the burden of paying for the peace with France.   They have been played out
of Vienna with French marches, and the trifling incident has helped on their
sadness.

The observer's vision being still bent on the train of vehicles and cavalry,
the point of sight is withdrawn high into the air, till the huge procession on
the brown road looks no more than a file of ants crawling along a strip of
garden-matting.   The spacious terrestrial outlook now gained shows this to
be the great road across Europe from Vienna to Munich, and from Munich
westerly to France.

The puny concatenation of specks being exclusively watched, the surface
of the earth seems to move along in an opposite direction, and in infinite
variety of hill, dale, woodland, and champaign.   Bridges are crossed, ascents
are climbed, plains are galloped over, and towns are reached, among them
Saint Polten, where night falls.

Morning shines, and the royal crawl is resumed, and continued through
Linz, where the Danube is reapproached, and the girl looks pleased to see
her own dear Donau still.   Presently the tower of Braunau appears, where
the animated dots pause for formalities, this being the frontier ; and MARIA
LOUISA becomes MARIE LOUISE and a Frenchwoman, in the charge of
French officials.

After many breaks and halts, during which heavy rains spread their gauzes over the scene, the roofs and houses of Munich disclose themselves, suggesting the tesseræ of an irregular mosaic. A long stop is made here.

The tedious advance continues. Vine-circled Stuttgart, flat Carlsruhe, the winding Rhine, storky Strassburg, pass in panorama beneath us as the procession is followed. With Nancy and Bar-le-Duc sliding along, the scenes begin to assume a French character, and soon we perceive Châlons and ancient Rheims. The last day of the journey has dawned. Our vision flits ahead of the cortège to Courcelles, a little place which must be passed through before Soissons is reached. Here the point of sight descends to earth, and the Dumb Show ends.

SCENE VI

COURCELLES

It is now seen to be a quiet roadside village, with a humble church in its midst, opposite to which stands an inn, the highway passing between them. Rain is still falling heavily. Not a soul is visible anywhere.

Enter from the west a plain, lonely carriage, travelling in a direction to meet the file of coaches that we have watched. It stops near the inn, and two men muffled in cloaks alight by the door away from the hostel and towards the church, as if they wished to avoid observation. Their faces are those of NAPOLÉON and MURAT his brother-in-law. Crossing the road through the mud and rain they stand in the church porch, and watch the descending drifts.

NAPOLÉON (stamping an impatient tattoo)

One gets more chilly in a wet March than in a dry, however cold, the devil if he don't! What time do you make it now? That clock doesn't go.

MURAT (drily, looking at his watch)

Yes, it does; and it is right. If clocks were to go as fast as your wishes just now it would be awkward for the rest of the world.

NAPOLÉON (chuckling good-humouredly)

How we have dished the Soissons folk, with their pavilions, and purple and gold hangings for bride and bridegroom to meet in, and stately ceremonial to match, and their thousands looking on! Here we are where there's nobody. Ha, ha!

MURAT

But why should they be dished, sire? The pavilions and ceremonies were by your own orders.

NAPOLÉON

Well, as the time got nearer I couldn't stand the idea of dawdling about there.

MURAT

The Soissons people will be in a deuce of a taking at being made such fools of!

NAPOLÉON

So let 'em. I'll make it up with them somehow.—She can't be far off now, if we have timed her rightly. (He peers out into the rain and listens.)

MURAT

I don't quite see how you are going to manage when she does come. Do we go before her towards Soissons when you have greeted her here, or follow in her rear? Or what do we do?

NAPOLÉON

Heavens, I know no more than you! Trust to the moment and see what happens. (A silence.) Hark — here she comes! Good little girl; up to time!

The distant squashing in the mud of a multitude of hoofs and wheels is succeeded by the appearance of outriders and carriages, horses and horsemen, splashed with sample clays of the districts traversed. The vehicles slow down to the inn. NAPOLÉON's face fires up, and, followed by MURAT, he rushes into the rain towards the coach that is drawn by eight horses, containing the blue-eyed girl. He holds off his hat at the carriage-window.

MARIE LOUISE (shrinking back inside)

Ah, Heaven! Two highwaymen are upon us!

THE EQUERRY D'AUDENARDE (simultaneously)

The Emperor!

The steps of the coach are hastily lowered, NAPOLÉON, dripping, jumps in and embraces her. The startled ARCHDUCHESS, with much blushing and confusion, recognizes him.

MARIE LOUISE (tremulously, as she recovers herself)

You are so much—better looking than your portraits—that I hardly knew you! I expected you at Soissons. We are not at Soissons yet?

NAPOLÉON

No, my dearest spouse, but we are together! (Calling out to the equerry.) Drive through Soissons—pass the pavilion of reception without stopping, and don't halt till we reach Compiègne.

He sits down in the coach and is shut in, MURAT laughing silently at the scene. Exeunt carriages and riders towards Soissons.

CHORUS OF IRONIC SPIRITS (aerial music)

First 'twas a finished coquette,
And now it's a raw ingénue.—
Blonde instead of brunette,
An old wife doffed for a new.
 She'll bring him a baby,
 As quickly as maybe,
And that's what he wants her to do,
   Hoo-hoo!
And that's what he wants her to do!

SPIRIT OF THE YEARS

What lewdness lip those wry-formed phantoms there?

IRONIC SPIRITS

Nay, Showman Years! With holy reverent air
We hymn the nuptials of the Imperial pair.

The rain thickens to a mist and obscures the scene.

SCENE VII

PETERSBURG. THE PALACE OF THE EMPRESS-MOTHER

One of the private apartments is disclosed, in which the Empress-mother and Alexander are seated.

EMPRESS-MOTHER

So one of Austrian blood his pomp selects
To be his bride and bulwark—not our own.
Thus are you coolly shelved!

ALEXANDER

      Me, mother dear?
You, faith, if I may say it dutifully!
Had all been left to me, some time ere now
He would have wedded Kate.

EMPRESS-MOTHER

How so, my son?
Catharine was plighted, and it could not be.

ALEXANDER

Rather you swiftly pledged and married her,
To let Napoléon have no chance that way.
But Anne remained.

EMPRESS-MOTHER

How Anne?—so young a girl!
Sane Nature would have cried indecency
At such a troth.

ALEXANDER

Time would have tinkered that,
And he was well-disposed to wait awhile;
But the one test he had no temper for
Was the apparent slight of unresponse
Accorded his impatient overtures
By our suspensive poise of policy.

EMPRESS-MOTHER

A backward answer is our country's card—
The special style and mode of Muscovy.
We have grown great upon it, my dear son,
And may such practice rule our centuries through!
The necks of those who rate themselves our peers
Are cured of stiffness by its potency.

ALEXANDER

The principle in this case, anyhow,
Is shattered by the facts: since none can doubt
Your policy was counted an affront,
And drove my long ally to Austria's arms,
With what result to us must yet be seen!

EMPRESS-MOTHER

May Austria win much joy of the alliance!
Marrying Napoléon is a midnight leap
For any Court in Europe, credit me,
If ever such there were!   What he may carve

Upon the coming years, what murderous bolt
Hurl at the rocking Constitutions round,
On what dark planet he may land himself
In his career through space, no sage can say.
One thing we may assume as certainty—
That he will never rest in righteous rule.

ALEXANDER

Well—possibly ! . . . And maybe all is best
That he engrafts his lineage not on us.—
But, honestly, Napoléon none the less
Has been my friend, and I regret the dream
And fleeting fancy of a closer tie !

EMPRESS-MOTHER

Ay ; your regrets are sentimental ever.
That he'll be writ no son-in-law of mine
Is no regret to me !   But an affront
There is, no less, in his evasion on't,
Wherein the bourgeois quality of him
Veraciously peeps out.   I would be sworn
He set his minions parleying with the twain—
Yourself and Francis—simultaneously,
Else no betrothal could have speeded so !

ALEXANDER

Despite the hazard of offence to one ?

EMPRESS-MOTHER

More than the hazard ; the necessity.

ALEXANDER

There's no offence to me.

EMPRESS-MOTHER

                There should be, then.
I am a Romanoff by marriage merely,
But I do feel a rare belittlement
And loud laconic brow-beating herein !

ALEXANDER

No, mother, no !   I am the Tsar—not you,
And I am only piqued in moderateness.
Marriage with France was near my heart—I own it—
What then ?   It has been otherwise ordained.

[A silence.

EMPRESS-MOTHER

Here comes dear Anne.   Speak not of it before her.

Enter the GRAND-DUCHESS, a girl of sixteen.

ANNE

Alas ! the news is that poor Prussia's queen,
Spirited Queen Louisa, once so fair,
Is slowly dying, mother !   Did you know ?

ALEXANDER (betraying emotion)

Ah !—such I dreaded from the earlier hints.
Poor soul—her heart was slain some time ago.

ANNE

What do you mean by that, my brother dear ?

EMPRESS-MOTHER

He means, my child, that he as usual spends
Much sentiment upon the foreign fair,
And hence leaves little for his folk at home.

ALEXANDER

I mean, Anne, that her country's overthrow
Let death into her heart.   The Tilsit days
Taught me to know her well, and honour her.
She was a lovely woman even then ! . . .
Strangely, the present English Prince of Wales
Was wished to husband her.   Had wishes won,
They might have varied Europe's history.

ANNE

Napoléon, I have heard, admired her once ;
How he must grieve that soon she'll be no more !

EMPRESS-MOTHER

Napoléon and your brother loved her both.

[Alexander shows embarrassment.

But whatsoever grief be Alexander's,
His will be none who feels but for himself.

ANNE

O mother, how can you mistake him so!
He worships her who is to be his wife,
The fair Archduchess Marie.

EMPRESS-MOTHER

         Simple child,
As yet he has never seen her, or but barely.
That is a tactic suit, with love to match!

ALEXANDER (with vainly veiled tenderness)

High-souled Louisa;—when shall I forget
Those Tilsit gatherings in the long-sunned June! . . .
Napoléon's gallantries deceived her quite,
Who fondly felt her pleas for Magdeburg
Had won him to its cause; the while, alas!
His cynic sense but posed in cruel play!

EMPRESS-MOTHER

Bitterly mourned she her civilities
When time unlocked the truth, that she had choked
Her indignation at his former slights
And slanderous sayings for a baseless hope,
And wrought no tittle for her country's gain.
I marvel why you mourn a frustrate tie
With one whose wiles could wring a woman so!

ALEXANDER (uneasily)

I marvel also, when I think of it!

EMPRESS-MOTHER

Don't listen to us longer, dearest Anne.

[Exit ANNE.

—You will uphold my judging by and by,
That as a suitor we are well quit of him,
And that blind Austria will rue the hour
Wherein she plucks for him her fairest flower!

The scene shuts.

SCENE VIII

PARIS.   THE GRAND GALLERY OF THE LOUVRE
AND THE SALON-CARRÉ ADJOINING

The view is up the middle of the Gallery, which is now a spectacle of much magnificence.   Backed by the large paintings on the walls are double rows on each side of brightly dressed ladies, the pick of Imperial society, to the number of four thousand, one thousand in each row; and behind these standing up are two rows on each side of men of privilege and fashion. Officers of the Imperial Guard are dotted about as marshals.

Temporary barriers form a wide passage up the midst, leading to the Salon-Carré, which is seen through the opening to be fitted up as a chapel, with a gorgeous altar, tall candles, and cross.   In front of the altar is a platform with a canopy over it.   On the platform are two gilt chairs and a priedieu.

The expectant assembly does not continuously remain in the seats, but promenades and talks, the voices at times rising to a din amid the strains of the orchestra, conducted by the EMPEROR'S Director of Music.   Refreshments in profusion are handed round, and the extemporized cathedral resolves itself into a gigantic café of persons of distinction under the Empire.

SPIRIT SINISTER

All day have they been waiting for their galanty-show, and now the hour of performance is on the strike.   It may be seasonable to muse on the sixteenth Louis and the bride's great-aunt, as the nearing procession is, I see, appositely crossing the track of the tumbril which was the last coach of that respected lady. . . . It is now passing over the site of the scaffold on which she lost her head. . . . Now it will soon be here.

Suddenly the heralds enter the Gallery at the end towards the Tuileries, the spectators ranging themselves in their places.   In a moment the wedding procession of the EMPEROR and EMPRESS becomes visible.   The civil marriage having already been performed, Napoléon and Marie Louise advance together along the vacant pathway towards the Salon-Carré, followed by the long suite of illustrious personages, and acclamations burst from all parts of the Grand Gallery.

SPIRIT OF THE PITIES

Whose are those forms that pair in pompous train
Behind the hand-in-hand half-wedded ones,
With faces speaking sense of an adventure
Which may close well, or not so?

RECORDING ANGEL (reciting)

First there walks
The Emperor's brother Louis, Holland's King;
Then Jérôme of Westphalia with his spouse;
The mother-queen, and Julie Queen of Spain,
The Prince Borghèse and the Princess Pauline,
Beauharnais the Vice-King of Italy,
And Murat King of Naples, with their Queens;
Baden's Grand-Duke, Arch-Chancellor Cambacérès,
Berthier, Lebrun, and, not least, Talleyrand.
Then the Grand Marshal and the Chamberlain,
The Lords-in-Waiting, the Grand Equerry,
With waiting-ladies, women of the chamber,
And others called by office, rank, or fame.

SPIRIT OF RUMOUR

New, many, to Imperial dignities;
Which, won by character and quality
In those who now enjoy them, will become
The birthright of their sons in aftertime.

SPIRIT OF THE YEARS

It fits thee not to augur, quick-eared Shade.
Ephemeral at the best all honours be,
These even more ephemeral than their kind,
So random-fashioned, swift, perturbable!

SPIRIT OF THE PITIES

Napoléon looks content—nay, shines with joy.

SPIRIT OF THE YEARS

Yet see it pass, as by a conjuror's wand.

Thereupon Napoléon's face blackens as if the shadow of a winter night
had fallen upon it. Resentful and threatening, he stops the procession and
looks up and down the benches.

SPIRIT SINISTER

This is sound artistry of the Immanent Will: it relieves the
monotony of so much good-humour.

NAPOLÉON (to the Chapel-master)

Where are the Cardinals? And why not here?

(He speaks so loud that he is heard throughout the Gallery.)

ABBÉ DE PRADT (trembling)

Many are present here, your Majesty ;
But some are feebled by infirmities
Too common to their age, and cannot come.

NAPOLÉON

Tell me no nonsense !   Half absent themselves
Because they *will* not come.   The factious fools !
Well, be it so.   But they shall flinch for it !
MARIE LOUISE looks frightened.   The procession moves on.

SPIRIT OF THE PITIES

I seem to see the thin and headless ghost
Of the yet earlier Austrian, here, too, queen,
Walking beside the bride, with frail attempts
To pluck her by the arm !

SPIRIT OF THE YEARS

Nay, think not so.
No trump unseals earth's sepulchres to-day :
We are the only phantoms now abroad
On this mud-moulded ball !   Through sixteen years
She has decayed in a back-garden yonder,
Dust all the showance time retains of her,
Senseless of hustlings in her former house,
Lost to all count of crowns and bridalry—
Even of her Austrian blood.   No : what thou seest
Springs of thy quavering fancy, stirred to dreams
By yon tart phantom's phrase.

MARIE LOUISE (sadly to Napoléon)

I know not why,
I love not this day's doings half so well
As our quaint meeting-time at Compiégne.
A clammy air creeps round me, as from vaults
Peopled with looming spectres, chilling me
And angering you withal !

NAPOLÉON

O, it is nought
To trouble you : merely, my cherished one,
Those devils of Italian Cardinals !—
Now I'll be bright as ever—you must, too.

Marie Louise

I'll try.

Reaching the entrance to the Salon-Carré amid strains of music the EMPEROR and EMPRESS are received and incensed by the CARDINAL GRAND ALMONERS. They take their seats under the canopy, and the train of notabilities seat themselves further back, the persons-in-waiting stopping behind the Imperial chairs.

The ceremony of the religious marriage now begins. The choir intones a hymn, the EMPEROR and EMPRESS go to the altar, remove their gloves, and make their vows.

Spirit Ironic

The English Church should return thanks for this wedding, seeing how it will purge of coarseness the picture-sheets of that artistic nation, which will hardly be able to caricature the new wife as it did poor plebeian Joséphine. Such starched and ironed monarchists cannot sneer at a woman of such a divinely dry and crusted line as the Hapsburgs!

Mass is next celebrated, after which the TE DEUM is chanted in harmonies that whirl round the walls of the Salon-Carré and quiver down the long Gallery. The procession then re-forms and returns, amid the flutterings and applause of the dense assembly. But Napoléon's face has not lost the sombre expression which settled on it. The pair and their train pass out by the west door, and the congregation disperses in the other direction, the cloud-curtain closing over the scene as they disappear.

ACT SIXTH

SCENE I

THE LINES OF TORRÈS VÉDRAS

A bird's-eye perspective is revealed of the peninsular tract of Portuguese territory lying between the shining pool of the Tagus on the east, and the white-frilled Atlantic lifting rhythmically on the west. As thus beheld the tract features itself somewhat like a late-Gothic shield, the upper edge from the dexter to the sinister chief being the lines of Torrès Védras, stretching across from the mouth of the Zezambre on the left to Alhandra on the right, and the south or base point being Fort S. Julian. The roofs of Lisbon appear at the sinister base, and in a corresponding spot on the opposite side Cape Roca.

It is perceived in a moment that the northern verge of this nearly coast-hemmed region is the only one through which access can be gained to it by land, and a close scrutiny of the boundary there reveals that means are being adopted to effectually prevent such access.

From east to west along it runs a chain of defences, dotted at intervals by dozens of circular and square redoubts, either made or in the making, two of the latter being of enormous size. Between these stretch unclimbable escarpments, stone walls, and other breastworks, and in front of all a double row of abattis, formed of the limbs of trees.

Within the outer line of defence is a second, constructed on the same principle, its course being bent to take advantage of natural features. This second rampart is finished, and appears to be impregnable.

The third defence is far off southward, girdling the very base point of the shield-shaped tract of country ; and is not more than a twelfth of the length of the others. It is a continuous entrenchment of ditches and ramparts, and its object—that of covering a forced embarkation—is rendered apparent by some rocking English transports off the shore hard by.

DUMB SHOW

Innumerable human figures are busying themselves like cheese-mites all along the northernmost frontage, undercutting easy slopes into steep ones, digging ditches, piling stones, felling trees, dragging them, and interlacing them along the front as required.

On the second breastwork, which is completed, only a few figures move.

On the third breastwork, which is fully matured and equipped, minute red sentinels creep backwards and forwards noiselessly.

As time passes three reddish-grey streams of marching men loom out to the north, advancing southward along three roads towards three diverse points in the first defence. These form the English army, entering the lines for shelter. Looked down upon, their motion seems peristaltic and vermicular, like that of three caterpillars. The division on the left is under Picton, in the centre under Leith and Cole, and on the extreme right, by Alhandra, under Hill. Beside one of the roads two or three of the soldiers are dangling from a tree by the neck, probably for plundering.

The Dumb Show ends, and the point of view sinks to the earth.

SCENE II

THE SAME.   OUTSIDE THE LINES

The winter day has gloomed to a stormful evening, and the road outside the first line of defence forms the foreground of the stage.

Enter in the dusk from the hills to the north of the entrenchment, near Calandrix, a group of horsemen, which includes MASSÉNA, in command of the French forces, FOY, LOISON, and other officers of his staff.

They ride forward in the twilight and tempest, and reconnoitre, till they see against the sky the ramparts blocking the road they pursue. They halt silently. MASSÉNA, puzzled, endeavours with his glass to make out the obstacle.

MASSÉNA

Something stands here to peril our advance,
Or even prevent it !

FOY

           These are the English lines—
Their outer horns and tusks—whereof I spoke,
Constructed by Lord Wellington of late
To keep his foothold firm in Portugal.

MASSÉNA

Thrusts he his burly, bossed disfigurements
So far to north as this?   I had pictured me
They lay much nearer Lisbon.   Little strange
Lord Wellington rode placid at Busaco
With this behind his back!   Well, it is hard
But that we turn them somewhere, I assume?
They scarce can close up every southward gap
Between the Tagus and the Atlantic Sea.

FOY

I hold they can, and do; although, no doubt,
By searching we shall spy some raggedness
Which customed skill may force.

MASSÉNA

           Plain 'tis, no less,
We may heap corpses vainly hereabout,
And crack good bones in waste.   By human power
This passes mounting!   What say you's behind?

LOISON

Another line exactly like the first,
But more matured.   Behind its back a third.

MASSÉNA

How long have these prim ponderosities
Been rearing up their foreheads to the moon?

LOISON

Some months in all.   I know not quite how long.
They are Lord Wellington's select device,
And, like him, heavy, slow, laborious, sure.

MASSÉNA

May he enjoy their sureness.   He deserves to.
I had no inkling of such barriers here.
A good road runs along their front, it seems,
Which offers us advantage. . . . What a night!

The tempest cries dismally about the earthworks above them, as the reconnoitrers linger in the slight shelter the lower ground affords.   They are about to turn back.

Enter from the cross-road to the right JUNOT *and some more officers. They come up at a signal that the others are those they lately parted from.*

JUNOT

We have ridden along as far as Calandrix,
Favoured therein by this disordered night,
Which tongues its language to the disguise of ours ;
And find amid the vale an open route
That, well manœuvred, may be practicable.

MASSÉNA

I'll look now at it, while the weather aids.
If it may serve our end when all's prepared
So good.   If not, some other to the west.

Exeunt MASSÉNA, JUNOT, LOISON, FOY, *and the rest by the paved crossway to the right.*

The wind continues to prevail as the spot is left desolate, the darkness increases, rain descends more heavily, and the scene is blotted out.

SCENE III

PARIS.   THE TUILERIES

The anteroom to the EMPRESS MARIE LOUISE's *bed-chamber, in which are discovered* NAPOLÉON *in his dressing-gown, the* DUCHESS OF MONTE-BELLO, *and other ladies-in-waiting,* CORVISART *the first physician, and the second physician* BOURDIER.

The time is before dawn.   The EMPEROR *walks up and down, throws himself on a sofa, or stands at the window.   A cry of anguish comes occasionally from within.*

NAPOLÉON *opens the door and speaks into the bed-chamber.*

NAPOLÉON

How now, Dubois?

VOICE OF DUBOIS THE ACCOUCHEUR (nervously)

> Less well, sire, than I hoped ;
I fear no skill can save them both.

NAPOLÉON (agitated)

> Good God !

Exit CORVISART *into the bed-room.   Enter* DUBOIS.

DUBOIS (with hesitation)

Which life is to be saved ?   The Empress, sire,
Lies in great jeopardy.   I have not known
In my long years of many-featured practice
An instance in a thousand fall out so.

NAPOLÉON

Then save the mother, pray !   Think but of her ;
It is her privilege, and my command.—
Don't lose your head, Dubois, at this tight time :
Your furthest skill can work but what it may.
Fancy that you are merely standing by
A shop-wife's couch, say, in the Rue Saint Denis ;
Show the aplomb and phlegm that you would show
Did such a bed receive your ministry.

> [Exit DUBOIS.

VOICE OF MARIE LOUISE (within)

 O pray, pray don't !   Those ugly things terrify me !   Why
should I be tortured even if I am but a means to an end !   Let
me die !   It was cruel of him to bring this upon me !

Exit NAPOLÉON *impatiently to the bed-room.*

VOICE OF MADAME DE MONTESQUIOU (within)

 Keep up your spirits, madame !   I have been through it myself, and I assure you there is no danger to you.   It is going on
all right, and I am holding you.

VOICE OF NAPOLÉON (within)

 Heaven above !   Why did you not keep those cursed sugar-
tongs out of her sight ?   How is she going to get through it if
you frighten her like this ?

VOICE OF DUBOIS (within)

If you will pardon me, your Majesty,
I must implore you not to interfere!
I'll not be scapegoat for the consequence
If, sire, you do!   Better for her sake far
Would you withdraw.   The sight of your concern
But agitates and weakens her endurance.
I will inform you all, and call you back
If things should worsen here.

Re-enter NAPOLÉON from the bed-chamber.   He half shuts the door, and remains close to it listening, pale and nervous.

BOURDIER

                    I ask you, sire,
To harass yourself less with this event,
Which may amend anon : I much regret
The honoured mother of your Majesty,
And sister too, should both have left ere now,
Whose solace would have bridged these anxious hours.

NAPOLÉON (absently)

As we were not expecting it so soon
I begged they would sit up no longer here. . . .
She ought to get along ; she has help enough
With that half-dozen of them at hand within—
Skilled Madame Blaise the nurse, and two besides,
Madame de Montesquiou and Madame Ballant——

DUBOIS (speaking through the doorway)

Past is the question, sire, of which to save !
The child is dead ; the while her Majesty
Is getting through it well.

NAPOLÉON

                    Praise Heaven for that !
I'll not grieve overmuch about the child. . . .
Never shall she go through this strain again
To lay down a dynastic line for me.

DUCHESS OF MONTEBELLO (aside to second lady)

He only says that now.   In cold blood it would be far otherwise.   That's how men are.

VOICE OF MADAME BLAISE (within)

Doctor, the child's alive !

(The cry of an infant is heard.)

VOICE OF DUBOIS (calling from within)

Sire, both are saved.

NAPOLÉON rushes into the chamber, and is heard kissing MARIE LOUISE.

VOICE OF MADAME BLAISE (within)

A vigorous boy, your Imperial Majesty. The brandy and hot napkins brought him to.

DUCHESS OF MONTEBELLO

It is as I expected. A healthy young woman of her build had every chance of doing well, despite the doctors.

An interval.

NAPOLÉON (re-entering radiantly)

We have achieved a healthy heir, good dames,
And in the feat the Empress was most brave,
Although she suffered much—so much, indeed,
That I would sooner father no more sons
Than have so fair a fruit-tree undergo
Another wrenching of such magnitude.

He walks to the window, pulls aside the curtains, and looks out. It is a joyful spring morning. The Tuileries' gardens are thronged with an immense crowd, kept at a little distance off the Palace by a cord. The windows of the neighbouring houses are full of gazers, and the streets are thronged with halting carriages, their inmates awaiting the event.

SPIRIT OF THE YEARS (whispering to Napoléon)

At this high hour there broods a woman nigh,
Ay, here in Paris, with her child and thine,
Who might have played this part with truer eye
To thee and to thy contemplated line !

NAPOLÉON (soliloquizing)

Strange that just now there flashes on my soul
That little one I loved in Warsaw days,
Marie Walewska, and my boy by her !—

She was shown faithless by a foul intrigue
Till fate sealed up her opportunity. . . .
But what's one woman's fortune more or less
Beside the schemes of kings!—Ah, there's the news!

A gun is heard from the Invalides.

CROWD (excitedly)

One!

Another report of the gun, and another, succeed.

Two! Three! Four!

The firing and counting proceed to twenty-one, when there is great suspense. The gun fires again, and the excitement is doubled.

Twenty-two! A boy!

The remainder of the counting up to a hundred-and-one is drowned in huzzas. Bells begin ringing, and from the Champ de Mars a balloon ascends, from which the tidings are scattered in hand-bills as it floats away across France.

Enter the PRESIDENT OF THE SENATE, CAMBACÉRÈS, BERTHIER, LEBRUN, *and other officers of state.* NAPOLÉON *turns from the window.*

CAMBACÉRÈS

Unstinted gratulations and goodwill
We bring to your Imperial Majesty,
While still resounds the superflux of joy
With which your people welcome this live star
Upon the horizon of our history!

PRESIDENT OF SENATE

All blessings at their goodliest will grace
The advent of this New Messiah, sire,
Of fairer prospects than the former one,
Whose coming at so apt an hour endues
The widening glory of your high exploits
With permanence, and flings the dimness far
That cloaked the future of our chronicle!

NAPOLÉON

My thanks; though, gentlemen, upon my soul
You might have drawn the line at the Messiah.
But I excuse you.—Yes, the boy has come;
He took some coaxing, but he's here at last.—
And what news brings the morning from without?
I know of none but this the Empress now
Trumps to the world from the adjoining room.

PRESIDENT OF SENATE

Nothing in Europe, sire, that can compare
In magnitude therewith to more effect
Than with an eagle some frail finch or wren.
To wit :· the ban on English trade prevailing,
Subjects our merchant-houses to such strain
That many of the best see bankruptcy
Like a grim ghost ahead.   Next week, they say
In secret here, six of the largest close.

NAPOLÉON

It shall not be !   Our burst of natal joy
Must not be sullied by so mean a thing :
Aid shall be rendered.   Much as we may suffer,
England must suffer more, and I am content.
What has come in from Spain and Portugal ?

BERTHIER

Vaguely-voiced rumours, sire, but nothing more,
Which travel countries quick as earthquake-thrills,
No mortal knowing how.

NAPOLÉON

                Of Masséna ?

BERTHIER

Yea.   He retreats for prudence' sake, it seems,
Before Lord Wellington.   Dispatches soon
Must reach your Majesty, explaining all.

NAPOLÉON

Ever retreating !   Why declines he so
From all his olden prowess ?   Why, again,
Did he give battle at Busaco lately,
When Lisbon could be marched on without strain ?
Why has he dallied by the Tagus bank
And shunned the obvious course ?   I gave him Ney,
Soult, and Junot, and eighty thousand men,
And he does nothing.   Really it might seem
As though we meant to let this Wellington
Be even with us there !

BERTHIER

                  His mighty forts
At Torrès Védras hamper Masséna,
And quite preclude advance.

NAPOLÉON

                 O well—no matter:
Why should I linger on these haps of war
Now that I have a son!

Exeunt NAPOLÉON by one door and by another the PRESIDENT OF THE SENATE, CAMBACÉRÈS, LEBRUN, BERTHIER, and officials.

CHORUS OF IRONIC SPIRITS (aerial music)

The Will Itself is slave to him,
And holds it blissful to obey!—
He said, " Go to; it is my whim

" To bed a bride without delay,
Who shall unite my dull new name
With one that shone in Caesar's day.

" She must conceive—you hear my claim?—
And bear a son—no daughter, mind—
Who shall hand on my form and fame

" To future times as I have designed;
And at the birth throughout the land
Must cannon roar and alp-horns wind!"

The Will grew conscious at command,
And ordered issue as he planned.

The interior of the Palace is veiled.

SCENE IV

SPAIN. ALBUERA

    The dawn of a mid-May day in the same spring shows the village of Albuera with the country around it, as viewed from the summit of a line of hills on which the English and their allies are ranged under Beresford. The landscape swept by the eye includes to the right foreground a hill loftier than any, and somewhat detached from the range. The green slopes behind and around this hill are untrodden—though in a few hours to be the sanguinary scene of the most murderous struggle of the whole war.

    The village itself lies to the left foreground, with its stream flowing behind it from the distance on the right. A creeping brook at the bottom of the heights held by the English joins the stream by the village. Behind the

stream some of the French forces are visible. Away behind these stretches
a great wood several miles in area, out of which the Albuera stream emerges,
and behind the furthest verge of the wood the morning sky lightens momently.
The birds in the wood, unaware that this day is to be different from every
other day they have known there, are heard singing their overtures with their
usual serenity.

DUMB SHOW

As objects grow more distinct it can be perceived that some strategic
dispositions of the night are being completed by the French forces, which the
evening before lay in the woodland to the front of the English army. They
have emerged during the darkness, and large sections of them—infantry,
cuirassiers, and artillery—have crept round to BERESFORD'S right without his
suspecting the movement, where they lie hidden by the great hill aforesaid,
though not more than half-a-mile from his right wing.

SPIRIT OF THE YEARS

A hot ado goes forward here to-day,
If I may read the Immanent Intent
*   From signs and tokens blent*
With weird unrest along the firmament
Of causal coils in passionate display.
—Look narrowly, and what you witness say.

SPIRIT OF THE PITIES

I see red smears upon the sickly dawn,
And seeming drops of gore.   On earth below
Are men—unnatured and mechanic-drawn—
Mixt nationalities in row and row,
*   Wheeling them to and fro*
In moves dissociate from their souls' demand,
For dynasts' ends that few even understand!

SPIRIT OF THE YEARS

Speak more materially, and less in dream.

SPIRIT OF RUMOUR

I'll do it. . . . The stir of strife grows well defined
Around the hamlet and the church thereby:
Till, from the wood, the ponderous columns wind,
Guided by Godinot, with Werlé nigh.
They bear upon the vill.   But the gruff guns
*   Of Dickson's Portuguese*
Punch spectral vistas through the maze of these! . . .
More Frenchmen press, and roaring antiphons
Of cannonry contuse the roofs and walls and trees.

SPIRIT OF THE PITIES

Wrecked are the ancient bridge, the green spring plot,
The blooming fruit-tree, the fair flower-knot!

SPIRIT OF RUMOUR

Yet the true mischief to the English might
Is meant to fall not there.   Look to the right,
And read the shaping scheme by yon hill-side,
Where cannon, foot, and brisk dragoons you see,
With Werlé and Latour-Maubourg to guide,
Waiting to breast the hill-brow bloodily.

BERESFORD now becomes aware of this project on his flank, and sends orders to throw back his right to face the attack.   The order is not obeyed. Almost at the same moment the French rush is made, the Spanish and Portuguese allies of the English are beaten back, and the hill is won.   But two English divisions bear from the centre of their front, and plod desperately up the hill to retake it.

SPIRIT SINISTER

Now he among us who may wish to be
A skilled practitioner in slaughtery,
Should watch this hour's fruition yonder there,
And he will know, if knowing ever were,
How mortals may be freed their fleshly cells,
And quaint red doors set ope in sweating fells,
By methods swift and slow and foul and fair!

The English, who have plunged up the hill, are caught in a heavy mist, that hides from them an advance in their rear of the lancers and hussars of the enemy.   The lines of the Buffs, the Sixty-sixth, and those of the Forty-eighth, who were with them, in a chaos of smoke, steel, sweat, curses, and blood, are beheld melting down like wax from an erect position to confused heaps.   Their forms lie rigid, or twitch and turn, as they are trampled over by the hoofs of the enemy's horse.   Those that have not fallen are taken.

SPIRIT OF THE PITIES

It works as you, uncanny Phantom, wist! . . .
Whose is that towering form
*   That tears across the mist*
To where the shocks are sorest?—his with arm
Outstretched, and grimy face, and bloodshot eye,
Like one who, having done his deeds, will die?

SPIRIT OF RUMOUR

He is one Beresford, who heads the fight
For England here to-day.

SPIRIT OF THE PITIES

He calls the sight
Despite itself!—parries yon lancer's thrust,
And with his own sword renders dust to dust!

The ghastly climax of the strife is reached ; the combatants are seen to be firing grape and canister at speaking distance, and discharging musketry in each other's faces when so close that their complexions may be recognized. Hot corpses, their mouths blackened by cartridge-biting, and surrounded by cast-away knapsacks, firelocks, hats, stocks, flint-boxes, and priming-horns, together with red and blue rags of clothing, gaiters, epaulettes, limbs, and viscera, accumulate on the slopes, increasing from twos and threes to half-dozens, and from half-dozens to heaps, which steam with their own warmth as the spring rain falls gently upon them.

The critical instant has come, and the English break. But a comparatively fresh division, with fusileers, is brought into the turmoil by HARDINGE and COLE, and these make one last strain to save the day, and their names and lives. The fusileers mount the incline, and issuing from the smoke and mist startle the enemy by their arrival on a spot deemed won.

SEMICHORUS I OF THE PITIES (aerial music)

They come, beset by riddling hail;
They sway like sedges in a gale;
They fail, and win, and win, and fail.   Albuera!

SEMICHORUS II

They gain the ground there, yard by yard,
Their brows and hair and lashes charred,
Their blackened teeth set firm and hard.

SEMICHORUS I

Their mad assailants rave and reel,
And face, as men who scorn to feel,
The close-lined, three-edged prongs of steel.

SEMICHORUS II

Till faintness follows closing-in,
When, faltering headlong down, they spin
Like leaves.   But those pay well who win Albuera.

SEMICHORUS I

Out of six thousand souls that sware
To hold the mount, or pass elsewhere,
But eighteen hundred muster there.

SEMICHORUS II

Pale Colonels, Captains, ranksmen lie,
Facing the earth or facing sky ;—
They strove to live, they stretch to die.

SEMICHORUS I

Friends, foemen, mingle ; heap and heap.——
Hide their hacked bones, Earth !—deep, deep, deep,
Where harmless worms caress and creep.

CHORUS

Hide their hacked bones, Earth !—deep, deep, deep,
Where harmless worms caress and creep.——
What man can grieve ? what woman weep ?
Better than waking is to sleep ! Albuera !

The night comes on, and darkness covers the battle-field.

SCENE V

WINDSOR CASTLE. A ROOM IN THE KING'S APARTMENTS

The walls of the room are padded, and also the articles of furniture, the stuffings being overlaid with satin and velvet, on which are worked in gold thread monograms and crowns. The windows are guarded, and the floor covered with thick cork, carpeted. The time is shortly after the last scene.

The KING is seated by a window, and two of Dr. WILLIS's attendants are in the room. His MAJESTY is now seventy-two ; his sight is very defective, but he does not look ill. He appears to be lost in melancholy thought, and talks to himself reproachfully, a hurried manner on occasion being the only irregular symptom that he betrays.

KING

In my lifetime I did not look after her enough——enough—enough ! And now she is lost to me, and I shall never see her more. Had I but known, had I but thought of it ! Gentlemen, when did I lose the Princess Amelia ?

FIRST ATTENDANT

The second of last November, your Majesty.

KING

And what is it now ?

FIRST ATTENDANT

Now, sir, it is the beginning of June.

KING

Ah, June, I remember! . . . The June flowers are not for me. I shall never see them; nor will she. So fond of them as she was. . . . Even if I were living I would never go where there are flowers any more! No: I would go to the bleak, barren places that she never would walk in, and never knew, so that nothing might remind me of her, and make my heart ache more than I can bear! . . . Why, the beginning of June?—that's when they are coming to examine me! *(He grows excited.)*

FIRST ATTENDANT *(to second attendant, aside)*

Dr. Reynolds ought not to have reminded him of their visit. It only disquiets him and makes him less fit to see them.

KING

How long have I been confined here?

FIRST ATTENDANT

Since November, sir; for your health's sake entirely, as your Majesty knows.

KING

What, what? So long? Ah, yes. I must bear it. This is the fourth great black gulf in my poor life, is it not? The fourth.

A signal at the door. The second attendant opens it and whispers.
Enter softly SIR HENRY HALFORD, DR. WILLIAM HEBERDEN, DR. ROBERT WILLIS, DR. MATTHEW BAILLIE, *the* KING'S APOTHECARY, *and one or two other gentlemen.*

KING *(straining his eyes to discern them)*

What! Are they come? What will they do to me? How dare they! I am Elector of Hanover! *(Finding Dr. Willis is among them he shrieks.)* O, they are going to bleed me—yes, to bleed me! *(Piteously.)* My friends, don't bleed me—pray don't! It makes me so weak to take my blood. And the leeches do, too, when you put so many. You will not be so unkind, I am sure!

WILLIS *(to Baillie)*

It is extraordinary what a vast aversion he has to bleeding—that most salutary remedy, fearlessly practised. He submits to leeches as yet, but I won't say that he will for long without being strait-jacketed.

KING (catching some of the words)

You will strait-jacket me?   O no, no!

WILLIS

Leeches are not effective, really.   Dr. Home, when I mentioned it to him yesterday, said he would bleed him till he fainted if he had charge of him!

KING

O will you do it, sir, against my will,
And put me, once your king, in needless pain?
I do assure you truly, my good friends,
That I have done no harm!   In sunnier years
Ere I was throneless, withered to a shade,
Deprived of my divine authority—
When I was hale, and ruled the English land—
I ever did my utmost to promote
The welfare of my people, body and soul!
Right many a morn and night I have prayed and mused
How I could bring them to a better way.
So much of me you surely know, my friends,
And will not hurt me in my weakness here!

                                        (He trembles.)

SPIRIT OF THE PITIES

The tears that lie about this plightful scene
Of heavy travail in a suffering soul,
Mocked with the forms and feints of royalty
While scarified by briery Circumstance,
Might drive Compassion past her patiency
To hold that some mean, monstrous ironist
Had built this mistimed fabric of the Spheres
To watch the throbbings of its captive lives,
(The which may Truth forfend), and not thy said
Unmaliced, unimpassioned, nescient Will!

SPIRIT OF THE YEARS

Mild one, be not too touched with human fate.
Such is the Drama: such the Mortal state:
No sigh of thine can null the Plan Predestinate!

HALFORD

We have come to do your Majesty no harm.
Here's Dr. Heberden, whom I am sure you like,
And this is Dr. Baillie.   We arrive
But to inquire and gather how you are,
Thereon to let the Privy Council know,
And give assurance for your people's good.

A brass band is heard playing in a distant part of Windsor.

KING

Ah—what does that band play for here to-day?
She has been dead and I so short a time! . . .
Her little hands are hardly cold as yet;
But they can show such cruel indecency
As to let trumpets play!

HALFORD

          They guess not, sir,
That you can hear them, or their chords would cease.
Their boisterous music fetches back to me
That, of our errands to your Majesty,
One was congratulation most sincere
Upon this glorious victory you have won.
The news is just in port; the band booms out
To celebrate it, and to honour you.

KING

A victory?   I?   Pray where?

HALFORD

          Indeed so, sir:
Hard by Albuera—far in harried Spain—
Yes, sir; you have achieved a victory
Of dash unmatched and feats unparalleled!

KING

He says I have won a battle?   But I thought
I was a poor afflicted captive here,
In darkness lingering out my lonely days,
Beset with terror of these myrmidons
That suck my blood like vampires!   Ay, ay, ay!—

No aims left to me but to quicken death
To quicklier please my son !—And yet he says
That I have won a battle !   O God, curse, damn !
When will the speech of the world accord with truth,
And men's tongues roll sincerely !

GENTLEMAN (aside)

Faith, 'twould seem
As if the madman were the sanest here !

The KING's face has flushed, and he becomes violent.   The attendants
rush forward to him.

SPIRIT OF THE PITIES

Something within me aches to pray
To some Great Heart, to take away
This evil day, this evil day !

CHORUS IRONIC

Ha-ha !   That's good.   Thou'lt pray to It :—
But where do Its compassions sit ?
Yea, where abides the heart of It ?

Is it where sky-fires flame and flit,
Or solar craters spew and spit,
Or ultra-stellar night-webs knit ?

What is Its shape ?   Man's counterfeit ?
That turns in some far sphere unlit
The Wheel which drives the Infinite ?

SPIRIT OF THE PITIES

Mock on, mock on !   Yet I'll go pray
To some Great Heart, who haply may
Charm mortal miseries away !

The KING's paroxysm continues.   The attendants hold him.

HALFORD

This is distressing.   One can never tell
How he will take things now.   I thought Albuera
A subject that would surely solace him.
These paroxysms—have they been bad this week ?   (To
    Attendants.)

FIRST ATTENDANT

Sir Henry, no.   He has quite often named
The late Princess, as gently as a child
A little bird found starved.

WILLIS (aside to apothecary)

I must increase the opium to-night, and lower him by a double
set of leeches since he won't stand the lancet quietly.

APOTHECARY

You should take twenty ounces, doctor, if a drop—indeed,
go on blooding till he's unconscious.   He is too robust by half.
And the watering-pot would do good again—not less than six
feet above his head.   See how heated he is.

WILLIS

Curse that town band.   It will have to be stopped.

HEBERDEN

The same thing is going on all over England, no doubt, on
account of this victory.

HALFORD

When he is in a more domineering mood he likes such
allusions to his rank as king. . . . If he could resume his walks
on the terrace he might improve slightly.   But it is too soon yet.
We must consider what we shall report to the Council.   There is
little hope of his being much better.   What do you think, Willis?

WILLIS

None.   He is done for this time!

HALFORD

Well, we must soften it down a little, so as not to upset the
Queen too much, poor woman, and distract the Council un-
necessarily.   Eldon will go pumping up bucketfuls, and the
Archbishops are so easily shocked that a certain conventional
reserve is almost forced upon us.

WILLIS (returning from the King)

He is already better.   The paroxysm has nearly passed.   Your opinion will be far more favourable before you leave.

The KING soon grows calm, and the expression of his face changes to one of dejection.   The attendants leave his side : he bends his head, and covers his face with his hand, while his lips move as if in prayer.   He then turns to them.

KING (meekly)

I am most truly sorry, gentlemen,
If I have used language that would seem to show
Discourtesy to you for your good help
In this unhappy malady of mine !
My nerves unstring, my friends ; my flesh grows weak :
" The good that I would do I leave undone,
The evil which I would not, that I do ! "
Shame, shame on me !

WILLIS (aside to the others)

Now he will be as low as before he was in the other extreme.

KING

A king should bear him kingly ; I, of all,
One of so long a line.   O shame on me ! . . .
—This battle that you speak of ?—Spain, of course ?
Ah—Albuera !   And many fallen—eh ?   Yes ?

HALFORD

Many hot hearts, sir, cold, I grieve to say.
There's Major-General Houghton, Captain Bourke,
And Herbert of the Third, Lieutenant Fox,
And Captains Erck and Montague, and more.
With Majors-General Cole and Stewart wounded,
And Quartermaster-General Wallace too :
A total of three generals, colonels five,
Five majors, fifty captains ; and to these
Add ensigns and lieutenants sixscore odd,
Who went out, but returned not.   Heavily tithed
Were the attenuate battalions there
Who stood and bearded Death by the hour that day !

KING

O fearful price for victory!   Add thereto
All those I lost at Walcheren.—A crime
Lay there! . . . I stood on Chatham's being sent:
It wears on me, till I am unfit to live!

WILLIS (aside to the others)

Don't let him get on that Walcheren business.   There will be
another outbreak.   Heberden, please ye talk to him.   He fancies
you most.

HEBERDEN

I'll tell him some of the brilliant feats of the battle.   (He goes
and talks to the KING.)

WILLIS (to the rest)

Well, my inside begins to cry cupboard.   I had breakfast
early.   We have enough particulars now to face the Queen's
Council with, I should say, Sir Henry?

HALFORD

Yes.—I want to get back to town as soon as possible to-day.
Mrs. Siddons has a party at her house at Westbourne to-night,
and all the world is going to be there.

BAILLIE

Well, I am not.   But I have promised to take some friends
to Vauxhall, as it is a grand gala and fireworks night.   Miss
Farren is going to sing "The Canary Bird."—The Regent's fête,
by the way, is postponed till the nineteenth, on account of this
relapse.   Pretty grumpy he was at having to do it.   All the
world will be *there*, sure!

WILLIS

And some from the Shades, too, of the fair sex.—Well, here
comes Heberden.   He has pacified his Majesty nicely.   Now we
can get away.

The physicians withdraw softly, and the scene is covered.

SCENE VI

LONDON. CARLTON HOUSE AND THE STREETS ADJOINING

It is a cloudless midsummer evening, and as the west fades the stars beam down upon the city, the evening-star hanging like a jonquil blossom. They are dimmed by the unwonted radiance which spreads around and above Carlton House. As viewed from aloft the glare rises through the skylights, floods the forecourt towards Pall Mall, and kindles with a diaphanous glow the hugh tents in the gardens that overlook the Mall. The hour has arrived of the Prince Regent's festivity.

A stream of carriages and sedan-chairs, moving slowly, stretches from the building along Pall Mall into Piccadilly and Bond Street, and crowds fill the pavements watching the bejewelled and feathered occupants. In addition to the grand entrance inside the Pall Mall colonnade there is a covert little "chair-door" in Warwick Street for sedans only, by which arrivals are perceived to be slipping in almost unobserved.

SPIRIT IRONIC

What domiciles are those, of singular expression,
Whence no guest comes to join the gemmed procession ;
That, west of Hyde, this, in the Park-side Lane,
Each front beclouded like a mask of pain ?

SPIRIT OF RUMOUR

Therein the princely host's two spouses dwell ;
A wife in each.   Let me inspect and tell.

The walls of the two houses—one in Park Lane, the other at Kensington—become transparent.

I see within the first his latter wife—
That Caroline of Brunswick whose brave sire
Yielded his breath on Jena's reeking plain,
And of whose kindred other yet may fall
Ere long, if character indeed be fate.—
She idles feasting, and is full of jest
As each gay chariot rumbles to the rout.
"I rank like your Archbishops' wives," laughs she ;
"Denied my husband's honours.   Funny me !"

Suddenly a Beau on his way to the Carlton House festival halts at her house, calls, and is shown in.

He brings her news that a fresh favourite rules
Her husband's ready heart; likewise of those
Obscure and unmissed courtiers late deceased,
Who have in name been bidden to the feast
By blundering scribes.

The Princess is seen to jump up from table at some words from her visitor, and clap her hands.

                         These tidings, juxtaposed,
Have fired her hot with curiosity,
And lit her quick invention with a plan.

PRINCESS OF WALES

Mine God, I'll go disguised—in some dead name
And enter by the leetle, sly, chair-door
Designed for those not welcomed openly.
There unobserved I'll note mine new supplanter!
'Tis indiscreet?   Let indiscretion rule,
Since caution pensions me so scurvily!

SPIRIT IRONIC

Good.   Now for the other sweet and slighted spouse.

SPIRIT OF RUMOUR

The second roof shades the Fitzherbert Fair;
Reserved, perverse.   As coach and coach roll by
She mopes within her lattice; lampless, lone,
As if she grieved at her ungracious fate,
And yet were loth to kill the sting of it
By frankly forfeiting the Prince and town.
"Bidden," says she, "but as one low of rank,
And go I will not so unworthily,
To sit with common dames!"—A flippant friend
Writes then that a new planet sways to-night
The sense of her erratic lord; whereon
The fair Fitzherbert muses hankeringly.

MRS. FITZHERBERT (soliloquizing)

The guest-card which I publicly refused
Might, as a fancy, privately be used! . . .
Yes—one last look—a wordless, wan farewell
To this false life which glooms me like a knell,
And him, the cause; from some hid nook survey
His new magnificence ;—then go for aye!

SPIRIT OF RUMOUR

She cloaks and veils, and in her private chair
Passes the Princess also stealing there—
Two honest wives, and yet a differing pair!

SPIRIT IRONIC

With dames of strange repute, who bear a ticket
For screened admission by the private wicket.

CHORUS OF IRONIC SPIRITS (aerial music)

A wife of the body, a wife of the mind,
A wife somewhat frowsy, a wife too refined:
Could the twain but grow one, and no other dames be,
No husband in Europe more steadfast than he!

SPIRIT OF THE YEARS

Cease fooling on weak waifs who love and wed
But as the unweeting Urger may bestead!—
See them withinside, douce and diamonded.

The walls of Carlton House open, and the spectator finds himself confronting the revel.

SCENE VII

THE SAME.   THE INTERIOR OF CARLTON HOUSE

A central hall is disclosed, radiant with constellations of candles, lamps, and lanterns, and decorated with flowering shrubs.   An opening on the left reveals the Grand Council-chamber prepared for dancing, the floor being chalked with arabesques having in the centre "G. III. R.," with a crown, arms, and supporters,   Orange-trees and rose-bushes in bloom stand against the walls.   On the right hand extends a glittering vista of the supper-rooms and tables, now crowded with guests.   This display reaches as far as the conservatory westward, and branches into long tents on the lawn.

On a dais at the chief table, laid with gold and silver plate, the Prince Regent sits like a lay figure, in a state chair of crimson and gold, with six servants at his back.   He swelters in a gorgeous uniform of scarlet and gold lace which represents him as a Field Marshal, and he is surrounded by a hundred-and-forty of his particular friends.

Down the middle of this state-table runs a purling brook crossed by quaint bridges, in which gold and silver fish frisk about between banks of moss and flowers.   The whole scene is lit with wax candles in chandeliers, and in countless candelabra on the tables.

The people at the upper tables include the Duchess of York, looking tired from having just received as hostess most of the ladies present, except those who have come informally, Louis XVIII. of France, the Duchess of Angoulême, all the English Royal Dukes, nearly all the ordinary Dukes and Duchesses; also the Lord Chancellor, the Speaker, the Chancellor of the Exchequer and other Ministers, the Lord Mayor and Lady Mayoress, all the more fashionable of the other Peers, Peeresses, and Members of Parliament, Generals, Admirals, and Mayors, with their wives. The ladies of position wear, almost to the extent of a uniform, a nodding head-dress of ostrich feathers with diamonds, and gowns of white satin embroidered in gold or silver, on which, owing to the heat, dribbles of wax from the chandeliers occasionally fall.

The Guards' bands play, and attendants rush about in blue and gold lace.

SPIRIT OF THE PITIES

The Queen, the Regent's mother, sits not here;
Wanting, too, are his sisters, I perceive;
And it is well. With the distempered King
Immured at Windsor, sore distraught or dying,
It borders nigh on an indecency
In their regard, that this loud feast is kept,
A thought not strange to many, as I read,
Even of those gathered here.

SPIRIT IRONIC

My dear phantom and crony, the gloom upon their faces is due rather to their having borrowed those diamonds at eleven per cent than to their loyalty to a suffering monarch! But let us test the feeling. I'll spread a report.

He calls up the SPIRIT OF RUMOUR, who scatters whispers through the assemblage.

A GUEST (to his neighbour)

Have you heard this report—that the King is dead?

ANOTHER GUEST

It has just reached me from the other side. Can it be true?

THIRD GUEST

I think it probable. He has been very ill all the week.

PRINCE REGENT

Dead? Then my fête is spoilt, by God!

SHERIDAN

Long live the King! (He holds up his glass and bows to the Regent.)

MARCHIONESS OF HERTFORD (the new favourite, to the Regent)

The news is more natural than the moment of it! It is too cruel to you that it should happen now!

PRINCE REGENT

Damn me, though; can it be true? (He provisionally throws a regal air into his countenance.)

DUCHESS OF YORK (on the Regent's left)

I hardly can believe it. This forenoon
He was reported mending.

DUCHESS OF ANGOULÊME (on the Regent's right)

On this side
They are asserting that the news is false—
That Buonaparté's child, the "King of Rome,"
Is dead, and not your royal father, sire.

PRINCE REGENT

That's mighty fortunate! Had it been true,
I should have been abused by all the world—
The Queen the keenest of the chorus too—
Though I have been postponing this pledged feast
Through days and weeks, in hopes the King would mend,
Till expectation fusted with delay.
But give a dog a bad name—or a Prince!
So, then, it is this new-come King of Rome
Who has passed or ever the world has welcomed him! . . .
Call him a king—that pompous upstart's son—
Beside us scions of the ancient lines!

DUKE OF BEDFORD

I think that rumour untrue also, sir. I heard it as I drove up from Woburn this evening, and it was contradicted then.

PRINCE REGENT

Drove up this evening, did ye, Duke. Why did you cut it so close?

DUKE OF BEDFORD

Well, it so happened that my sheep-shearing dinner was fixed for this very day, and I couldn't put it off. So I dined with them there at one o'clock, discussed the sheep, rushed off, drove the two-and-forty miles, jumped into my clothes at my house here, and reached your Royal Highness's door in no very bad time.

PRINCE REGENT

Capital, capital.　But, 'pon my soul, 'twas a close shave!

Soon the babbling and glittering company rise from supper, and begin promenading through the rooms and tents, the REGENT setting the example, and mixing up and talking unceremoniously with his guests of every degree. He and the group round him disappear into the remoter chambers; but many concentrate in the Grecian Hall, which forms the foreground of the scene, whence a glance can be obtained into the ball-room, now filled with dancers.

The band is playing the tune of the season, "The Regency Hornpipe," which is danced as a country-dance by some thirty couples; so that by the time the top couple have danced down the figure they are quite breathless. Two young lords talk desultorily as they survey the scene.

FIRST LORD

Are the rumours of the King of Rome's death confirmed?

SECOND LORD

No.　But they are probably true.　He was a feeble brat from the first.　I believe they had to baptize him on the day he was born.　What can one expect after such presumption—calling him the New Messiah, and God knows what all.　Ours is the only country which did not write fulsome poems about him. "Wise English!" the Tsar Alexander said drily when he heard it.

FIRST LORD

Ay!　The affection between that Pompey and Caesar has begun to cool.　Alexander's soreness at having his sister thrown over so cavalierly is not salved yet.

SECOND LORD

There is much besides.　I'd lay a guinea there will be a war between Russia and France before another year has flown.

FIRST LORD

Prinny looks a little worried to-night.

SECOND LORD

Yes.　The Queen don't like the fête being held, considering the King's condition.　She and her friends say it should have been put off altogether. But the Princess of Wales is not troubled that way. Though she was not asked herself she went wildly off and bought her people new gowns to come in. Poor maladroit woman! . . .

Another new dance of the year is started, and another long line of couples begin to foot it.

That's a pretty thing they are doing now. What d'ye call it?

First Lord

"Speed the Plough." It is just out. They are having it everywhere. The next is to be one of those foreign things in three-eight time they call Waltzes. I question if anybody is up to dancing 'em here yet.

"Speed the Plough" is danced to its conclusion, and the band strikes up "The Copenhagen Waltz."

Spirit Ironic

Now for the wives. They both were tearing hither,
Unless reflection sped them back again;
But dignity that nothing else may bend
Succumbs to woman's curiosity,
So deem them here. Messengers, call them nigh!

The PRINCE REGENT, having gone the round of the other rooms, now appears at the ball-room door, and stands looking at the dancers. Suddenly he turns, and gazes about with a ruffled face. He sees a tall, red-faced man near him—LORD MOIRA, one of his friends.

Prince Regent

Damned hot here, Moira. Hottest of all for me!

Moira

Yes, it is warm, sir. Hence I do not dance.

Prince Regent

H'm. What I meant was of another order;
I spoke it figuratively.

Moira

O indeed, sir?

Prince Regent

She's here. I heard her voice. I'll swear I did!

MOIRA

Who, sir?

PRINCE REGENT

Why, the Princess of Wales. Do you think I could mistake those beastly German Ps and Bs of hers?—She asked to come, and was denied; but she's got here, I'll wager ye, through the chair-door in Warwick Street, which I arranged for a few ladies whom I wished to come privately. (He looks about again, and moves till he is by a door which affords a peep up the grand staircase.) By God, Moira, I see *two* figures up there who shouldn't be here—leaning over the balustrade of the gallery!

MOIRA

Two figures, sir. Whose are they?

PRINCE REGENT

She is one. The Fitzherbert is t'other! O I am almost sure it is! I would have welcomed her, but she bridled and said she wouldn't sit down at my table as a plain "Mrs." to please anybody. As I had sworn that on this occasion people should sit strictly according to their rank, I wouldn't give way. Why the devil did she come like this? 'Pon my soul, these women will be the death o' me!

MOIRA (looking cautiously up the stairs)

I can see nothing of her, sir, nor of the Princess either. There is a crowd of idlers up there leaning over the bannisters, and you may have mistaken some others for them.

PRINCE REGENT

O no. They have drawn back their heads. There have been such damned mistakes made in sending out the cards that the biggest w—— in London might be here. She's watching Lady Hertford, that's what she's doing. For all their indifference, both of them are as jealous as two cats over one tom.

Somebody whispers that a lady has fainted up-stairs.

That's Maria, I'll swear! She's always doing it. Whenever I hear of some lady fainting about upon the furniture at my presence, and sending for a glass of water, I say to myself, There's Maria at it again, by God!

Spirit Ironic

Now let him hear their voices once again.

The REGENT starts as he seems to hear from the stairs the tongues of the two ladies growing louder and nearer, the PRINCESS pouring reproaches into one ear, and MRS. FITZHERBERT into the other.

Prince Regent

'Od seize 'em, Moira; this will drive me mad!
If men of blood must mate with only one
Of those dear damned deluders called the Sex,
Why has Heaven teased us with the taste for change?—
God, I begin to loathe the whole curst show!
How hot it is! Get me a glass of brandy,
Or I shall swoon off too.   Now let's go out,
And find some fresher air upon the lawn.
Here Moira, Yarmouth; quick and come along.

Exit the PRINCE REGENT, with LORDS MOIRA and YARMOUTH.   The band strikes up " La Belle Catarina," and a new figure is formed.

Spirit of the Years

Phantoms, ye strain your powers unduly here,
Making faint fancies as they were indeed
The Mighty Will's firm work.

Spirit Ironic

                    Nay, Father, nay;
The wives prepared to hasten hitherward
Under the names of some gone down to death,
Who yet were bidden.   Must they not be here?

Spirit of the Years

There lie long leagues between a woman's word—
" She will, indeed she will!"—and acting on't.
Whether those came or no, thy antics cease,
And let the revel wear it out in peace.

Enter SPENCER PERCEVAL the Prime Minister, a small, pale, grave-looking man, and an Under-Secretary of State, meeting.

Under-Secretary

Is the King of Rome really dead, and the gorgeous gold cradle wasted?

PERCEVAL

O no, he is alive and waxing strong :
That tale has been set travelling more than once.
But touching it, booms echo to our ear
Of graver import, unimpeachable.

UNDER-SECRETARY

Your speech is dark.

PERCEVAL

          Well, a new war in Europe.
Before the year is out there may arise
A red campaign outscaling any seen.
Russia and France the parties to the strife—
Ay, to the death !

UNDER-SECRETARY

       By Heaven, sir, do you say so ?

Enter CASTLEREAGH, a tall, handsome man with a Roman nose, who,
seeing them, approaches.

PERCEVAL

Ha, Castlereagh.   Till now I have missed you here.
This news is startling for us all, I say !

CASTLEREAGH

My mind is blank on it !   Since I left office
I know no more what villainy's afoot,
Or virtue either, than an anchoret
Who mortifies the flesh in some lone cave.

PERCEVAL

Well, happily that may not last for long.
But this grave pother that's just now agog
May reach such radius in its consequence
As to outspan our lives !   Yes, Bonaparte
And Alexander—late such bosom-friends—
Are closing to a mutual murder-bout
At which the lips of Europe will wax wan.
Bonaparte says the fault is not with him,
And so says Alexander.   But we know
The Austrian knot began their severance.

And that the Polish question largens it.
Nothing but time is needed for the clash.
And if so be that Wellington but keep
His foot in the Peninsula awhile,
Between the pestle and the mortar-stone
Of Russia and of Spain, Napoléon's brayed.

SPIRIT OF RUMOUR (to the Spirit of the Years)

Permit me now to join them and confirm,
By what I bring from far, their forecasting?

SPIRIT OF THE YEARS

I'll go.   Thou knowest not greatly more than they.

The SPIRIT OF THE YEARS enters the apartment in the shape of a pale,
hollow-eyed gentleman wearing an embroidered suit. At the same time
re-enter the REGENT, LORDS MOIRA, YARMOUTH, KEITH, LADY HERTFORD,
SHERIDAN, the DUKE OF BEDFORD, with many more notables. The band
changes into the popular dance, "Down with the French," and the characters
aforesaid look on at the dancers.

SPIRIT OF THE YEARS (to Perceval)

Yes, sir; your text is true.   In closest touch
With European courts and cabinets,
The imminence of dire and deadly war
Betwixt these east and western emperies
Is lipped by special pathways to mine ear.
You may not see the impact: ere it come
The tomb-worm may caress thee (Perceval shrinks); *but*
    believe
Before five more have joined the shotten years
Whose useless films infest the foggy Past,
Traced thick with teachings glimpsed unheedingly,
The rawest Dynast of the group concerned
Will, for the good or ill of mute mankind,
Down-topple to the dust like soldier Saul,
And Europe's mouldy-minded oligarchs
Be propped anew; while garments roll in blood
To confused noise, with burning, and fuel of fire.
Nations shall lose their noblest in the strife,
And tremble at the tidings of an hour!

(He passes into the crowd and vanishes.)

PRINCE REGENT (who has heard with parted lips)

Who the devil is he?

PERCEVAL

One in the suite of the French princes, perhaps, sir?—though his tone was not monarchical. He seems to be a foreigner.

CASTLEREAGH

His manner was that of an old prophet, and his features had a Jewish cast, which accounted for his Hebraic style.

PRINCE REGENT

He could not have known me, to speak so freely in my presence!

SHERIDAN

I expected to see him write on the wall, like the gentleman with the Hand at Belshazzar's Feast.

PRINCE REGENT (recovering)

He seemed to know a damn sight more about what's going on in Europe, sir (to Perceval), than your Government does, with all its secret information.

PERCEVAL

He is recently over, I conjecture, your Royal Highness, and brings the latest impressions.

PRINCE REGENT

By Gad, sir, I shall have a comfortable time of it in my regency, or reign, if what he foresees be true! But I was born for war; it is my destiny!

He draws himself up inside his uniform and stalks away. The group dissolves, the band continuing stridently, "Down with the French," as dawn glimmers in.

Soon the REGENT'S guests begin severally and in groups to take leave.

SPIRIT OF THE PITIES

Behold To-morrow riddles the curtains through,
And labouring life without shoulders its cross anew!

M

CHORUS OF THE YEARS (aerial music)

Why watch we here?   Look all around
Where Europe spreads her crinkled ground,
From Osmanlee to Hekla's mound,
                              Look all around!

Hark at the cloud-combed Ural pines;
See how each, wailful-wise, inclines;
Mark the mist's labyrinthine lines;

Behold the tumbling Biscay Bay;
The Midland main in silent sway;
As urged to move them, so move they.

No less through regal puppet-shows
The rapt Determinator throes,
That neither good nor evil knows!

CHORUS OF THE PITIES

Yet It may wake and understand
Ere Earth unshape, know all things, and
With knowledge use a painless hand,
                              A painless hand!

Solitude reigns in the chambers, and the scene shuts up.

Printed in Great Britain by R. & R. CLARK, LIMITED, *Edinburgh.*